# The Celtic
# Book of Names

# The Celtic Book of Names

Traditional Names From
Ireland, Scotland, and Wales

D. J. CONWAY

A Citadel Press Book
Published by Carol Publishing Group

11/99

A Citadel Press Book
Published by Carol Publishing Group
Citadel Press is a registered trademark of Carol Communications, Inc.

Editorial, sales and distribution, and rights and permissions inquiries should be addressed to Carol Publishing Group, 120 Enterprise Avenue, Secaucus, N.J. 07094.

In Canada: Canadian Manda Group, One Atlantic Ave, Suite 105, Toronto, Ontario M6K 3E7

Carol Publishing Group Books may be purchased in bulk at special discounts for sales promotion, fundraising, or educational purposes. Special editions can be created to specifications. For details, contact Special Sales Department, Carol Publishing Group, 120 Enterprise Avenue, Secaucus, N.J. 07094.

Manufactured in the United States of America
10 9 8 7 6 5 4 3 2 1

Library of Congress Cataloging-in-Publication Data

Conway, D.J. (Deanna J.)
        The Celtic Book of names / D. J. Conway
                p.   cm.
        "A Citadel Press book."—T.p. verso.
        Includes bibliographical references (p. ).
        ISBN 0–8065–2096–5 (pbk.)
        1. Names, Personal—Celtic Dictionaries. 2. Names, Personal—
Ireland Dictionaries. 3. Names, Personal—Scotland Dictionaries.
4. Names, Personal—WalesDictionaries. I. Title.
CS2377C66    1999
929.4′0941—dc21
                                                                99–22594
                                                                    CIP

# Contents

# Introduction

The term Celts historically covers the cultures of Ireland, Scotland, Wales, Cornwall, the Isle of Man, and Brittany, who were all once closely related. However, in this book, I will cover only the names in Ireland, Scotland, and Wales, the three countires whose descendants make up a large portion of the citizens in the United States.

The most ancient tales of the Celtic warrior-tribes can be found in the legends of India. These say that the Celts came out of the East, but no one knows their exact point of origin. By the ninth century B.C.E. the Celtic peoples appeared in recorded Mediterranean history as they swept out of the mountainous area around the Black Sea. They slowly forced their way into Gaul, the Iberian Peninsula, northern Italy, the Balkans, and Asia Minor, finally settling in Brittany, Britain, and Ireland. The name Celt actually comes from the Roman word *Keltoi.*

Although all the tribes were not of the same ethnic stock, they did speak dialects of the same language and had many of the same religious customs and tribal laws. The Celts were experts in metal, built roads and chariots, and were quite proficient in agriculture and animal husbandry. However, their greatest expertise was as warriors, both men and women. They were paid high prices as mercenaries and bodyguards in such civilizations as Byzantium.

At the height of their power, about 500 B.C.E. according to the history writer Nora Chadwick, they controlled large stretches of land from the British Isles to Turkey. Except for Wales, Scotland,

and Ireland, they were eventually conquered by the more disciplined armies of Rome.

Scotland was held by the non-Celtic race called the Picts until the Irish King Fergus Mor mac Eirc brought his followers to that country in about 500 C.E. King Fergus was not abandoning Ireland; rather, he was expanding his kingdom. His kingdom of Dal Riada was merely an extension of his Irish holdings. The Celts in Scotland intermarried with the Picts who were already there.

Although Scotland and Ireland maintained a common language (including a similarity in names and customs) until the fifteenth century when the English conquered Scotland, Wales remained isolated. Thus, the Welsh language developed into a much different tongue from the others, a language is that more similar to the one spoken in Brittany. Welsh legends also differ from the similar ones of Ireland and Scotland, although there is mention of intermarrying and communicating with the Irish. Contact with the Anglo-Saxons, Norse Vikings, and French Normans affected the Celtic Gaelic language and the names used in Ireland, Scotland, and Wales even more.

Many first names became surnames, especially in Ireland and Scotland. In Ireland, for example, O'Brien means "son of Brien" and mac Cumaill means "son of Cumaill," while in Scotland, MacLeod means "son of Leod." In Irish either "mac" or "o" denotes "son of." In Scotish, "mac" denotes "son of." In Welsh "ap" denotes lineage. It also was customary to refer to the head of a clan as "the Bruce" or "the MacLeod," for example.

With personal names whose spelling radically differs from the pronunciation, I have included the correct pronunciation wherever possible. In cases where I am not certain of the pronunciation, I do not give any. I also do not include any accent marks on any of the Gaelic spelling. An accent mark missed or placed in the wrong place completely changes the pronunciation of the name. The pronunciation rules for Gaelic are very complicated, made more difficult by the fact that ancient Gaelic was slightly different from the modern version. In fact, each of these Celtic countries had ancient and medieval forms of their language before the modern tongue evolved. Therefore, I suggest any reader interested in further study in this area should consult a competent Gaelic dictionary of the Celtic country of choice.

In Irish names, the letter "c" is always pronounced as a hard "k," which has led to some confusion in the spelling. The "c" in the word Celtic also is pronounced as a hard "k," unless you are speaking of a basketball team in Boston.

In the text I often use the words "Gaelic" and "Celtic" in conjunction with certain names. These words refer to the fact that the words or names in question would be recognized, at least nominally, in any of the three countries. Otherwise, I use the words "Irish Gaelic" or "Scottish Gaelic" for names or words recognized within a specific form of the Gaelic language.

Lest someone take offense by my reference to monasteries started by women, let me assure the reader this was so in Ireland. The very early Celtic Church was quite different from its later Romanized form. In the Celtic Church women, as well as men, established monasteries where both men and women lived and worked. The religious members of these monasteries were allowed to marry and have children, as were abbots and bishops of that time. The Celtic Church continued in this form until the Roman church authorities forced it to change its policies governing the lives of its members.

I hope you enjoy the snippets of history and mythology sprinkled liberally throughout this book. Perhaps it will give you a greater understanding of your own ancestral background.

DANA NI CONNMHAIGH

# Part 1
# First Names

# Ireland

## Female Names

**Abaigeal** (AB-I-gel)  *Father's joy.* This is a Hebrew name adopted by the Irish. A variant is ABAIGH (AB-ee).

**Aedammair**  Derived from the word *aedh*, meaning "fire." Tradition says that this was the name of the first woman to take the veil of a nun under Saint Patrick. She is said to have established a nunnery at Drom Dubhain near Clogher in County Tyrone. Her feast day is February 18. A variant spelling is AODHAMAIR.

**Affrica**  *Pleasant, agreeable.* Rather than being connected with the continent as many people suppose, this Irish name was actually the name of a twelfth-century queen of the Isle of Man. Variant spellings are AFRICA and AIFRIC.

**Agata**  *Good.* A variant of the Greek name Agatha.

**Aghna** (EE-nuh)  *Gentle, pure.* This is the Irish version of Agnes. A variant is AIGNEIS ([AG]-NESH).

**Aideen**  The wife of Oscar, Finn mac Cumhail's grandson. She died of grief when her husband was killed at the Battle of Gabhra.

**Ailbhe** (AL-vyuh)  Either a female or male name. This name comes from the Celtic *albho*, which means "white." Some sources list the meaning as "noble" or "bright." In Irish legends, two important women had this name; Ailbe Gruadbrecc ("Freckled" or "Red-and-White Cheeks") was the wife of Finn mac Cumaill and the daughter of King Cormac mac Airt; the other Ailbe was the daughter of Midir, a fairy king. A variant is AILBE (AL-fe).

3

**Aileen** (A-leen)   *Light.* This is the Irish version of Ellen. Variant spellings are AILEY and EIBHLIN.

**Ailidh** (A-lee)   *Kind or noble.*

**Ailis** (AY-lish)   This name became popular during the Norman invasions of Ireland and comes from the French name Aliz, which means "noble" or "kind." Other sources list this as a form of the name Adelaide.

**Aimiliona** (a-mil-EE-nuh)   *Industrious.* This is the Irish version of the Teutonic name Amelia.

**Aine** (AN-yuh or AW-nee)   *Joy.* A moon goddess and the patroness of cattle and crops, Aine was later considered to be the fairy queen of the *sidhe* (underground fairy palace) at Knockaine. At one time she was celebrated at Midsummer Eve. A variant spelling is AINA.

**Aingeal** (AN-gel)   *Messenger.* This is the Irish spelling for the word angel.

**Airmid** (AIR-mit)   She was the daughter of the great physician Dian Cecht and one of the Tuatha De Danann. She was an expert in the use of herbs for medicinal purposes.

**Aisling** (AH-shleeng)   The Old Irish *aislinge* means "vision-or-dream." At one time this was a man's name, but is now popular among women. In many old Irish tales, the *speir-bhean* (vision-woman) brought humans closer to the Otherworld. During the eighteenth century many Irish poets wrote Aisling poems. A variant of this name is AISLINN.

**Aithne** (ATH-nyuh)   *Fire.*

**Alana**   *Attractive, fair, peaceful.* A variant is ALAINA.

**Alastrina** (al-is-TREE-nah)   *Defends mankind.* Variants are ALASTRIONA and ALASTRINE.

**Alma**   *Good.*

**Andraste**   *Victory.* A British war goddess worshipped by Queen Boadicia. Since many Celtic deities were known beyond the immediate area of their worship, the Irish Celtics likely knew of her.

**Anu** (AW-noo or AN-oo)   The mother goddess of the Tuatha De Danann, or early settlers in Ireland, was called Anu or Ana (AW-nee). As the goddess of fertility, cattle, good health, prosperity, and plenty, fires were lit in her honor at Midsummer's Eve. Another variant of this name is ANANN.

**Aodhnait** (EH-nat)   This is an ancient Irish name whose meaning is unknown.

**Aoibheann** (EE-vuhn)  *Fair form* or *beautiful sheen.* This is listed as the name of Saint Enda of Aran and his sisters. AOIBHIN is a variant.

**Aoibhell**  This was the name of a fairy woman said to live at Craig Liath in Munster. At one time she was the mistress of Dubhlainn. She is the *bean-sidhe,* or banshee, of the O'Brien family, and is said to play beautiful music on her harp as a warning of approaching death.

**Aoife** (EE-fe or EE-fa)  In Old Irish this means "beautiful-or-radiant." In the story of the hero Cu Chulainn's martial arts training, Aoife was the fiercest warrior woman working with the goddess Scota, the master of the martial arts. She was also Scota's sister. After Cu Chulainn defeated Aoife in a war that arose between the sisters, they had a love affair which produced the hero's only son, Connla. Another Aoife was the foster-daughter of Bodh Dearg, who became the second wife of Lir. A variant is AIFE.

**Arienh** (A-reen)  *Pledge.*

**Artis**  Some sources list the meaning as "noble," while others give "lofty hill."

**Badb** (BIBE)  This name has been translated as "boiling, battle raven," and "scald-crow." Badb was a war goddess and the wife of a little-known war god named Net. She was also sister of Morrigan, Anu, and Macha, and was part of the triad of important Irish goddesses. She was associated with the Cauldron of Life, wisdom, inspiration, and enlightenment. A variant spelling is BADHBH.

**Bairbre** (BAR-bruh)  An Irish version of the Greek name Barbara, which means "savage, uncouth; a barbarian." A variant is BAIBIN (BAB-een).

**Bairrfhionn**  Listed as either a female or male name, it means "fair-haired." Variant Irish spellings are BARRFIND, BAIRRE, BARRE, and BARRON.

**Banba**  One of the three goddesses of sovereignty whom Amerigin met when his people invaded Ireland. According to very ancient Irish legends, Ireland was first called "the island of Banba of the women."

**Bean Mhi** (BEN-vee)  *Lady of Meath.* A variant is BENVY.

**Beare**  This was the name of a Spanish princess who married Eoghan Mor. A peninsula on the southwest tip of Ireland is named for her.

**Bebhinn** (BAY-vin or BEH-vin)  This name comes from a combination of the Old Irish words *be* meaning "woman" and *binn* meaning "white or fair lady; sweet, melodious." Several early Irish queens had this name, as did many later saints. Alternate spellings are BEVIN and BEFIND.

**Becuma**   A woman from the Otherworld who married Conn Cetchathach, but who lusted after his son Art.

**Berrach**   *Pointed* or *sharp*. Berrach Bred (Freckled Berrach) was the daughter of Cas Cuailgne of Ulster and the third wife of Finn mac Cumaill. She bore him three sons, Faelan, Aedh, and Uillen. A variant spelling is BEARRACH.

**Binne** (BEE-ne)   The name of several fairy women in old stories, this name comes from the Old Irish *binn* meaning "sweet, melodious."

**Blair**   A Celtic word that means "from the plain."

**Blathnat** (BLA-nat)   The Old Irish *blath,* meaning "flower" is the source of this name. The original Blathnat was the daughter of Midir, king of the Gaelic Underworld. She helped the hero Cu Chulainn steal her father's magic cauldron. In another legend, Blathnat, daughter of Mend, was married against her will to Cu Roi, a king of west Munster. Because of her love for Cu Chulainn, she revealed the secret of her husband's defenses, then went with the hero after Cu Roi was killed. However, Ferchertne, her dead husband's bard, caught up with the couple, grabbed Blathnat, and jumped over a cliff to his death with her. Variants are BLATHNAID, BLAITHIN (BLAW-heen), and BLANAID.

**Blinne**   A diminutive form of the name Mo-Ninne (MONINNA). The first recording of this name appears in the time of Saint Patrick, when a Moninna or Blinne established a nunnery, first at Faughart, in County Louth, then on Beggerin Island in County Wexford. Although she was baptized by Patrick, the nunnery was under the rule of Saint Ibhar, a rival of Patrick's.

**Boann** (BOO-an)   A goddess connected with healing and water, Boann was mother of Angus mac Og by the god the Dagda. She was particularly connected with the River Boyne. She was known as She of the White Cows. Other Celtic river goddesses were Siannan (River Shannon), Sabrina (R. Severn), Sequana (R. Seine), Deva (R. Dee), Clota (R. Clyde), Verbeia (R. Wharfe), and Brigantia (R. Braint and R. Brent).

**Breck**   Derived from the Irish word for "freckled."

**Breena** A Celtic word for "dark hair."

**Brenda** Derived from the Irish word for "raven." This is a feminine version of the male name Brendan. A variant is BRENNA.

**Bretta** *From Britain.* Variants are BRETT, BRIT, BRITTANY, and BRITA.

**Briana** (BREE-a-na) This name is a female form of Brian, which may come from the Celtic Gaelic *brig,* meaning "high, noble." Some sources list the meaning as "strong," and say it is a variant of BRIGHID. Variants of this name are BREANNE, BRINA, BREANNA, BREANN, BRIONA, BRYNA, BRYANA, and RIANA.

**Brid** (BREED) An ancient Celtic goddess name which means "power, renown, mighty" or "High Goddess." A daughter of the Dagda, Brighid was associated with February 1, a holy day called Imbolc. She had an all-female priesthood at Kildare, where an ever-burning fire was kept. She was associated with healing, poetry, smithcraft, inspiration, learning, and agriculture. Sometimes this goddess was called the Triple Brigids, the Three Mothers, and the Three Blessed Ladies of Britain. Later, the Christians turned this goddess into Saint Brighid because the people refused to stop worshipping her. The first Christian female community was established in Ireland in her name at Kildare. Variants of this name are BRIDE, BRIDGET, BRIGID, BRIGIT, BERGET, BRIDEY, BRYG, and GITTA.

**Brina** Some sources list the meaning of this name as "protector," while others say it means "speckled."

**Britta** Some sources list the meaning as "speckled," while others list this name as a version of Bretta. A variation is BRIT.

**Bronach** *Sorrowful.* A Saint Bronach is said to have lived in Kilbroney, County Down. The National Museum of Ireland has her crosier, and her bell is housed in the Roman Catholic church in Rostrevor. Her feast day is April 2.

**Bryg** (BREE) This name is a variant of the name BRIGHID. Thirteen early Irish saints had this name.

**Caelfind** (KAYL-fin) Derived from *caol* meaning "slender," and *fionn,* meaning "fair." Several Irish saints had this name, the best known of which was a daughter of a descendant of Fergus, son of Ros, son of Rudraighe. Her feast day is February 3. A variant Irish spelling is CAOILAINN.

**Caer Ibormeith** She was a powerful shapeshifter and the daughter of Ethal Anubal. Angus mac Og fell in love with her.

**Cahan**    Derived from *cath* meaning "battle" or "a warrior." A female or male name. A Cathan was abbess of Kildare. A variant Irish spelling is CATHAN.

**Caillech** (CALL-yach or KEE-lek)    A goddess known in both Ireland and Scotland, she was frequently called the Veiled One. A teacher of the arts of war, she was viewed as a Destroyer aspect of the Goddess.

**Caireach** (KEE-rek)    This name is associated with the Kelly and Madden families of Ireland, whose women had a patron saint named Cairech Dergain.

**Caireann** (KAW-ran)    Legends of the O'Neill family and of the High Kings of Ireland were said to begin with Caireann Chasdubh (Dark Curly Hair), who was the mother of Niall of the Nine Hostages. A variant of this name is CAIRENN (kaw-REEN).

**Cait** (KAYT)    A variant of the name CAITRIONA. Irish history lists several women with the name CAITILIN, one of which was Caitilin, daughter of MacSweeney and wife of O'Doherty (died in 1530). Another was Caitilin, daughter of Domnall and wife of Tadg (died in 1592). Variants are CAITLIN (kayt-LEEN), and CAILIN (kay-LEEN or KAY-leen).

**Caitriona** (kaw-TREE-a-na)    The Anglo-Saxons brought the name Catherine to Ireland, and the people adopted it under this spelling. Catariona, daughter of O'Duigenan, was buried at the monastery of Donegal in 1525. Variants are CAITIN (kayt-TEEN), and TRIONA (TREE-a-na).

**Caoilfhionn** (KEE-lin)    *Slender* or *fair.* A variant spelling is KEELIN.

**Caoimhe** (KEE-vy)    *Beauty, grace.* This name is connected to an obscure virgin saint who lived in Killeavy, County Down. Her feast day is November 2.

**Casidhe**    From a word meaning "clever." A variant spelling is CASIE.

**Cathasach**    *Brave.* A variant spelling is CASIE.

**Ceara** (KE-a-ra)    The Old Irish spelling is CERA, which means "bright red." One of the legendary invaders of ancient Ireland was Nemed, whose wife's name was Cera. This was also the name of three Irish saints, one of which was Saint Cera of Killahear, County Monaghan. Her celebration day is September 9.

**Cellach**    *Bright-headed.* Either a male or female name, most commonly given to males.

**Cessair** (KAH-seer)    Irish legends say that Noah would not allow fifty women and three men onto the ark, so these people went to Ireland. One of these women was Noah's granddaughter, Cessair. All of these people, except the man Finian, drowned in the flood.

**Ciannait** (KEE-nat or KIN-nat)   An ancient Irish name. Variants are KEENAT and KINNAT.

**Ciar** (KEE-ar or KEER)   The Old Irish word *ciar* means "dark" or "black." Stories from Kilkeary tell of a Saint Ciar, whose feasts days are January 5 and October 16. This saint lived in Kilkeary, County Tipperary, and founded a monastery at Kilkeary. Variants of this name are CIARA (KEE-a-ra), CEIRE, KIERA, and KEARA.

**Cliodhna** (KLEE-a-na)   CLIDNA, a variant spelling, was listed in old legends as one of the three beautiful daughters of the poet Libra, who lived in Tir Tarrngaire (The Land of Promise) with the god Manannan mac Lir. The modern Irish spelling of this name is CLIONA.

**Clodagh** (KLOH-da)   The name of the river Cloideach in County Waterford and another river in County Tipperary, this has become a popular name for girls in Ireland.

**Cochrann** (KAW-kran)   The Old Irish word *coch* means "red," possibly a red-haired woman. The story of Cochrann, who was the mother of Diarmaid, a handsome and irresistible young man, is found in the tales of Finn mac Cumaill.

**Colleen**   Derived from the Celtic word for "girl."

**Conchobarre**   A feminine version of the name Conchobar. A variant is CONCHOBARRA (KON-kho-var-ah).

**Congalie**   A feminine version of an Ulster chieftain named Conall.

**Cori**   Derived from the word meaning "from the hollow."

**Creidne**   A woman warrior of the Fianna.

**Cristen** (KRIS-teen)   An Irish version of the Latin name Christian.

**Cuimhne**   An Otherworld woman who helped Mongan get back his wife from Brandubh, who had kidnapped her.

**Dairine** (daw-REE-ne)   This was the name of an ancient princess, the younger daughter of Tuathal Teachtmar, king of Tara. It is probably derived from the Old Irish *daire,* meaning "fruitful" or "fertile." Another Dairine was the daughter of Bobh Dearg.

**Dallas**   *Wise.* Variants are DALLYS, DALISHYA, and DALYCE.

**Damhnait** (DEV-nat)   Some sources list the meaning as "poet," while others list it as "fawn." One saint with this name was Saint Damhnat of Tedavnet, County Monaghan, who founded a monastery for women in the sixth century. Her crosier, now in the National Museum in Dublin, was once used to test oaths for lying. Her feast day is June 13. A variant is DAMHNAT.

**Dana**   This name comes from two different sources. One means "from Denmark," the other is a version of the name of the goddess DANU.

**Danu**   This was the name of the major Irish Mother Goddess and ancestress of the Tuatha De Danann (People of the Goddess Danu). The name means "wealth, abundance." The goddess Danu is similar to and might be the same as the goddess Anu, although there is no general agreement on this. Danu was connected with the powers of wells, prosperity, magic, and wisdom. Variants are DANA and DANANN.

**Darby**   From the word meaning "free."

**Darcy**   An Old French name meaning "d'Arcy" or "from Arcy." It was brought to Ireland by the French Norman invaders.

**Daron**   Derived from the word meaning "great." This is a feminine version of the name Darren. Variants are DARYN, DARONICA, and DARNELLE.

**Dealla** (DAWL-la)   This name belonged to a female companion of the woman leader, Cessair. She was one of fifty women turned away from the ark by Noah. Those women and three men then went to Ireland.

**Dearbhail** (DER-vahl)   May mean "daughter of Fal (Ireland)" or "daughter of a poet." Another source lists the meaning as "true desire." A Saint Deirbhile is said to have founded a sixth century convent in Fallmore, County Mayo. Variants are DERBAIL and DEIRBHILE.

**Dechtire** (deck-TIER-a)   In ancient Irish legends, Dechtire was the great-granddaughter of Angus mac Og, the half-sister of King Conchobar, and the mother of the hero Cu Chulainn.

**Decla**   A feminine version for the name Declan.

**Deirdre** (DYEER-dre)   May come from an old word for woman. However, the usual meaning is given as "sorrowful." A very early Irish tale, found in *The Exile of the Sons of Uisliu,* tells of the great beauty, Deirdre. She was the daughter of Feidlimid, a storyteller associated with King Conchobar. Before her birth, the druid Cathbad predicted her beauty and the troubles she would bring to Ulster. Promised to Conchobar mac Nessa, King of the Ulstermen,

Deirdre was deeply in love with Naoise, the son of Usliu. The couple fled to Scotland, but were lured back to Ireland by false promises of forgiveness by Conchobar. Naoise was slain, and after a year of marriage to Conchobar, Deirdre killed herself. Interlocked pine trees grew up from the couple's graves. Variants of this name are DERDRIU (a very old spelling), DIERDRE, DEDRE, and DEIDRA.

**Delaney** *Descendant of the challenger.*

**Delbchaem** The daughter of Morgan, king of Coinchend. Because a prophecy said that when she married her mother would die, she was kept guarded by monsters. However, Art got through all the obstacles and took her for his wife.

**Derry** Derived from the Irish word meaning "redhead."

**Dervil** (DER-uh-vil) Probably derived from the Old Irish name of DERBAIL, which may have come from *der* meaning "daughter" and *Fal,* a very ancient name for Ireland. This was a traditional name among the McDermotts. Derbail was also the name of several early Irish princesses. A variation is DERVLA (DAYR-vla).

**Devin** Either a male or female name. Variations are DEVANY and DEVYN.

**Devnet** One source lists this name as from the Old Irish *damnat,* meaning "little doe," while another lists the meaning as "poet." There was a legendary queen of Munster by this name, who is considered the ancestor of the O'Cahills, O'Flynns, and O'Moriartys. One of the modern spellings is DAMHNAIT (DOW-net).

**Doireann** (DAHR-an or DOHR-en) The Old Irish name was DOIREND, which may have meant "daughter of Finn." There are two legendary women of this name; one the daughter of Midir, the fairy king; the other the granddaughter of the god Dagda.

**Doirind** Some sources think this name means "daughter of Finn," that is, *Der Finn.* Legends say that Doirind was one of three daughters of Midhir Yellow-Mane. She and her sisters were married to the sons of Lughaid Menn, king of Ireland. A variant is DAIRINN.

**Doneele** A feminine version of the male name Don, taken from the Irish god of the Underworld.

**Donnfhlaidh** *Brown princess.* This name is rarely found in Irish histories. However, Dunlaith, daughter of Fogartach, died in 773, and a Dunflaith, daughter of King Flaithbertach, died in 798. A variant spelling is DUNFLAITH.

**Druantia** (Druh-AN-tee-a or druh-an-TEE-a)  A Gaelic-Celtic goddess known as Queen of the Druids and Mother of the tree calendar, the ancient method by which the Celts divided their year.

**Duana**  A Gaelic word meaning "song." A variant is DUBHAIN.

**Dubh**  A druidess who drowned the rival for her husband's affection, her name comes from the Old Irish word *dub*, meaning "dark." Her husband shot her with his sling, and she fell into a pool that was thereafter called Dubhlinn or Dublin.

**Dubheasa** (doo-VAH-sa)  The Old Irish words of *dub* meaning "dark" and *ess* meaning "waterfall." It means "dark woman of the waterfall."

**Dubh Lacha**  She was the wife of Mongan, who was born on the same night as she. She was kidnapped by Brandubh and rescued with the help of Cuimhne.

**Eabha** (AY-va)  The name of one of the wives of the legendary Nemed, an ancient immigrant to Ireland. It is the Old Irish spelling for the name Eva.

**Eachna** (AK-na)  Derived from the Old Irish *ech* meaning "horse." An ancient story tells of a woman by this name who was one of the most beautiful and clever women in the world.

**Eadan** (AH-dan)  Derived from the old name of Etan. Etan was the woman that the hero Cu Chulainn loved.

**Eadaoin** (eh-DEEN)  *Happy friend.*

**Earlene**  *Pledge.*

**Eavan** (E-van)  Several ancient Irish princesses had this name, which comes from the Old Irish *aibinn*, meaning "fair form."

**Ebliu**  Some sources say this name derives from another name of the sun goddess, while others think it comes from the Old Irish word *oiph*, meaning "beauty, sheen, radiance." Legends tell of Eibhliu, daughter of Guaire, who married Mairid, king of Munster. After a time she fell in love with his son Eochaid and persuaded him to run off with her. When they stopped at a spring well in Ulster, it overflowed, killing Eochaid and all but three of his family. Variants are EIBHLIU, EBLENN, and EIBHLEANN.

**Echna**  Derived from the Old Irish word *ech*, meaning "horse." Irish history tells of an Echna, daughter of Muiredach mac Finnachta, king of Leinster, who was one of the world's wisest women.

**Edana**  *Ardent or flame.* Possible variants are ETHNA, EDA, and EITHNA.

**Eibhlin** (eh-y-LEEN)    Light. Variants are EIBHLHIN, EILY, EBLIU, and AIBHILIN.

**Eibhlin** (ay-LEEN)    *Light.* Changed from the French name Aveline, which was brought to Ireland by Norman invaders. It was very popular among Irish nobility in the Middle Ages. A variant Irish spelling of this name is AIBHILIN.

**Eileen**    An Irish version of Helen. Variants are ELAN and ILENE.

**Eilinora** (EL-eh-nohr)    This is another Greek name meaning "light" whose spelling changed in the Irish version. Variants are LEAN (LEHN), and EILEANOIR.

**Eilis** (AY-leesh or EH-leesh)    *Consecrated to God.* This is an Irish form of the medieval Norman-French name Isabel and the English name Elizabeth. The famous blind harper Turlough O' Carolan wrote a song praising the beauty of Eilis nic Diarmada Rua.

**Eithne** (AY-he-ne or ETH-nuh)    *Kernel* or *seed.* The first Eithne in Irish mythology was the mother of the god Lugh. This was also the name of the wives of Conn of the Hundred Battles and Cormac mac Airt, as well as many legendary queens. There are also eight saints having this name.

**Elatha** (AHL-a-hah)    A female or male name that means "art" or "craft."

**Elva** (AL-va)    Old tales say she was the sister-in-law of the god Lugh.

**Emer** (EE-mer or ah-VAIR)    The most famous woman in Irish mythology having this name was the daughter of Forgall the Wily and the wife of the hero Cu Chulainn. Before Emer, the daughter of Forgall Manach, would agree to marry the hero, she made Cu Chulainn answer a series of riddles. She did this because she refused to marry before her sister Fial or before Cu Chulainn had won his reputation. When Cu Chulainn returned from studying the martial arts under Scota in Scotland, he carried off Emer along with two loads of gold and silver from her father's fortress. Legend says Emer had the six gifts of womanhood; beauty, voice, sweet speech, needlework, wisdom, and chastity. A variant of this name is EIMER.

**Ena**    Derived from the Celtic word meaning "fire." A variant is ENAT.

**Erin**    *Peace.* This name for Ireland comes from an ancient goddess whose name was Eriu. Eriu was one of the three queens of the Tuatha De Danann and a daughter of the Dagda. Variants are ERINA and ERIU (ERR-I-oo).

**Erlina**    A Gaelic name that means "girl from Ireland."

**Ernine**    Derived from *iarn,* meaning "iron." Either a male or female name. Legend lists a virgin daughter of Archenn with this name. Her feast day is February 28.

**Etan** (eh-TAIN)    This spelling refers to the daughter of the great Tuatha De Danann physician Dian Cecht who became the wife of the god Ogma.

**Etaoin** (AY-deen)    Probably comes from the Old Irish word *et* meaning jealousy. Etaoin was a traditional name in the families O'Connor, O'Hara, and O'Flannagan. Variants of this name are EADAOIN and ETAN.

**Ethniu**    In ancient legend, Ethniu was the daughter of the Fomor Balor of the Evil Eye. The Fomorians ruled in Ireland before the Tuatha De Danann came. In an attempt to create peace between the two races, she married Cian, the son of Dian Cecht. A variant of the name EITHNE.

**Fainche** (FAN-chuh)    Records tell of an early Saint Fainche of Rossory, County Fermanagh. Although she was courted by Oengus mac Natfraich, king of Cashel, she managed to get her sister to marry him, while she established a monastery on the shore of Lough Erne. Her feast day is January 1.

**Fallon**    *Grandchild of the ruler.* Variants are FALEN and FALLAN.

**Fand**    In legends of Ireland and the Isle of Man, Fand was a goddess of healing and pleasure who married the sea god Manannan mac Lir.

**Fedelm**    Some very famous women in Irish history had this name. The most interesting was Fedelm Noichrothach (Nine-Times Beautiful), daughter of Conchobhar mac Nessa, king of Ulster. Variant spelling is FEIDHELM (FAY-delm).

**Fenella**    A feminine version of the name Finn. A variant is FIONNGHUALA.

**Fethnaid**    Ancient legends tell of a Fethnaid who was the daughter of Fidach, who himself was a bard of the Tuatha De Danann. Fethnaid was an accomplished harp player, whose death was considered to be one of the three great losses of the Tuatha De Danann. A variant is FETHNAT.

**Fianait** (FYAN-it or FEE-nat)    This is an Old Irish word for "deer." Two early Irish saints had this name. A variant is FIONNAIT.

**Fidelma** (fee-DEL-ma) This name is derived from the Old Irish name of FEDELM. Several women in Irish mythology and history bore this name, as well as six Irish saints. The modern Irish spelling is FEIDHELM (FAY-delm).

**Finnsech** *Fair or blonde lady.* Two Irish saints had this name, Saint Finnsech of County Meath, whose celebration day is February 17 and Saint Finnsech of County Tyrone, whose feast day is October 13. A variant is FINNSEACH.

**Fiona** (FYUN-a or FEE-nuh) Derived from the word *finn,* meaning "fair, brilliant, white." A male or female name. Variants are FINNA and FIONN.

**Fionnabhair** (fyuhn-OOR) The Irish equivalent of the Welsh Gwenhwyfar (Guinevere), this name comes from the Old Irish *finn,* meaning "bright, fair" and *siabhre,* meaning "fairy" or "phantom." The daughter of the legendary King Aillil and Queen Maeve or Medb of Connacht had this name. A variant is FIONUIR.

**Fionnuala** (fin-NOO-a-la or fin-NOO-la) Derived from two Old Irish words, *finn,* meaning "bright, fair," and *guala,* meaning "shoulders." In ancient legends, Fionnuala was the daughter of Lir and Aobh; she and her brothers were turned into swans by their stepmother. During the Middle Ages this was a popular feminine name in the families of O'Brien, O'Connor, and McDermott. Variants of this name are FINOLA, FIONNGUALA, FIONNULA, and GWENETH. FENELLA is commonly used in Scotland, while FINVOLA is used in County Derry, Ireland. A nickname is NUALA (NOO-a-la).

**Flann** (FLAHN) Both a female and male name, this comes from the Old Irish *flann,* meaning "blood red." It has been the name of a great many queens, kings, poets, saints, and abbots in Ireland. Variants are FLANNACAN and FLANNA.

**Flannery** Derived from the Irish for "redhead."

**Flidais** An Irish goddess of forests, woodlands, and wild creatures. A powerful shapeshifter, she was said to ride in a chariot drawn by deer.

**Fodla** SOVEREIGNTY. In very ancient legends, Fodla was a goddess with Banba and Eriu who were all given the honor of naming Ireland.

**Fuamnach** She was the wife of Midir, the fairy king, and very jealous of his other wife Etain. To get rid of Etain, she used magic to turn her into a fly.

**Geileis** (GAY-leesh)   The name of several Irish princesses, it comes from the Old Irish name Gelgeis, which in turn comes from the words *gel,* meaning "shining, bright" and *geis,* meaning "swan."

**Glenna**   From a Gaelic word meaning "glen" or "valley." A variant is GLYNIS.

**Gobnait** (GOHB-nit)   This is a feminine version of the male name of a legendary Irish smith. It comes from the Old Irish word *gobha,* meaning "a smith." A very early female saint and abbess of Munster had the name GOBNAT, and once directed her bees against an attacking army and defeated them. The O'Herlihy family kept her beehive for many years as a holy relic. Her feast day is February 11.

**Gormlaith** (GOORM-la)   Derived from *gorm,* meaning "splendid," and *flaith,* meaning "queen, sovereignty." Some sources list the meaning as "blue princess" or "illustrious princess." Many queens of the Middle Ages also had this name. A variant is GORMGHLAITH (GOR-em-lee).

**Grania** (GRAW-nya)   The name of an ancient Irish grain goddess, this name comes from the word *grainne* or *gran,* meaning "grain" or "seed." Another source lists the meaning as "she who inspires terror." The legendary Grainne, who was betrothed to the elderly Finn mac Cumhaill, chose instead to elope with the irresistible Diarmaid. Variants of this name are GRANNA, GRAIN, and the modern GRAINNE (GRAW-ne).

**Granuaile**   An actual Irish woman who lived from 1530 until 1603. During the time of Elizabeth I, Grania Mhaol Ni Mhaolmhaigh (Grace O'Malley) was a seafaring chieftainess from the clan O'Malley of Clare, who fought against the English queen's forces. Both a wife and a mother, she sailed her own fleet of ships in pirate raids against English ships, frustrating Sir Richard Bingham who fought against her for years. A strong defendant of Irish customs and rights, she was popular with the Irish people. Finally, she met with Elizabeth I at Greenwich and was granted a charter that freely allowed her to sail the Western Seas.

**Grianne** (GROH-nyuh)   *Sun* or *sun goddess.* There is a hill near Pallas Green in County Limerick called Cnoc Greine. Legend says that this is the Otherworld seat of Grian, the sun goddess and daughter of Finn.

**Guennola**   Derived from the Celtic word meaning "white."

**Ina**  The Irish version of Agnes.

**Isibeal** (ISH-a-behl or i-se-BEL)  An Irish derivation of the Norman French name Isabel.

**Isleen** (ish-LEEN)  *Vision.* A variant is ISLENE.

**Ite** (EE-te)  Since this name comes from the Old Irish *ite,* meaning "thirst or devouring," the sixth century saint Ite, abbess of Killeedy in County Limerick, believed her name meant the thirst for divine love. She founded a monastery at Killeedy, where she died in 570. She wrote a famous lullaby to the baby Jesus. Her life is celebrated on January 15. Variants are IDE and ITA.

**Jilleen**  Derived from the Latin name Juliane or Julius, it means "youthful."

**Kacey**  A variant spelling of the name CASIE.

**Kaitlin**  A variant spelling of the name CAITLIN.

**Keara**  *Saint.* A variant of the name CIARA.

**Keavy**  *Gentleness, beauty, grace.*

**Keelin**  *Slender, fair.* Variants are KEELY and KEELIA.

**Keena**  Derived from the Irish word for "brave."

**Kelly**  Derived from a Gaelic word meaning "warrior woman." At the ancient shrine of the goddess Brigit at Kildare, there were sacred priestesses and warrior women who were called *kelles.* It is possible that the name and surname Kelly came from these priestesses.

**Kenna**  A version of the male name Kenneth. A variation is KEN-NICE.

**Kennocha** (ken-OH-kuh)  *Beauty.*

**Kerry**  Derived from a Gaelic word for "dark."

**Kevyn**  *Beautiful.* A variation is KEVA.

**Kiley**  Derived from the word for "attractive." Variants are KYLI and KYLEE.

**Labhaoise** (LAU-ee-shuh)  The Irish version of the Teutonic name Louisa, which means holiness.

**Laoise**  This name is possibly the same as LUIGSECH, a name derived from that of the god Lugh. The female version means "radiant girl." Records list a Saint Luigsech or Laoise, whose feast day is May 22.

**Lasair** (LOH-seer)  Popular in early Ireland, this name derives from the Old Irish word *lassa,* meaning "flames." Several female saints and queens bore this name, among them Saint LASSA of Meath, whose feast day is February 18.

**Lasairfhiona**    Derived from the words *lasair,* meaning "flame" and *fion,* meaning "wine." Historical records list many women of this name. A variant is LASAIRIONA.

**Lavena**    Derived from the Celtic word for "joy."

**Lebharcham**    The foster-mother of Deirdre and a female messenger who worked for Conchobar mac Nessa.

**Liadan** (LYAH-dan)    Probably means "gray lady." This ancient Irish name was held by two saintly women. One was a poetess and nun who loved the poet Cuirithur. According to legend, the other, the mother of Saint Ciaran of Seir, conceived her son after a falling star dropped into her mouth while she was sleeping.

**Luiseach** (LEE-sak)    A feminine name derived from the name of the god Lugh. It means "bringer of the light." This was also the name of an early female saint, whose holy day is celebrated on May 22. A variant is LUIGHSEACH.

**Mab** (MEEV)    A goddess and fairy queen, her name means "drunk woman." Some sources list the meaning as "wolf queen." A goddess of war, she was also said to be a Mother Goddess, who blessed kings through her fairy drink called "red mead." Later she was considered to be a queen of Connacht, a warrior queen of the Ulster cycle of stories. A variant spelling is MABH.

**Macha** (MAH-ka)    The goddess Macha whose name translates as "crow" or "battle," was one of three war goddesses of the Tuatha De Danaan. Her female warrior companions were Badb and Morrigan. Called the Mother of Life and Death, Macha was a protectress in war as in peace. There was also a Saint Macha of Killiney, whose feast day is February 6. Variants are MANIA and MENE.

**Maeve** (MAYV)    Some sources list this name as meaning "fragile," but it is more likely a variant of the name MEDB.

**Maire** (MAW-re or MAW-zhe or MEH-ree)    Because this name is derived from the name Mary, Irish girls were not given this name before the seventeenth century, as it was considered to be too sacred. Mael Muire (devotee of Mary) was used instead for both girls and boys. Maire ni Scolai, who was born in Dublin in 1909, collected, interpreted, and performed tradition Irish songs; she died in Galway in 1985. Variants are MOIRA, MAURA, and MAIRIN (maw-REEN).

**Mairead** (MAW-rayt or MAW-reed)    A form of the Greek name Margaret, which is derived from the Greek *margaron,* meaning "pearl," this name became popular in Ireland after the eleventh century, when Saint Margaret was queen of the Scots. Irish-language nicknames are PEIG and PEIGI.

**Margo** (MOHR-gaw)   This name comes from Old Irish legends of the fairy Margo, who was the mother of the beautiful woman Etain.

**Margreg**   An Irish version of the Latin name Margareta. This name became popular in Ireland after the marriage of Malcolm III of Scotland to Margareta of the Hungarian Court. The queen later became Saint Margaret. A variant is MAIRGHREAD.

**Maureen**   Derived from the Celtic word for "great."

**Mavelle**   From the Celtic word for songbird. A variant is MAVIE.

**Meagan**   A variation of MEDB.

**Meara**   *Merry.*

**Medb**   *Intoxicating* or *she who makes men drunk.* This name is very ancient and comes from the Old Irish name of Medb. The goddess of the kings of Tara was Medb Lethderg (Maeve of the Red Side). She was said to have been the consort of nine successive Irish kings, among them Conn of the Hundred Battles, his son Art, and Art's son Cormac mac Airt. Variants of this name are MEDB, MAEDHBH, and the modern spelling MEADHBH.

**Mell** (MAHL)   From the word *mall,* meaning "lightning." The sister of Saint Kevin had this name and was said to have been the mother of seven saints. A variant is MELLA (MAH-la).

**Melva**   Derived from the Celtic word for "chief."

**Meriel**   *Shining sea.* Variants are MERIOL and MURIEL.

**Mess Buachalla**   The translation of this name is "Cowherd's Fosterchild." It was the name of the the daughter of Etain and Cormac, king of Ulster. However, Cormac had the baby thrown out because he tired of Etain. The child was rescued by cowherds and later became the mother of Conaire by a birdman.

**Moina**   *Mild.* A variant is MOYNA.

**Moira**   Derived from the Celtic word for "great." A variant of the name MOR.

**Mona** (MOH-na)   Stemming from the word *muad,* meaning "noble, good," this modern spelling comes from the old Irish name of MUADNAT. January 6 is the feast day of Saint Muadnat of Drumcliffe. The modern Irish version is MUADHNAIT (MOO-uh-nit).

**Moninne**   Another version of the name Blinne. One Saint Moninne worked at the hospital at Kildare in the time of Saint Brighid where she healed the sick and gave generously to the poor. Later she moved to Killevy, County Armagh, where she established a community at the foot of Slieve Gullion. Her feast day is July 6.

**Mor** (MOHR)   One of the most popular Irish female names until the nineteenth century, Mor comes from the Old Irish word *mor*, which means "great" or "tall." The original Mor in ancient stories is considered to be the ancestress of the royal houses of Munster. She was a sun goddess whose throne is in the western seas of Ireland. Variations of this name are MOIRE, MORIN, and MOYA.

**Moriath**   The daughter of a Gaulic king, she was wooed and won by Craiftine.

**Morna**   From the word *muirne,* meaning "beloved."

**Morrigan** (MOHR-ee-gan)   Called the Great Queen, this Irish goddess was a war deity, although she never actually took part in battle. She was associated with crows and ravens (into which she often shapeshifted), magic, fate, and death. She always appeared fully armed and carried two spears. In later tales, Morrigan became the queen of the Fairies. Variant spellings are MORRIGHAN and MORGAN.

**Muadhnait**   Derived from the word *muad,* meaning "noble, good." A Saint Muadnat founded a monastery at Drumcliffe, County Sligo. Her feast day is January 6.

**Muireann** (MEER-an or MOHR-in)   Derived from the word *muir,* meaning "sea," or it may mean "sea-white" or "sea-fair." This name has been connected with some very important legendary Irish women. Muireann was the wife of Finn mac Cumhail's son Oisin. There was also a Queen Muireann, considered to be the ancestor of the kings of Connacht. Four abbesses of Kildare also had this name.

**Muirgheal** (MOHR-e-guhl)   Another name that means "sea-bright" or "sea-fair." A variant is MUIRGEL.

**Muirin** (MEER-een)   Derived from the words *muir,* meaning "sea," and *gein* meaning "birth," or "born of the sea," this name first appeared in a sixth century legend of a 300-year-old mermaid who was caught in Lough Neagh by fishermen of Saint Comgall. They had her baptized, thus causing her death, but ensuring her entry into heaven. Other versions of this name are MUIRGEN and MUIRENN.

**Muiriol** (MEER-ol)   The name of several early queens of Leinster, this name is derived from the Old Irish name MUIRGEL, which in turn comes from *muir,* meaning "sea" and *gel,* meaning "bright, shining."

**Muirne** (MEER-ne)   An ancient name meaning "high-spirited." Muirne Munchaem (Lovely-Shouldered Muirne) was the name of Finn mac Cumaill's mother.

**Murine**   The sister-in-law of Lugh and the mother of Fionn. Unable to protect Fionn after his father's death, Murine left him in the care of a druidess and a woman warrior.

**Myrna**   Derived from the Irish word for "beloved."

**Nainsi**   The Irish spelling of the name Nancy, which means "grace."

**Naomh**   The word in Irish means "a saint."

**Narbflaith**   *Noble princess.* Listed in records as the name of a series of princesses. This was also recorded as the name of a wife of an abbot of Trim, County Meath.

**Neala**   The female version of the name Niall, which means "champion."

**Nessa** (NES-ah)   An ancient legendary Irish name, Nessa was the mother of Conchobar mac Nessa, who was the great king of Ulster. Originally this woman was called ASSA, meaning "gentle." However, after she returned home one day to find her twelve foster-fathers murdered by a band of outlaws, she became a woman warrior so she could avenge their deaths. She then changed her name to Nessa or Niassa, meaning "ungentle."

**Nevina**   A feminine form of the name Nevin, which means "worshipper of the saint." A well-known Irish saint was named Nevin.

**Nia**   A variant of the welsh name Niamh. A variant spelling is NYA.

**Niamh** (NEE-av)   *Brightness, radiance, luster.* In ancient Irish mythology, Niamh was a goddess who helped heroes at death. Several legendary women bore the name Nia, the Old Irish version of this popular name. One of these women, Niamh Cinn Oir (Niamh of the Golden Head) was a princess of Tir-Nan-Og, or Land of Youth who took Oisin, Finn mac Cumhaill's son, to the Otherworld.

**Nila**   A feminine version of the male names Neil and Niall. A variant is NYLA.

**Nola**   A shortened version of FIONNULA. A variant is NUALA.

**Nora** (NOH-ra)   This classic Irish name for females is a version of the Latin name Honoria, which means "honor."

**Noreen**  The Irish spelling of the name Nora or Eleanor.

**Odarnat**  Derived from the word for "otter" or the word for "sallow female." One saint with the feast day of November 13 had this name, but nothing is known of her. Variants are ODHARNAIT and ORNAIT.

**Odharnait** (OHR-nat)  Some sources list the meaning as "pale, olive-colored," while others say this name is a variant of ODARNAT. Another variant is ORNA.

**Oilbhe** (OL-iv)  The Irish spelling of the name OLIVE.

**Onora**  A version of the name HONORA.

**Oona**  A variant of the name UNA. Other variants are OONAGH and ONA.

**Orghlaith** (OHR-e-lath)  From a word meaning "golden lady." Variants are ORLAITHE and ORLA.

**Oriana**  Derived from the word "golden."

**Orla** (OHR-la)  Derived from the Old Irish *or*, meaning "gold," and *flaith*, meaning "queen." In twelfth-century records, this name was the fifth most popular for females. Both the sister and a niece of Brian Boru bore this name. The king of Breifne had a daughter named Orlaith. During the Middle Ages, the name Orla was very popular in Ireland. The modern spelling is ORLAITH.

**Ornice**  *Olive-colored.*

**Padraigin** (PAH-dri-geen)  Derived from the Latin word for "noble," this is a feminine form of the male name Padraig.

**Payton**  A form of the male name Patrick or Padraig.

**Quincy**  *Fifth.*

**Ranait** (RAN-eh)  Derived from the word for "prosperity, grace."

**Reganne**  Derived from the word for "royal." A variant is REGEEN.

**Richael**  Some sources list this name as meaning saint.

**Rigru Roisclethan**  The queen of Benn Edair, a place in the Otherworld. When Conn Cetchathach was about to kill her son at Tara, she appeared as a wailing woman.

**Riley**  *Valiant.* A variant is RILEIGH.

**Riomthach**  One of the five sisters of Saint Colman of County Cork had this name. The church that Saint Colman founded was known as *Cill Inghean Leinin* (Church of the Daughters of Lenine, who was the saint's father). A variant is RIOFACH.

**Riona**  From the word for "saint."

**Rionach** (REE-un-nak)   From the Old Irish name of RIGNACH, which means "queenly." Legends tell of a Queen Rionach who was the ancestress of the families of O'Neill, MacLoughlin, O'Donnell, O'Gallagher, and O'Gromley. Other versions of this name are RIOGHNACH and RIONA.

**Rori**   Derived from the word meaning "famous," or "brilliance."

**Ros** (ROHS)   There is some confusion over the origin of this name. It may come from the Germanic *hros,* meaning "horse," or the English word "rose." It has been a traditional name in the families O'Kane and O'Murray for centuries. Versions of this name are ROISIN (row-SHEEN) and ROISE.

**Rowena**   Derived from the word meaning "white mane" or "white hair."

**Ryann**   The feminine version of the name Ryan. It means "little ruler."

**Rylee**   A variant of the name RILEY. Another variant form is RYLYN.

**Sadhbh** (SAH-eev or SAYV)   The similar Old Irish name of Sadb may mean "sweet" or "goodness." Daughters of Queen Medb of Connacht, of King Brian Boru, and of Conn of the Hundred Battles all had this name. The Sadbh of ancient legends was the mother of Oisin by Fionn. She was enchanted into the form of a deer and could only have her human shape when she was within the dun of the Fianna. Variants are SIVE, SADHBBA, SADBH, SABHBH, and SABHA (SE-va).

**Saoirse**   A male or female name. This name comes from an Irish word *saor,* meaning "freedom or liberty."

**Saorla** (SAYR-la)   Comes from the Old Irish name Saerlaith, which is derived from *saer,* meaning "noble," and *flaith,* meaning "queen."

**Saraid**   *Clear, bright.*

**Scathach** (SKAW-hak)   Derived from *scath* meaning "shadow, shade." The goddess Scathach, also known as SCOTA and SCATHA, was considered to be an Underworld deity in the old legends. She also was a warrior woman and prophetess who lived in Albion (Scotland), probably on the Isle of Skye, where she taught the martial arts. She taught the Ulster hero Cu Chulainn there.

**Sceanbh**   The wife of the harper Craiftine, her betrayal with Cormac caused the harper to try to kill Cormac.

**Seana**   A variant of the names SINE and SHAUNA.

**Seanait** (SHAY-nat)   A variant spelling of the Old Irish name SEGNAT, which comes from *seig,* meaning "a hawk."

**Searlait** (SHEHR-let)   The Irish spelling of the French Norman name Charlotte. It means "petite, feminine."

**Seosaimhthin** (SHOH-sa-veen)   The Irish spelling of the name Josephine, meaning "God will add." A variant spelling is SEO-SAIMHIN.

**Shanley**   The hero's child. A variant is SHANLEIGH.

**Shannon** (SHAH-non)   This is the name of the longest river in Ireland, which takes its name from the goddess Siannan (or Siann), the granddaughter of Manannan Mac Lir, the sea god. Although this is a popular first name in the United States, it is not used as a first name in Ireland. A variant spelling is SHANNA.

**Shea**   A variant spelling of the Irish word *sidhe* (shee), which means "fairy palace." Variants are SHAE and SHEALY.

**Sierra**   Derived from the word meaning "black." A variant is SEARA.

**Sile** (SHEE-la)   Also written as SHEELA, this is an Irish form of Cecilia. The Franks brought the name to Ireland, where it became very popular during the medieval period.

**Sine** (SHEE-na)   In County Derry this is a variation of the name SINEAD. This name is an Irish form of the French names Jeanne and Jeanette. Variants are SINA, SEENA, SHEENA, SHENA, SINA, SHANA, SHAUNA, SHAY, SHONA, SHONDA, SHAWNDA, SHONTA, and SHUNTA.

**Sinead** (shi-NAYD)   This is an Irish version of the French Norman names Jonet and Jeanne.

**Siobhan** (shi-VAWN)   Another Irish version of the French Norman name Jeanne, this name is a feminine version of John. Variant spellings are SIBAN, SHIBAHN, and SIOBHANIN (SHI-vawn-EEN).

**Siomha** (SHEE-va)   A version of an Old Irish name Sithmaith, which comes from *sith,* meaning "peace," and *maith,* meaning "good." An eighth-century abbess of Clonburren had this name.

**Slaine** (SLAY-nye or SLAHN-nuh)   A medieval name used by the Mac-Namaras and O'Briens meaning "good health."

**Sloane**   *Warrior.*

**Sorcha** (SOO-ruh-ka or SOHR-e-khuh)   This comes from the old word *sorchae,* meaning "bright, radiant." This name has remained popular in Ireland from the Middle Ages.

**Taillte**   In Irish legend Tailtiu was the foster-mother of the god

Lugh, and daughter of a Spanish king who married Eochaid of the Tuatha De Danann. An Earth Goddess, she was connected with fertility, peace, and prosperity. Connected with Lughnassadh (Lugh) on August 1, she and Lugh were later honored by games in honor of the dead at Mag Taillten in County Meath. The last time these celebrations were held with public approval was in 1168. The town is now known as Teltown on the River Blackwater. Until the eighteenth or nineteenth centuries "Teltown Marriages" were held in the ring-fort of Rath Dugh. If the couple did not want to continue the marriage at the end of a year and a day, they returned to the fort, stood with their backs to each other, and walked away. Variants are TAILLTIU and TAILTIU.

**Tara** (TAH-ra)   Tara was the traditional seat of Irish kingship. Some sources list the meaning of this name as "tower." The legendary Teamair, wife of Eremon who led the Sons of Mil (Irish ancestors) originally gave her name to the sacred hill of Tara.

**Teamhair** (TOHR)   Probably means "eminence" or "elevated place." Some sources list this name as a version of the name Tara.

**Tierney**   From the word meaning "noble." A variant is TIERNAN.

**Tipper**   *Water pourer.*

**Tlachtga**   A daughter of Mog Ruith, she traveled throughout the world with her father and learned all his magic. She was connected with prophecy and foretelling. Druids lit their Samhain (October 31) fires on her mound twelve miles from Tara.

**Toireasa** (toh-REH-suh)   An Irish form of the name Teresa, meaning "harvester."

**Treasa**   *Strength.* Although this name has been used as an equivalent of the name Teresa, it has no connection. Variants are TREISE and TOIREASA.

**Trevina**   *Prudent.* A feminine version of Trevor. A variant is TREVA.

**Troya**   Derived from the Irish word for "foot soldier."

**Tullia**   *Peaceful, quiet.* Variants are TULIA and TULLIAH.

**Tuiren**   An Otherworld woman who was Fionn's aunt and married to Iollan, one of the Fianna.

**Uathach**   The daughter of Scathach, her name means "specter." She became the mistress of Cu Chulainn after her husband died.

**Ula**   *Sea jewel.* Variants are ULI and ULICIA.

**Una** (OO-na)   Derived from the old word *uan,* meaning "lamb."

Other sources list the meaning as "unity." In Old Irish legends, a king of Locklainn had a daughter by this name. The mother of Conn Cetchathach (Conn of the Hundred Battles) had this name. The O'Carroll family also had a *bean sidhe* (banshee) with this name.

## MALE NAMES

**Abban** (A-bahn or ah-BAN)    *Little abbot.* Saint Abban mac ua Cormaic is said to have been associated with a church at Adamstown in County Wexford. His feast day is March 16.

**Adair**    *From the ford by the oak trees.* A variant is ADARE.

**Adamnan**    *The timid one.* One of the great abbots of Iona had this name. He was born near Raphoe in 624. When he returned briefly to Ireland during the crisis with the Saxon raiders, he was able to negotiate the release of sixty Irish captives and an end to the raids. He became abbot of Iona in 679 and died in 704. His celebration day is September 23. Variants are AWNAN, ADOMNAN, and ADHAMHAN.

**Aed**    Derived from the word *aedh,* meaning "fire." In early Ireland it was a very common name for men. Several early saints, including Aedh mac Bricc of Rahugh, County Westmeath, had this name. Four Ui Neill High Kings also had this name.

**Aedan** (EH-thahn)    A diminutive form of AED. The saint Aodhan of Ferns went to Wales and studied under Saint David. There he performed many miracles, including healing the lame and blind son of a British king. When he returned to Ireland, he established a monastery at Ferns in County Wexford. His celebration day is January 31.

**Aeducan**    A quite common diminutive form of Aed in medieval Ireland. The last of the great Munster poets was Aodhagan O' Raithile, born in Kerry in 1670. He was buried at Muckross Abbey. A variant is AODHAGAN.

**Ahern**    *Lord of the horses.*

**Aidan** (AY-duhn)    *Fiery.* This is another name derived from *aedh,* meaning fire.

**Ailbhe** (AL-vyuh or AL-fe)    A male or female name that comes from the Celtic *albho,* meaning "white." There was a Saint Ailbe, who lived in the sixth century and was said to have been raised by a wolf. His holy day is September 12.

**Ailbhis** (AL-vis)    The name of a sixth century Irish saint, this name may be a form of AILBHE.

**Ailill**    Ailill mac Matach was the name of a legendary king of Connacht and the husband of Medb. The arguments with his wife over the merits of their bulls caused the famed epic, *The Cattle Raid of Cooley.*

**Ailin** (A-lin or ay-LEEN)    Possibly derived from the Old Irish word *ail* meaning noble.

**Aindrea** (AHN-dree-ah)    The Irish version of the name Andrew.

**Alan**    *Handsome* or *peaceful.*

**Alaois** (A-leesh)    An Irish version of a Norse name meaning "mighty battle."

**Alastar** (AH-lah-star)    An Irish version of the Greek name Alexander. This name came to Ireland from Scotland, where the modern version is Alasdair.

**Alpin**    *Attractive.*

**Alsandair**    The Irish form of Alexander.

**Amargein** (aw-VEER-een)    Derived from the words *amar,* meaning "singing" or "song," and *gein,* meaning "birth." The legendary Amargein was the druid, poet, and judge of the Sons of Mil, the ancestors of the Irish. His magic helped his invading people to overcome the Tuatha De Danann. This is a traditional name in the family O'Clery.

**Amhlaoibh** (A-leev)    An Irish form of a Norse name meaning "ancestral relic."

**Aodh** (EH or AY)    Derived from the word *aed,* meaning "fire," this was another name of the god Dagda. A common male name in early Ireland, this was the name of six High Kings and twenty Irish saints.

**Aodhan** (EH-dawn or AY-dawn)    A version of the Old Irish name Aedan, this name also comes from the word for "fire." Twenty-one early Irish saints bore this name.

**Aonghus** (AYNG-guhs)    Derived from *oen,* meaning "one," and *gus,* meaning "vigor." This is the mythological name of Oengus, a Tuatha De Danann god of youth and love, who was the son of the goddess Boann and the god Dagda. His golden harp made irresistibly sweet

music, and his kisses turned into birds that carried messages of love.
Legend says he had a fairy palace (*brugh*) on the banks of the River
Boyne. A legendary hero and the ancestor of the O'Briens and Mac-
Namaras was Oengus Tirech. Five saints also had this name.

**Ardal** (AHR-dawl)    From the Old Irish words *art*, meaning "bear,"
and *gal*, meaning "fury," or "valor." Ardal was a traditional name in
the families MacMahon, O'Connelly, MacCabe, McKenna, and
MacArdle. Other versions are ARTEGAL and ARTHGALLO.

**Ard-Greimne**    *High power.* He was the father of Scathach and Aoife,
who taught the martial arts on the Isle of Skye.

**Arlen**    Pledge. Variant forms are ARLAND and ARLYN.

**Art**    Derived from the word *art*, meaning "bear." Not a nickname
for the English Arthur, this was an ancient Irish Celtic male name,
derived from the same word. One man with the name Art was the
son of Conn Cetchathach. He was banished from Ireland by his
stepmother Becuma who desired him. After a perilous quest, he
won the hand of Delbchaem, daughter of King Morgan. This was a
traditional name among the families O'Hara, MacMurrough,
O'Connor, O'Mulloy, O'Rouke, O'Neill, MacKiernan, and O'Keeffe.
A variant is ARTAGAN.

**Artur** (AR-toor)    First recorded in the ninth century in Ireland, this
is a form of the British masculine name Arthur. Variants are ARTAIR,
ARTHUR, ARTUS, and ARTH.

**Bain**    A shortened version of Bainbridge, which means "fair bridge."

**Baird**    *Bard, poet, traveling minstrel.* A variant is BARD and BAIRDE.

**Bairre** (BAW-re)    A form of the names Bearach and Finnbarr, this is
also used as a separate name.

**Bairrfhionn** (BAR-fin)    A male or female name meaning "fair-haired."
Several male Irish saints had this name, including Barrfhionn of Kil-
barron, County Donegal. Diminutives of this name are BAIRRE,
BARRE, and BARRA.

**Banning**    *Fair and small.*

**Barram**    A version of the name BARRFHION, as is BARRFIND.

**Barry**    *Spearman.*

**Beacan** (BE-kawn or BA-kawn)    Derived from *bec*, meaning "little,"
and *an* (a diminutive), it was the name of a saint who founded one
of the monasteries in Westmeath in the sixth century. His feast day
is May 26.

**Beagan**  *Small.*

**Bearach** (BA-rak)  From the Old Irish word *berach*, meaning "pointed" or "sharp." Many Irish saints were named Berach, including the patron saint of the O'Hanlys, whose holy day is celebrated on February 15.

**Bearchan** (BAR-uh-hawn or BAR-uh-kawn)  This is a diminutive form of the name Bearach. In early Ireland this was another common name of saints.

**Bearnard**  The Irish form of the name Barney, which means "having the courage of a bear."

**Beircheart** (BEHR-khart)  An Anglo-Saxon name adopted by the Irish. It means "bright army."

**Belenus**  A sun and fire god, this Irish god was similar to the Greek Apollo and closely connected to the druids. His name can be seen in the word Beltane, the name of an ancient festival held on May 1. On Beltane, cattle were driven between bonfires for purification and fertility. Some sources say his Irish name was Bile.

**Benen** (BEH-non)  *Blessed.* A variant is BEINEON.

**Bevan**  *Youthful warrior.*

**Blaine**  *Thin or lean.*

**Blair**  *Plain or field.*

**Blathmac** (BLAW-vak)  Derived from the words *blath*, meaning "flower," and *mac*, meaning "son," this name was popular during the early days in Ireland.

**Bodb** (BOVE)  Bodb the Red was a son of the Dagda and eventually succeeded his father as king of the Tuatha De Danann. He was primarily connected with southern Ireland, the Galtee Mountains, and Lough Dearg. At Lough he had a *sidhe*, or underground fairy palace.

**Bogart**  *Bog* or *marshland.*

**Bowie** (BOO-ee)  *Yellow-haired.* A variant form is BOWEN.

**Brady**  *Spirited.* A variant form is BRADAIGH.

**Bram**  The Irish form of the name Abraham. A variant is ABRACHAM.

**Bran** (BRAWN)  A name found in both Irish and Welsh myths, this name is derived from the word *bran*, meaning "raven." This was a very popular name during the Middle Ages, and was traditional among the O'Byrnes.

**Brandubh** (BRAWN-doov)  From the Old Irish words *bran*, meaning "raven," and *dubh,* meaning "black." This was the name of a seventh-century king of Leinster and two saints with feast days on February 6 and June 3.

**Breandan** (BRAWN-dan)   Possibly derived from the Welsh word *brenhin,* meaning "king" or "prince." *The Voyage of Saint Brendan* is the story of an eighth-century Irish saint who sailed the Atlantic Ocean in a *curragh* (leather-clad boat) and reached North America. His holy day is May 16. Variations of this name are BREANAINN (BREH-neen), BRENDIS, BRANNON, and BRYN.

**Breasal** (BREE-sal)   Hi Breasil was another name for Tir-Nan-Og, or Fairyland. It was sometimes described as a land across the west sea where part of the Tuatha De Danann retreated, a place where the old were made young again. As a personal name it would mean "land of the young," or "land of the blessed."

**Breck**   *Freckled.* Variant forms are BREC and BREXTON.

**Bress**   The son of Elathan of the Fomors who married the goddess Brighid. The Fomors were a sea-dwelling race who opposed the Tuatha De Danann over Ireland and lost.

**Bret**   A name derived from the country Brittany.

**Brian** (BREE-an)   May come from the Celtic word *brig,* meaning "high, noble." In ancient Irish myth, Brian was one of the three sons of the goddess Danu, who was the head of the Tuatha De Danann. Later, Brian Boru, who ruled Ireland from 1002 until 1014, was a historical High King who defeated the Vikings at the battle of Clontarf. This is a traditional name among such families as the O'Connors, MacDonaghs, MacGoverns, O'Kellys, and MacMahons.

**Bricriu**   A mischief-maker at the court of Conchobar, where he instigated a rivalry among the heroes Cu Chulainn, Conall, and Loegaire.

**Brody**   *Ditch or man from the muddy place.*

**Brogan**   There is no agreement on the meaning of this name. Although several saints bore this name, the most interesting one was Brogan, scribe to Saint Patrick during his meeting with the Fianna. A variant is BROCCAN.

**Caeoimhin**   *Gentle.* A variant spelling is sometimes listed as CAEMGEN.

**Cahan**   A male or female name derived from *cath,* meaning "battle" or "warrior." The first Cathan mentioned in Irish tales was the grandson of Niall of the Nine Hostages.

**Cailean** (CAL-lan)   A Gaelic word meaning "child." Probably connected with the name Colin.

**Cairbre** (KAHR-bre)   In ancient legends, Cairbre was one of the Sons of Mil to settle in Ireland. Later there were two well-known saints who bore this name.

**Cairell**   Several Irish saints had this name. Saint Cairell of Tir Rois helped found the monastery at Lynally, County Westmeath. His special day is June 13. A variant is COIREALL.

**Cairpre** (KAIR-pre)   The legendary Cairpre was the chief bard of the Tuatha De Danann and the son of the god Ogma. Cairpre Liffechair wiped out the Fianna at the Battle of Gabhra where he killed Fionn's grandson.

**Calbhach**   Derived from a word meaning "bald," this name was popular among certain Irish families, including the O'Donnells.

**Caley**   An alternate Irish form of the name Caleb.

**Calhoun**   *Narrow woods.* Variant spellings are COILLCUMHANN and COLQUHOUN.

**Callough** (KAHL-uh)   *Bald.* Other forms of this name are CALVAGH and CALBHACH (KAHL-ahkh).

**Callum**   *Dove.* It comes from the name Columba.

**Caoilte** (KWEEL-te)   In legends, Cailte was a member of Finn mac Cumaill's renowned warrior band. He was said to have returned from the Otherworld to tell Saint Patrick the true stories of Finn mac Cumaill and other Irish Pagan heroes.

**Caoimhin** (kwee-VEEN)   This name comes from the Old Irish name of Caemgen, which is derived from the words *caem,* meaning "gentle," and *gein,* meaning "birth." A seventh-century Saint Caemgen is said to have founded the monastery at Glendalough in County Wicklow. His day is June 3.

**Caolan** (KWEE-lahn)   *Slender.*

**Carlin**   A Gaelic name meaning "little champion." A variant is CARLEY.

**Carney**   Some sources list the meaning as "warrior," while others say it means "victorious." Variant forms are CEARNACH, CAR, and KEARN.

**Carrick**   *Rock.* Variant spellings are CAROOQ and CARRAIG.

**Casey**   *Brave.*

**Cass** (KAHS)   From the word *cas,* meaning "curly." In early Ireland this was a popular male name. A man bearing this name is said to have been one of the ancestors of the families O'Brien, MacNamara, and O'Grady.

**Cassidy**   Some sources say this name comes from a word meaning "clever," while others say it means "curly hair."

**Cathair** (KAH-heer)   Some sources list this name as meaning "battle-lord." The legendary ancestor of the Leinstermen, Cathair Mar, was said to have fathered thirty-three sons and reigned for fifty years. A variant is CATHAOIR.

**Cathal** (KA-hal or KOH-hal)   Derived from the Old Irish word *cath*, meaning "battle," this name means "strong in battle." During the Middle Ages this was a popular name. The families MacManus, Maguire, and MacDonagh used this as a traditional name.

**Cathaoir** (KAH-heer)   *Warrior.* A variant form is CATHAIR (KA-heer).

**Cathbad**   The legendary name of the druid and son of Conchobar mac Nessa. He prophesied Cu Chulainn's warrior valor and the sorrow that Deirdriu would cause Conchobar of Ulster.

**Cavan**   Comes from the name CAOIMHIN. A variant is CAVIN.

**Ceallach**   *Bright-headed.* This name was borne by several Leinster rulers, as well as Irish saints. Saint Ceallach of Killala, County Mayo, was the son of King Connacht. Variants are CELLACH and KELLY.

**Ceallachan** (CAL-a-kawn)   There is some dispute over the meaning of this name. Some sources give the meaning as "one who frequents churches," others give it as "one who is warlike."

**Cearbhall** (KAHR-e-val or KEE-a-ruhl)   The Old Irish spelling of this name was Cerball or Cerbhall. Several early kings of Ossory and Leinster bore this name, which has become traditional among the O'Dalys.

**Cedric**   *Chieftain.*

**Chad**   A Celtic name meaning "defender."

**Chullain** (KUHL-in)   A mythic name that comes from CU CHULLAIN.

**Cian** (KEE-an or KEEN)   From the word *cian*, meaning "ancient, enduring." In the ancient legends of the Tuatha De Danann, Cian was the son of the god of healing, Dian Cech. He married Ethniu, the daughter of Balor the Fomor and became the father of the hero-god Lugh. Variants are CIANAN (KEE-nahn), KIAN, KEON, and KEAN.

**Ciaran** (KEER-an)   Derived from *ciar*, meaning "dark," and *an*, a diminutive. September 6 is the feast day of a sixth-century Saint Ciaran who founded the monastery of Clonmacnoise.

**Ciarrai** (KEH-ehr-ee)  The masculine version of the Irish county Kerry used as a name.

**Cillene**  May be derived from *cill,* meaning "church." A Saint Cillene was said to have made all the wine in the castle of Count Eulfus disappear when he was refused a drink. He made the wine reappear after an apology was given. A variant is KILLIAN.

**Cillian** (KEEL-yan)  A variant of CEALLACH, this name means "war or strife."

**Cinaed**  Some sources say that this name was borrowed into Old Irish from the Picts of Scotland. Records tell of several men with this name who were killed in battle with the Cruithne, among them Cinaedh Cairgge, son of Cathasach; Cinaedh, son of Conchobhar; and Cinaedh, son of the king of the Dal nAraidhe of the North.

**Cinneide** (kih-NEE-juh)  An old Irish spelling of the name Kennedy, which means "helmeted head."

**Clancy**  *Red-headed fighter.*

**Cleary**  Derived from a word meaning "learned."

**Cluny**  From a word that means "meadow."

**Coinneach** (KUH-nukh or KI-nek)  The Old Irish spelling of this name was Cainnech, which comes from *cain,* meaning "good, beautiful." The city of Kilkenny takes its name from a sixth-century Saint Cainnech who founded monasteries in Ireland and Scotland. This saint's feast day is October 11.

**Coireall** (kohr-EE-ahl)  The Irish version of the name Cyril, which means "lord."

**Collin**  A variant of the Irish names CHULAINN and CULIN.

**Colm** (KUHL-uhm)  Derived from the Latin word *columba,* meaning "dove." One of the most important Irish saints, along with Patrick, was Colm Cille, "dove of the church," who was born into the royal Ui Neill clan and lived in the sixth century. He was banished to Scotland for copying a book without the owner's permission. Once in Scotland, Colm Cille founded the monastery on Iona. His feast day is June 9.

**Colman** (KOHL-mawn)  A diminutive name derived from the name COLM. Early Irish records reveal more than 200 Irish saints bearing this name.

**Coman** (KOH-mahn)  *Bent.*

**Comhghall** (KOH-gahn or CO-en)  *Fellow hostage.* The birth of Saint

Comhghall of Bangor was predicted sixty years before by Saint Patrick. He founded a monastery at Bangor in around 555, which eventually housed 4,000 monks. It became known as The Vale of the Angels. His feast day is May 10. A variant is COMGAL.

**Conaire** (KAW-nir-re)    Possibly comes from the words *cu* (con), meaning "wolf, hound," and *aire,* meaning "farmer, landowner." One of the most notable Irishmen to bear this name was Conaire Mess Buachalla (Big Conaire), a High King of Tara who appears in the tale, *The Destruction of Da Derga's Hostel.* Legend says this Conaire was the son of a princess and a bird-man. Variants are CONOR, CONLAN, and CONROY.

**Conall** (KAW-nal)    Derived from the word *cu,* meaning "hound," or "wolf." Some sources list the meaning as "strong as a wolf." Many Irishmen of legend bore this name, including the fabled hero of Ulster, Conall Cernach.

**Conan** (KOH-nawn)    Derived from the Celtic word *kuno,* meaning "great, high." Some sources list the meaning as "hound" or "wolf," or "wisdom." Six Irish saints had this name. The most famous Conan was Conan mac Morna, a member of Finn mac Cuhaill's warrior band. The original Conann was the son of the Tuatha De Danann woman Febar and a Fomor king. A variant is CONANN.

**Conchobar** (KON-kho-var or KROO-ar)    This name is derived from *cu,* meaning "hound" or "wolf," and *cobar,* meaning "desiring," thus meaning "wolf-lover" or "lover of hounds." The most famous man with this name was Conchobar mac Nessa, king of the Ulaid (Ulstermen), whose royal seat was at Emhain Macha. His jealousy led to the treacherous death of Naoise and the suicide of his lover Deirdre. A variant is CONCHOBHAR.

**Conlaed**    Some sources say this name is derived from *connla,* meaning "prudent" or "chaste," and *aed,* meaning "fire." Saint Conlaed was the first bishop to serve at Kildare over the monks after the monastery admitted men. His feast day is May 3. A variant is CONLAODH.

**Conlaoch** (CON-la)    The son of Cu Chulainn and the warrior woman Aoife.

**Conley** (KAWN-lay)    The most famous person with this rare, old name was Conlaed, a sixth-century bishop of Kildare. He was head of the school that taught manuscript illumination. His feast day is May 3. A variant is CONLETH (KOHN-leth).

**Conn** (KOHN)  Another ancient Irish name derived from *cu,* meaning "wolf" or "hound." The most famous man bearing this name was Conn Cethchathach (Conn of the Hundred Battles), who was a High King. The families O'Neill, O'Donnell, O'Rourke, O'Flaherty, and O'Dowd claim this Conn as an ancestor.

**Connacht**  An Irish county.

**Connla**  A legendary name that means "son of Conn." A variant spelling of CONLAOCH.

**Connlaio**  A variant of the names CONLEY and CONLETH.

**Connlaoi** (KOHN-lee)  *Chaste fire.* Variants are CONNOLLY and CON-LETH.

**Conor** (KAW-nor)  Derived from the name CONCHOBAR, *cu,* meaning "wolf" or "hound," and *cobar,* meaning "desiring." Conchobar mac Nessa was the king of Ulster who appears in the epic, *The Cattle Raid of Cooley.*

**Conri** (KAWN-ree)  This is one of the earliest recorded names of Irish men and comes from *cu,* meaning "hound" or "wolf" and *ri,* meaning "king." A variant is CONROY.

**Conway**  From a word meaning "hound or wolf of the plain."

**Corc**  Born Conall mac Luigthig and fostered by the witch Fedelm, Corc received his name after his ear was magically singed red during a ritual. He went to the court of the King of the Picts and married the king's daughter before returning to Ireland to found his own dynasty at Femhen.

**Corcoran**  *Ruddy* or *red.* A variant name of the legendary CORC.

**Cormac** (KAWR-mak)  Some sources say this name is derived from the words *corbaid,* meaning "defile," and *mac,* meaning "son," while others list the meaning as "charioteer." Several legendary and historical men bore this name. Another popular name in early Ireland, this was the name of many kings, bishops, and saints.

**Corrigan**  From a word meaning "spearman." Variant spellings are COREY and CORRIN.

**Cosgrove**  Derived from a word meaning "victor" or "champion."

**Cowan**  Some sources list the meaning of this name as "hillside hollow."

**Coyle**  Derived from a word meaning "leader in battle."

**Craiftine**  He was a harper to Labraid Longseach. His harp was made of a wood that had retained a secret about the king.

**Craig**  *A steep rock* or *crag*. A variant is CRAIGEN.

**Credne**  The bronze-smith god of the Tuatha De Danann and one of the triad of smiths. He helped Dian Cecht make the silver arm for Nuada.

**Criofan** (KREE-fan)  Derived from the Old Irish name of CRIMTHANN, meaning "a fox." Ten of Finn mac Cumaill's warriors were named Criofan. Saint Crimathann has a feast day on May 23.

**Criostoir** (KRIS-ter)  The Irish version of the name Christopher, which means "Christ bearer."

**Crofton**  *A small town with little houses and fields.*

**Cu Chulainn** (KOO KUHL-in)  One of the greatest heroes of Irish legends was Cu Chulainn, whose birth name was Setanta. After he killed the watchdog of Culann, a smith, he assumed the dog's duties for a time and was given the name Cu Chulainn, which means "hound of Culann." He studied the martial arts under the goddess Scathach on the Isle of Skye. Other early names which begin with *cu* (dog) are Cu Maige (Hound of the Plain), Cu Mara (Hound of the Sea), and Cu Coigriche (Hound of the Border). Cu was a common title of Celtic chieftains.

**Cu Roi**  The full name of this king of Munster was Cu Roi mac Daire. He had great Otherworld powers. Because she loved Cu Chulainn, his wife Blanaid helped the hero kill Cu Roi.

**Cu Uladh** (koo-ULL-uh)  *Hound of Ulster.* Variants are COOLEY and CULLO.

**Cuirithir**  A poet, Cuirithir loved a woman named Liadin, but she refused to marry him and became a nun instead.

**Culann**  A variant of CU CHULAINN. The Culann of Irish legend was an Irish chief. Cu Chulainn served him for a time as payment for killing his dog. A variant is CULIN.

**Culley**  Some sources give the meaning of this name as "woods."

**Cumhea** (kuhm-EH)  *Hound of the plains.* Variants are COOEY, CUU-LAGH, COOLEY, CULLO, and COVEY.

**Cunningham**  Possibly means "village of the milk pail."

**Curran**  Derived from a word meaning "hero." A variant is CURREY.

**Dagda**  This god was primarily called the Good God, but he had other titles, such as All-father, Great God, Lord of Life and Death, and High King of the Tuatha De Danann. As the master of all trades and lord of perfect knowledge, the Dagda was said to have four great palaces in the depths of the earth and under the hollow hills. The most important of his children were Brighid, Aongus, Midir, Ogma, and Bodb the Red. His great cauldron, called the Undry, supplied unlimited food, while his living oak harp caused the seasons to change in perfect order. A variant spelling is DAGHDA.

**Daibhead** (DEH-vid or da-VEECH)    The Irish spelling of the name David, this name was mainly used among the cleric, not the general population. Several Irish saints with connections to Wales bore this name. Variants are DAIBHEID and DAIGHI.

**Daigh**    *Flame or fire.* Saint Daigh of Inishkeen became a famous craftsman at Bangor and Clonmacnoise. He worked in metals. His feast day is August 18.

**Daimine**    Derived from the word *dam,* meaning "deer" or "ox." Daimin Daimairgit, king of Airgialla, died in 564. A variant is DAIMHIN.

**Daire** (DEH-ruh or DI-re)    An Old Irish word that meant "fruitful" or "fertile." This name may once have applied to an ancient fertility deity or bull-god. The Brown Bull of Cooley was owned by Daire mac Fiachna. Daire's refusal to loan his bull to Queen Medb was part of the cause of the fight between the Ulstermen and the men of Ireland. Other variants are DARY and DARRAGH.

**Daithi** (DAH-hee)    *Swiftness or nimbleness.*

**Daley**    Some sources give the meaning as "an assembly," while others say it means "a valley." Variant forms are DAWLEY and DALE.

**Damhlaic** (DAW-lik)    The Irish version of the name Dominic.

**Daray**    An Irish adaptation of the French-Norman name D'aray, which means "dark."

**Darren**    Derived from a word meaning "great."

**Dearg**    *Son of the Dagda.*

**Declan** (DEK-lawn)    This was the name of a sixth-century Irish saint who founded a monastery at Ardmore in County Waterford. His feast day is July 24.

**Delaney**    *Descendant of the challenger.*

**Delano**    Some sources say this name means "dark."

**Demne**    When Fionn was tutored by Finneces, he took this name.

**Dempsey**    *Proud.*

**Dermot**    Derived from a word meaning "free from envy" or "free man." Other forms are DERMOD, DARBY, and DARCY.

**Derry** *Red-headed.* Derry also is a city in Northern Ireland.

**Desmond** (DEZ-mond)   This came from a surname that was itself based on an ancient name for South Munster. A variant spelling is DEMOND.

**Desmumhnach**   This name means "man of Muman," which was a tribe or territory in the Cork area of Munster in the centuries just before the Anglo-Norman invasion of Ireland. The name is associated with the families Mac Carthy and FitzGerald.

**Devin**   Derived from a word that means "poet."

**Devine**   *Ox.* An older spelling is DAIMHIN.

**Devlin**   *Brave or fierce.* A variant is DEVLYN.

**Diancecht** (DI-an-ket)   He was the great physician of the Tuatha De Danann whose healing skills were unparalleled. His sons were Miach, Cian, Cethe and Cu; his daughter was Airmid.

**Diarmaid** (DEER-mit)   The legendary Diarmaid belonged to the warrior band of Finn mac Cumaill. He had a beauty mark on his forehead that caused any woman who saw it to fall madly in love with him. At one time this was a traditional name in the families McCarthy, McDermott, O'Brien, and O'Connor. It was the name of several Irish kings. DIARMAIT or DIARMUID is the old form of this name.

**Digby**   *A town with a ditch or dike.*

**Dillon**   Derived from a word meaning "loyal" or "faithful."

**Dinsmore**   Some sources give the meaning of this name as "fortified hill."

**Doherty**   *Harmful.*

**Dolan**   Derived from a word meaning "dark-haired." A variant is DOLYN.

**Domnall**   *World-mighty.* A very popular name in ancient Ireland. No less than five High Kings bore this name. Variant spellings are DONAL and DOMHNALL.

**Don**   The Irish lord of the Underworld or Land of the Dead.

**Donahue**   *Dark hued.* This name is related to DON, the Irish god of the Underworld.

**Donal** (DON-al or DOH-nal)   This name comes from the Old Irish name Domnall, which is derived from the words *domun,* meaning "world," and *gal,* meaning "ardor" or "valor." Five High Kings had this name, including Domnall Ilchelgach (Donal of the Many Treacheries), an ancestor of the O'Neills and MacLoughlins.

**Donn** (DON or DOWN)   Derived from the Old Irish word DONN, which means both "brown" and "chief." In ancient myths, Donn was the god of the dead or the Underworld, who was said to live on an island off the coast of Munster. This was a popular name in the families Maguire and Kennedy until the end of the nineteenth century. Variant forms are DONNAN (DUN-ahn) and DONNAGAN.

**Donnchad** (DUN-uh-khuh)   *Brown lord.* One Donnchad was the son of Brian Boru who died in Rome in 1064. Another Donnchad, son of Flann Sinna, was High King in the early 900s.

**Donnell**   Related to the names DONAL and DOMNAL. Other forms are DONEAL and DONNELLY.

**Donovan**   *Dark or brown warrior.* A variant is DONVAN.

**Dooley**   Derived from a word meaning "dark hero."

**Doran**   *Stranger* or *exile.* An older spelling is DEORADHAIN.

**Dougal**   A version of DUBGALL or DUBHGHALL (DOO-gal or DOO-ahl). It means "dwells by the dark stream."

**Dow**   *Dark-haired.* An older spelling is DUBG.

**Driscol**   *Interpreter.* A variant is DRISCOLL.

**Dubaltach**   *Black-jointed* or *dark-limbed.* Dubultach Mac Fir Bisigh was a famous historian and genealogist in the latter part of the sixteenth century. Variant spellings are DUBHALTACH and DUALTACH.

**Dubgall** (DOO-ahl)   *Dark or black foreigner.* It referred to the Vikings, especially those from Denmark, who came to Dublin in 850. However, the Irish frequently used the name for their own as well. A variant is DUBGHALL.

**Dubhan** (DUH-ven or DUH-wen)   *Dark.* Other forms are DOWAN, DUGGAN, DUANE, DWAYNE, and DUBHAGAIN.

**Dubhdara** (doov-DAW-ra)   Comes from the ancient words *dub,* meaning "dark," and *dara,* meaning "oak," thus meaning "dark man of the oak."

**Dubhghlas**   This name is compounded of two words, *dubh,* meaning "black," and *glas,* meaning "blue." It has always been more popular in Scotland than in Ireland. However, the first president of Ireland was Douglas Hyde, born at Castlerea, County Roscommon, in 1860. Anglicized as Douglas.

**Dugan**   Variants of the name are DUBHAN and DUGGAN.

**Dwayne**   Another name derived from "dark." Variants are DUWAIN and DUANE.

**Ea** (EH)   A form of the name AODH.

**Eachan**   *Horseman.*

**Eamon** (EH-mon or AY-mon)   This is an Irish version of the Anglo-Saxon Edmund, introduced into Ireland by the Anglo-Normans. He was also the founder of the Fianna Fail Party for an independent Ireland. A variant is AIMON.

**Eanna**   Some sources claim this name means "birdlike." A number of legendary heroes bore this name. A variant is ENNAE.

**Earnan**   *Knowing* or *experienced.*

**Egan** (EE-gan)   Derived from "ardent or fiery." An older spelling is AEDHAGAN (EH-uh-gahn). Variants are EGON and EAGON.

**Eibhear** (EH-ver)   Probably means "strong as a bear."

**Eimhin** (EH-veen)   A male or female name, derived from the word *eim,* meaning "prompt" or "ready." Saint Eimhin, one of six sons of Eoghan mac Murchad of the royal house of Munster, turned to religion and founded a monastery in County Kildare where he was buried in 689. His feast day is December 22. A variant is EMINE.

**Eion**   A form of the name IAN. Variants are EANN and EIN.

**Eireamhon** (AY-ra-vohn)   A form of the Old Irish legendary name EREMON. At one time this name was traditonal among the McSweeneys and O'Hallorans.

**Eirnin**   A male or female name, possibly derived from *iarn,* meaning "iron." There are sixteen Irish saints bearing this name.

**Elatha** (AHL-a-hah)   A male or female name that means "art" or "craft."

**Elcmar**   Legends say that he was the original owner of Brugh Na Boinne, an underground fairy palace where the god Angus mac Og later lived.

**Enan** (EH-nahn)   The name of an obscure Irish saint. A variant is EANAN.

**Eochaid** (OH-kad)   Derived from the word *ech,* meaning "horse," this name may mean "horse rider." In early Irish history, horses were a sign of nobility and kingship. Therefore, several early kings bore this name. The modern Irish version is Eochaidh.

**Eocho** (OH-koh)   This was a nickname for Eochaid, which later became a name itself. Both the O'Hallinan and O'Quinn families have an ancestor by the name of Eocho mac Tairdelbaig.

**Eoghan** (oh-GAHN or OHN)   The name of several early kings and saints, this name is derived from *eo,* meaning "yew," and *gein,* meaning "birth." Variants are EOIN and EOGAN.

**Eoin** (OH-en)   The Irish version of the name Johannes. Eoin Mac-Neill was a patriot and scholar who helped found the Gaelic League in 1893. He later became Minister of Education in the first government of the Irish Free State.

**Erc**   Possibly means "battle boar." A variant is EARC.

**Eremon**   He fought Eber, his brother, to see who should become king of Ireland. All later Irish kings claimed descent from him.

**Erin**   An alternate name for Ireland, derived from the goddess Eriu. It means "peace." A variants is ERYN.

**Esras**   The ancient legends say that the Tuatha De Danann came from four cities, one of which was Gorias. Esras was the master of wisdom in Gorias; he later gave Lugh the victory spear, one of the treasures of the Tuatha De Danann.

**Evan**   An Irish form of the name John.

**Eveny**   A name used primarily in County Derry and connected to the name Aibhne.

**Fallon**   A variant of the name FAOLAN. A variant is FALLAMHAIN.

**Faolan** (FEH-lahn or FAY-lawn)   From the word *faol,* meaning "wolf," and the diminutive form *an.* This name was borne by fourteen Irish saints and ten warriors who belonged to the band of Finn mac Cumaill. One clergyman, the grandson of the king of Leinster, for a time was a missionary in Scotland. His feast day is January 9. Variants are FAELAN and FELAN.

**Farrell**   *Heroic.*

**Fearghus** (FAHR-gus or fay-REES)   A popular name of legend and history, it is derived from *fer,* meaning "man," and *gus,* meaning "strength, vigor." Fergus Wine-Mouth (Fergus Finbel) was a legendary poet.

**Fechine**   Some sources say this name derives from *fiach,* meaning "raven," while others believe it comes from an old word meaning "battle." Five Irish saints bore this name. A variant is FECHIN.

**Feidhlim** (FELL-em)   A male or female name that means "fortunate, lucky" or "ever good." One saint of this name was Feidhlimidh of County Cavan, whose feast day is August 9. In early times, at least three kings of Munster bore this name. Prince Phelim O'Neill led an uprising in Ulster in 1641 and was executed in 1653. A variant is FEIDHLIMIDH.

**Fercetrniu**   He was the poet of King Cu Roi, whose wife had caused the King's death. When the poet discovered this, he leaped over a cliff, taking the traitorous wife with him to her death.

**Fergal**    A popular early Irish name, it means "manly" or "valorous." A variant spelling is FEARGHAL.

**Fergus** (FER-guhs)    A common name in early Ireland, it means "the strength of a man." Fergus mac Roich was king of Ulster before Conchobhar took over. He made a pact with Cu Chulainn to never engage him in single combat, an agreement that led to the defeat of Medb and Ailill's army. A form of FEARGHUS.

**Ferris**    A form of the name Peter. A variant is FARRIS.

**Fiachra** (FEE-uh-khruh)    Some sources list this name's meaning as "battle-king," while others believe it means "eagle." The sea god Lir's son by his first wife Aobh had this name. He, his two brothers, and one sister were turned into swans by the jealous second wife. Their tale is told in *The Children of Lir.* Some sources list the name as FIACHNA. Variants are FEARY and FIACH.

**Finghin** (FIN-jin)    A variant of the names FIONN and FIONNBARR. Others are FINEEN, FINNIN, FIONAN, FINIAN, and FINBAR.

**Finlay**    *Blond-haired soldier.* Variants are FINDLEY and FINLEA.

**Finneces**    The poet who lived by the River Boyne and guarded the salmon of knowledge for seven years. He planned to eat the salmon himself to gain all knowledge, but his pupil Fionn mac Cumhail tasted the salmon first. A variant is FINEGAS.

**Finnegan**    *Light-skinned.*

**Finnian**    Derived from the word *finn,* meaning "fair, pale-colored." Several Irish saints had this name. A variant spelling is FINNEN.

**Fionn** (FYUHN)    Comes from the Old Irish *finn,* meaning "bright, fair." The most legendary holder of this name was Fionn mac Cumaill, a hero, warrior, poet, and the leader of a band of warriors called the Fiana. A traditional name in the families O'Dempsey and O'Driscoll. Variants are FIANN and FINIAN.

**Fionnbharr** (FIN-ver or FYUHN-var)    Derived from *finn,* meaning "bright, fair," and *barr,* meaning "hair." Eight Irish saints, including Saint Finnbarr of Cork and Barra in the Outer Hebrides, bore this name. A variant is FINNBARR.

**Fionntan** (FIN-tan or FYUN-tawn)    Derived from the Old Irish word *finn,* meaning "bright, fair," this name is known in legends as Fintan. The most legendary man to have this name was the consort of Cessair and the only man to survive the great flood. For thousands of years after this flood, Fintan lived on as a salmon, an eagle, and a hawk. This was also the name of seventy-four Irish saints.

**Fiontan**  Some sources say the meaning of this name is "white ancient," while others say it means "white fire." More than seventy Irish saints had this name.

**Fitzroy**  *Son of Roy.*

**Flann** (FLAHN)  A male or female name, it is derived from *flann,* meaning "blood red." Flann is listed in Irish history and legend as the name of kings and queens, poets, scholars, abbots, and saints. Variants and names derived from this name are FLAINN, FLOINN, FLANNAN, FLANAGAN, FLANNAGAIN, FLYNN, FLOINN, and FLANNERY.

**Flynn**  Some sources give the meaning of this name as "son of the red-headed man."

**Gaeth** (GAYTH)  An ancient name that means "intelligent, skillful."

**Gair**  *Small.* Other spellings are GEIR and GAER.

**Galbraith**  In old Ireland, this name meant "Scotsman."

**Galen**  Some sources list the meaning as "small but lively," while others say it means "calm."

**Gallagher**  Derived from the word for "eager helper."

**Galloway**  In Ireland at one time this name referred to a Scotsman from Galloway, Scotland. A variant spelling is GALWAY.

**Galvin** (GAHL-vin)  This name is derived from the Old Irish *gelbann,* meaning "a sparrow."

**Gannon**  *Light-skinned.*

**Garban**  Derived from *garb,* meaning "rough." Several saints bore this name, including Saint Garbhan whose feast day is July 9.

**Garett**  *Brave spearman.*

**Garvey**  Derived from a word meaning "rough place." Variant is GAIRBITH.

**Gaynor**  *Son of the fair-skinned man.* A variant is GAINOR.

**Gearard** (GEHR-ed)  *Spear-brave.* The Irish version of the Norse-Viking name Gearoid.

**Gearoid** (GAHR-ohd)  This comes from the ancient name Gelgeis, which itself comes from *gel,* meaning "shining." Another source believes this name to mean "spear-might" and says it came from the Anglo-Normans. This was popular in the Fitzgerald family. Variants are GEARALT and GARALT.

**Genty**  Derived from a word meaning "snow."

**Ghilchrist**  *Servant of Christ.* Variants are GILCHRIST, GIOLLA CHRIOST, GIL, GILLEY, and GILVARRY.

**Gillean**  *Servant of Saint John.* A variant is GILLAN.

**Gillespie**  *Son of the bishop's servant.* A variant is GILLIS.

**Gilmore**  Derived from words meaning "devoted to the Virgin Mary."

**Giolla Deacair**  An Otherworld champion who owned a horse that could not be ridden. The hero Conan managed to mount this horse but it carried him away to Tir Tairngire, and Fionn had to rescue him.

**Gilroy**  *Devoted to the king.* Another spelling is GILDRAY.

**Gilvarry**  *Servant of Saint Barry.* An older spelling is BHEARAIGH (GIL-a VER-ee).

**Giolla Bhrighde** (GIL-a BREED)  From words meaning "servant of the goddess Brighid" or "Saint Brigid."

**Giolla Chriost** (GIL-a KREEST)  *Servant of Christ.*

**Giolla Dhe** (GIL-a DEH)  *Servant of God.*

**Glaisne** (GLAS-nee)  A name commonly used in Ulster.

**Glen**  *Glen or narrow valley.*

**Glenville**  *Village in the glen.*

**Gobban** (GOH-ban)  This name is derived from Goibniu, the name of the ancient god of smithcraft, who worked for the Tuatha De Danann. Later legends say that one Gobban Saor built the Round Towers and could make a sword with three blows of his hammer. There were several saints of this name, including Gobban of Killamery, County Kilkenny, whose feast day is December 6. A variant is GOBAN.

**Goffraidh** (GO-free-y)  This is a variant of the Old German name Godfrey brought to Ireland by the Vikings and which means "God's peace." In 950 records state that a Gothfrith plundered Kells with the Vikings.

**Goibniu**  Known in both Ireland and Wales, this god of blacksmiths was one of a triad of craftsmen. The others were Luchtaine the wright and Credne the brazier. Similar to the Greek Vulcan, Goibniu forged all the weapons for the Tuatha De Danann. These weapons never missed their mark and the wounds they made were always fatal. The ale he brewed also gave the Tuatha De Danann their invulnerability.

**Gordan**   A name more widely used in Ulster. It means "hero."

**Gorman**   Derived from a word meaning "dark" or "swarthy." Either a male or female name. Gorman mac Airtri, king of Munster, died in 821. A variant is GORMAIN.

**Grady**   Derived from a word meaning "noble" or "illustrious." Another spelling is GRADLEIGH.

**Greagoir**   The Irish version of the name Gregory. A variant is GRIOGHAR.

**Guaire**   A common name in early Ireland, it means "noble or proud." It is recorded that Guaire, son of Dungalach, an O'Brien king, died in 787.

**Guthrie**   *Windy place.*

**Guy**   *Sensible.*

**Hagen**   *Youthful* or *young.*

**Haley**   Derived from a word meaning "ingenious."

**Hannraoi** (HAN-ree)   The Irish version of the Norse name Henry. It means "ruler of an estate."

**Harkin**   Derived from an old word meaning "dark red."

**Hogan**   A name similar to Hagen, it means "youth."

**Hoyt**   Derived from a word meaning "spirit" or "mind."

**Hurley**   From a word meaning "sea tide."

**Iarlaith** (YAR-lath)   Saint Iarlaith, born in Tuam, was ordained in 468 and built his first monastery and school at Cloonfush. Variants are IARLAITHE and IARFHLAITH.

**Ibor**   Derived from *iobar,* meaning "yew tree." The best known holder of this name was Saint Ibor of Beggerin Island, who opposed Saint Patrick because he was a "foreigner." His feast day is April 23. A variant is IOBHAR.

**Imar**   This is probably the name Ivarr borrowed from the Norse-Vikings who invaded Ireland. A variant is IOMHAR.

**Innis**   *From the island.* Variants are INNES and INISS.

**Irv**   *Handsome.* A variant is IRVING.

**Iuchar and Iucharba**   The two brothers of Brian mac Tuirenn, who killed Cian, Lugh's father.

**Jarlath** (JAR-leth)   The most famous man to bear this name in Irish history was a sixth-century saint who taught Saint Brendan the Navigator. Following a prophecy to drive eastward until his chariot wheel broke, he did so, and built a church at Tuam. This church became one of the greatest centers of learning and the arts. The modern Irish spelling is IARLAITH (YAR-lath or YAHR-le).

**Kacey** An alternate spelling of the name CASEY.

**Kane** From a Gaelic word meaning "tribute."

**Kavan** *Handsome.* A variant is KAVENAUGH.

**Keallach** *Little Kelly.* A variant is KILLIAN.

**Keary** *Dark or dark-haired.*

**Keefe** From a word meaning "handsome or loved."

**Keegan** *Little and fiery.* Variants are KEAGEN and KEGAN.

**Keelan** Derived from a word meaning "slender."

**Keeley** *Handsome.* Other forms are KEALEY and KEALY.

**Keenan** *Little Keene.* Other spellings are KEANAN and KIENAN.

**Kellen** *Mighty warrior.* Variants are KAELAN, KAEL, KAILEN, KALLEN, KAYLEN, KAYLAN, KEALAN, and KELAN.

**Keller** From a word meaning "little companion."

**Kelvin** *A narrow river.* A variant is KELVYN.

**Kendrick** From a word meaning "son of Henry." Another spelling is KEONDRIC.

**Kennard** *Brave chieftain.* A variant is KENNER.

**Kennedy** (KI-ne-dee) Possibly derived from *cenn,* meaning "head," and *etig,* meaning "ugly," this name means either "helmeted head" or "ugly head." The Old Irish spelling was CENNETIG. The father of Brian Boru, High King of Ireland, was Cennetig mac Lorcain.

**Kenneth** Variant of CINAED. A variant is KENNET.

**Kenyon** *White or blond hair.* A variant is KENYAN.

**Kermit** Some sources say this name is a variant of the name DERMOT, while others think it means "son of Diarmaid."

**Kerry** From a word meaning "dark hair," it possibly means "son of the dark one." A variant spelling is KEARY.

**Kerwin** *Small and dark.* Variants are KERVIN and KERWYN.

**Kildare** An Irish county.

**Kilian** (KIL-yan) The Old Irish name was Cillene, which may have come from *cell,* meaning "church." Among the saints bearing this name was an abbot of Iona in Scotland. Variants of this name are CILLENE, KILLIAN, and KILLY.

**Korey** A variant spelling of the name CORRIGAN.

**Kyele** *A narrow piece of land* or *one from the strait.* Variants are KYLE and KIEL.

**Labhras** (LAU-rahsh)    The Irish form of the name Laurence, which means "laurel."

**Labraid**    *Speaker.* Labraid Longsech is the legendary ancestor of the people of Leinster. A variant is LABHRAIDH.

**Labras**    *A laurel bush.* A variant is LABHRAS.

**Laegaire**    Possibly means "calf-herd." Several kings and princes bore this name, including Laegaire, son of Niall, who ruled when Patrick arrived in Ireland in 432. This king had two wives, Feidlim and Aeife. The king of the Cinell-Coirpri, who died in 812, was another Laegaire. A variant is LAOGHAIRE.

**Laisrean**    Derived from *laisre,* meaning "flame." A variant is LAISREN.

**Laoire** (LAY-re)    The Old Irish spelling of this name was LAEGAIRE, which may have come from a word meaning "calf-herder." A king of Tara and two saints bore this name.

**Larkin**    *Rough and fierce.*

**Laughlin**    *Servant of Saint Secundinus.* Variants are LANY, LEACH-LAINN, and LOUGHLIN.

**Lawler**    From an Irish word meaning "mutterer."

**Leachlainn** (LEKH-len)    Other forms of the name are LAUGHLIN and LOCHLAINN.

**Leary**    A variant of both LAOIRE and LAEGAIRE.

**Lee**    *Meadow.* A variant spelling is LAOIDHIGH.

**Lennan** (LAN-awn)    From an Old Irish word that means "lover" or "sweetheart." This name was most common in County Clare. A variant is LEANNAN.

**Liam** (LEE-am)    Short for Uilliam, this is an Irish form of the name William, which was introduced into Ireland by the Anglo-Norman invaders.

**Lir**    The father of Manannan mac Lir. His second wife turned his other four children into swans.

**Lochlainn** (LOCH-lan or LOX-lin)    Derived from an Irish word for the land of the Vikings. During the Middle Ages, this was a popular name in the families MacTeague, MacCabe, Malone, and MacCann. Variants are LAKELAND and LAUGHLIN.

**Loegaire**    Cu Chulainn's charioteer who went with the hero to Mag Mell to rescue its queen from abductors. Another tale says he died from a spear meant for the hero.

**Logan**    Derived from a word meaning "meadow" or "from the hollow."

**Lomman** (LO-man)   Derived from the word *lomm,* meaning "bare." Saint Lomman of Trim, County Meath, was the first bishop of the church Patrick founded at Trim. His feast day is October 11.

**Lonan** (LYO-nawn)   This name comes from *lon,* meaning "blackbird," and the diminutive *an.* Saint Lonan Finn (feast day of January 22) and seven other early Irish saints had this name.

**Lorcan** (LOR-kawn)   From the word *lorc,* meaning "fierce" or "cruel," and the diminutive *an.* Lorcan was the name of several early Irish kings.

**Luchtaine**   The god of carpentry for the Tuatha De Danann and a member of the trio of smiths. A variant is LUCHTA.

**Lugaid**   The son of Cu Roi and Blanaid, he was known as the Son of Three Dogs because his mother had lain with three men who had *cu* in their names. When Lugaid cut off Cu Chulainn's head, the sword slipped and cut off his own hand.

**Lugh** (LOO)   Derived from the word *lugu,* meaning "light," this was the name of a Celtic sun god, who was also known by the titles the Many Skilled, the Shining One, and Lugh of the Long Arm. In Welsh mythology, Lugh was known as LLEU. Nicknames are LUGHAN (LOO-awn) and LUGHNA (LOO-na).

**Lughaidh** (LOO-ee)   An Irish version of the French-Norman name Louis, which means "renowned warrior."

**Lunn**   *Warlike.* Variants are LONN and LUN.

**Lynch**   From a word meaning "mariner." A variant is LINCH.

**Macallister**   *Son of Alistair.* A variant is MCALLISTER.

**Macarthur**   *Son of Arthur.* A variant is MCARTHUR.

**MacBride**   From the Irish meaning "son of the follower of Saint Brighid."

**Maccoy**   *Son of Hugh.* A variant is MCCOY.

**Maccrea**   Derived from the Irish meaning "son of grace." Variants are MCCREA and MCCRAE.

**MacDara** (mahk-DAH-ra)   Derived from the words *mac,* meaning "son," and *dara,* meaning "oak," this name means "son of the oak" and may have originally designated a child born to a Druid or a Pagan priestess. The Irish patron of fishermen is Saint Mac Dara of Connemara, whose holy days are September 28 and July 16.

**Mackenzie**   *Son of Kenzie.* A variant is MCKENZIE.

**Mackinnley**   *Son of the learned ruler.* A variant is MCKINNLEY.

**Maclean** Derived from "son of Leander." Variants are MCLEAN and MACLAINE.

**Macklin** *Son of Flann.* A variant is MACLAND.

**Macmahon** *Son of Mahon.* A variant is MCMAHON.

**MacMurra** Possibly a variant of MACMURRAY. Another variant is MAC-MAUREADHAIGH.

**Macmurray** *Son of Murray.* A variant is MCMURRAY.

**Mael Coluim** Literally means "servant or devotee of Colm." This name was more popular in Scotland than in Ireland, although there was a Maelcoluim ua Canannain, king of Cinel-Conall, who died in 956. A variant is MAEOLCHOLUIM.

**Maelduine** His mother was a nun raped by his father Ailill. He made a skin boat and sailed among the Blessed Islands in search of his father's murderers.

**Mael Iosu** More commonly used at one time among the clergy, this name means "devotee of Christ." Mael Isu ua Brolchain was a religious lyric poet who died in 1086.

**Maghnus** (MAKH-nus) A variant of the name MANUS or the Norse-Viking MAGNUS; it means "great."

**Mahon** *Bear.*

**Mairtin** (MAHR-teen) The Irish version of the name Martin. The name means "warlike one."

**Maitias** (muh-THY-uhs) The Irish version of the name Mathias.

**Maitiu** (MATH-yoo) The Irish form of the name Matthew.

**Mal** The Irish shortened version of many names that begin with "mal."

**Malachy** (MA-la-kee) An anglicization of the Irish *mael*, meaning "servant or devotee," such as Mael Maedoc and Mael Sechlainn. Saint Malachy of Armagh was a twelfth-century church reformer whose feast day is November 3. Variants are MAELACHLAINN and MILOS.

**Malone** *Church-going.* A variant is MALONEY.

**Malvin** The Irish form of the name Melvin. A variant is MALVYN.

**Manannan mac Lir** (mah-NAN-awn or mah-NAN-awn mac leer) The chief Irish sea god, he was the son of the sea god Lir. A skilled shapeshifter, he dressed primarily in a green cloak and a gold headband. The Isle of Man (the Isle of Manannan) and the Isle of Arran in the Firth of Clyde (Scotland) were specifically under his protection. Legend says that at Arran Manannan he had a beautiful palace called Emhain of the Apple Trees. The chief food of the Tuatha De Danann were the pigs belonging to this god, said to constantly renew themselves after they were eaten. This pork kept the Tuatha De Danann from aging. A great warrior, he had many magical weapons; the spears Yellow Shaft and Red Javelin; the swords named The Retaliator, Great Fury, and Little Fury. His armor protected any wearer from wounds and could make them invisible at will. He used his boat Wave Sweeper to journey from Ireland to his islands and back. He was a deity of weather-forecasting, magic, commerce, and all things to do with the sea.

**Mannix**    Comes from an Irish word meaning "monk." A variant is MAINCHIN (MAN-e-kheen).

**Manus** (MA-nuhs)    Derived from the Latin *magnus,* "great," this name was taken from the Norse, who had borrowed it from Carolus Magnus, the Latin form of Charlemagne, a French emperor. A variant is MANNUSS.

**Maolruadhan** (mal-ROO-ahn)    *Servant of Saint Ruadhan.* A variant is MELRONE.

**Marcan** (MOR-kawn)    From the word *marc,* meaning "horse," and the diminutive *an.*

**Mathghamhain** (ma-HOHN)    An Old Irish word meaning "bear," this was the name of a brother of Brian Boru. It used to be traditional in the families of O'Connor, O'Brien, and O'Farrell.

**Mayo**    This is the name of a County in Ireland, as well as meaning "yew-tree plain."

**Meallan** (MAHL-an)    Derived from the word *mall,* meaning "lightning," and the diminutive *an.*

**Meilseoir** (MEL-shyahr)    The Irish version of the name Melchior. It means "king."

**Mel**    There is no recorded meaning for this name, although it appears in historical records. Saint Mel was the bishop and patron of Ardagh, County Limerick and was a nephew of Saint Patrick.

**Mellan**    This name appears to be derived from an early word for "lightning." Saint Mellan founded a church at Kilrush, County Meath and became a bishop, an event prophesied by Patrick. His feast day is January 28.

**Melvin**    Derived from the Irish word meaning "armored chief." Variants are MELWYNN and MAL.

**Merril** *Bright sea.* A variant is MERYL.

**Merritt** From the word meaning "valuable" or "deserving." A variant spelling is MERITT.

**Miach** A son of the Tuatha De Danann physician Dian Cecht. He was slain by his father when he and his sister Airmid restored Nuada's physical hand.

**Micheal** (MEE-kal) Very simply the Irish form and spelling of the name Michael.

**Midir** (MY-tir) A fairy king and another deity of the Underworld, he was connected with the Isle of Falga (Isle of Man) where he had his palace. He owned three wonderful cows and a magic cauldron. A variant spelling is MIDHIR.

**Miles** Although many sources list the origin of this name as connected to the Latin *miles,* meaning "soldier," it is more likely associated with the historical Sons of Mil. A variant is MYLES.

**Mochaomhog** A priest who cared for the swan-children of Lir. He made silver chains to hang around their necks so people could identify them as enchanted humans.

**Monahan** *Monk.* A variant is MONOHAN.

**Mongan** The son of Manannan mac Lir and Caintigerna. Manannan took him to the Otherworld to learn magical skills that later helped him to become a king and overcome his enemies. Some tales say he was the reincarnation of Finn mac Cumhail.

**Monroe** A name derived from the mouth of the Roe River in Ireland.

**Morann** (MOOR-an) The meaning of this name is uncertain, although it is connected with the ancient name of MORAND. Several of Finn mac Cumaill's warriors had this name, as did a legendary judge who never gave a wrong verdict.

**Morc** The son of Dela, a Fomor king.

**Morfessa** A master of great wisdom who lived in Falias, one of the four cities from which the Tuatha De Danann came. He gave the Tuatha De Danann the Stone of Fal, the inauguration stone for making a king.

**Morgan** Possibly a male name based on the war goddess Morrigan. Some sources list the meaning as "lives by the sea."

**Moss** An Irish shortened form of the name Maurice or Morris.

**Muireadhach** (MUR-e-thekh) Derived from *muiredach,* meaning "lord, master." Other sources list its meaning as "sea lord." Many

kings, princes, and saints bore this name. An abbot of Monaster-
boice, County Louth, who died in 922, bore this name. Variants are
MURRY, MURRAY, MUIREDACH, and MUIRIOCH.

**Muirios** (MEER-ees)   A modern spelling of the Old Irish name MUIR-
GIUS, derived from *muir,* meaning "sea," and *gus,* meaning "strength,
vigor." This was the name of several kings of Connacht and a traditional name among the families McDonagh and McDermott.

**Mundy**   A name taken from those who live in Reamonn, Ireland.

**Murchadh** (MUR-kha or MOOR-uh-ka)   Derived from *muir,* meaning
"sea," and *cath,* meaning "warrior." A favorite name of the families
O'Brien, O'Flaherty, O'Connell, and O'Donovan. Several early Irish
warriors and kings were also named Murchadh. Variants are MUR-
ROUGH, MURPHEY, MURCHACH, and MURPHY.

**Murtagh**   Variants of the name MURDOCK. A variant is MURTAUGH.

**Naoise**   The legendary Naoise was the son of Uisliu and served Conchobhar mac Nessa, king of the Ulaidh. He fell in love with
Deirdre, the young maiden promised to the king, and had to flee
for his life. Later the couple returned under a promise of forgiveness, but Naoise was ambushed and killed. A variant is NAOISI.

**Neasan** (NESH-ahn)   A variant of the name NESSA (Conchobar mac
Nessa).

**Nechtan**   The husband of the goddess Boann and the keeper of a
magic well of knowledge around which grew nine hazel trees.

**Nemhglan**   The bird-like being who was the father of Conaire Mess
Buachalla by a human woman. He gave his son instructions on how
to become the next High King.

**Nevan**   *Holy.* A variant is NAOMHAM (NAU-ahn).

**Niall** (NEE-al)   Possibly derived from the word *nel,* meaning "cloud."
One of the most famous kings of Tara was named Niall Noigiallach
(Niall of the Nine Hostages). He was the founder of the Ui Neill
dynasty and the ancestor of both the Irish O'Neills and the Scottish
MacNeils. He gained the kingship by agreeing to kiss an ugly hag,
who then turned into a beautiful young woman. Actually, she was
the disguised goddess of sovereignty. A traditional male name in the
families O'Neill, O'Donnell, O'Higgins, O'Quinn, O'Kelly, O'Boyle,
and O'Doherty. A nickname is Niallan (NEE-a-lahn). Variants are
NYLE, NIALL, NEAL, and NEALY.

**Nolan**   *Famous* or *noble.* Variants are NOLAND and NOLIN.

**Nuada**    Known in both Ireland and Wales, this god lost his hand in battle and had to step down as king, for the laws demanded that a king of the Tuatha De Danann be perfect. Thereafter he wore a flexible silver hand made for him by the physician Dian Cecht, until Dian Cecht's son Miach and his daughter Airmid replaced the physical hand by magic. He had an invincible sword, one of the four great treasures of the Tuatha De Danann that they brought with them to Ireland. He was killed at the second battle of Mag Tuired.

**Odran**    Some sources say this name is derived from the word *odhar,* meaning "dun-colored," while others say the meaning comes from the old name for "otter." Although several Irish saints bore this name, the most famous was the charioteer for Saint Patrick. Variants are ODHRAN and ORRIN.

**Oengus**    A variant of AONGHUS. Another variant spelling is AENGUS.

**Ogma**    Known as Sun-Face and Honey-Mouthed, Ogma was similar to the Greek hero Herakles or Hercules. He carried a huge club and was the champion of the Tuatha De Danann. Legend says this deity also created the Ogham script alphabet. He married Etan, one of the daughters of Dian Cecht, and had several children. Ogma was a deity of eloquence, poets and writers, magic, inspiration, and the arts.

**Oilibhear** (OH-li-vehr)    An Irish form of the Norse name Oliver, which means "ancestral relic."

**O'Neil**    *Son of Neil.*

**Oisin** (oh-SHEEN)    Derived from the Old Irish *oisin,* meaning "fawn" or "deer," Oisin was the son of Finn mac Cumaill and the woman Sadb, who had been turned into a deer. This Oisin dallied with Niamh, daughter of Aengus Tirech, king of Munster. When she suddenly died, her father challenged Finn and the Fianna to fight. Instead, Finn paid Niamh's weight in both gold and silver to Aengus. The variant is OISSINE, a name borne by two saints, whose feast days were January 1 and May 1. Anglicized as Ossian.

**Oistin** (OHS-teen)    The Irish version of the name Austin. The name means "venerable."

**Oran** (OHR-an)    From the old word *odran,* meaning "otter." May 8 is the feast day of Saint Odran, patron of Waterford, Ireland.

**Oscar** (OHS-car)    Possibly means "one who loves deer" and comes from the word *os,* meaning "deer." He was the son of Oisin. A traditional name in the families MacLoughlin, Maguire, and O'Connor.

**Owain**   Some sources give the meaning as "born to nobility," while others say this name means "young warrior." Variants are OWEN and UAINE.

**Owney**   An old Irish name that means "elderly." A variant is ONEY.

**Padraig** (PAH-drig or PAH-dreek)   Taken from the Latin name Patricius, meaning "noble." The most notable holder of this name was Saint Patrick, the patron saint of Ireland. This name was not used for children before 1700 as it was considered to be too sacred. Instead, children were given such names as Gilla Patraic (servant of Patrick) or Mael Patraic (devotee of Patrick). The feast day of this saint is March 17. Variants are PADDY, PADRAIC, and PATRAIG.

**Parlan**   Some sources say this is the Irish form of the name Bartholomew, which means "plowman." However, in Irish legend, the Partholon was the first race of invaders to arrive in Ireland. Variants are PATHOLON and PARTHALAN (PAR-ha-lahn).

**Patterson**   The Irish version of "son of Pat."

**Peadar** (PA-der)   The Irish version of the name Peter. Several early saints bore this name, including one whose celebration day is June 4.

**Phelan**   Derived from a word meaning "wolf." A variant of the name FAOLAN.

**Piaras** (PEER-as or PEE-a-ras)   This is the Irish form of the French Norman name Piers. Variants are PERAIS and FERUS.

**Piran**   *Prayer.* The Irish saint of miners had this name.

**Proinnsias** (PRON-shee-as)   The Irish version of the name Francis (of Assissi). This was not a popular name until recently.

**Quigley**   Derived from a word meaning "from the maternal side."

**Quillan**   *Cub.* Variant is QUILLON.

**Quinlan**   Some sources give the meaning as "strong," while others say this name means "well shaped." A variant is QUINLIN.

**Quinn**   An Irish variant of the name CONN. The old spelling is CUINN.

**Raegan**   *Little king.* Variants are REAGAN, REEGEN, and REGAN.

**Rafer**   Derived from a word meaning "rich, prosperous." Variants are RAFFER and RAFFERTY.

**Ragallach**   A king of Connacht, he abandoned his infant daughter because of a prophecy that said he would die at his daughter's hands.

**Raghnall** (RAN-al)   Another name borrowed from the Norse-Vikings, it means "mighty power." Among the Norse slain in the battle of Tara in 850 was a Raghnall mac Amlaib.

**Regan**   A form of RAEGAN. A variant is RIAGAN.

**Reilly** *Valiant.* A variant of this name is spelled RILEY.

**Remann** (RYEH-mon or RAY-moon) This is the Irish version and spelling of the Old German name Raymond, which is a compound of *ragan,* meaning "counsel," and *mund,* meaning "protection." The Anglo-Normans brought this name to Ireland when they invaded. A variant is REAMONN.

**Renny** The Irish version of the French name Rene, meaning "small but strong." A variant is RAIGHNE.

**Rian** (REE-an) This is derived from the Old Irish word *ri,* or "king," and is the source for the surname Ryan, which is used as a first name in the United States. Variants are RIGAN (REE-an) and RIGAN.

**Riddock** *Smooth field.* Variants are REIDHACHADH and RIDDOC.

**Riocard** (REE-kard) An Irish variation of the Anglo-Norman name Richard.

**Riordan** (REER-dawn) Derived from the word *rigbarddan,* meaning "royal poet."

**Roarke** *Famous ruler.* Variants are ROARK, RUARC, RUARK, RORKE, RUAIDHRI, and ROURKE.

**Rodhlann** (ROH-lan) An Irish version of the name Roland, which means "fame of the land."

**Rogan** *Red-headed.* Variants are RUADHAGAN, ROWE, ROWEN, ROWYN, ROWIN, ROWAN, and RUADHAN.

**Roibhilin** (RO-bin) A diminutive of the name Robert, this is the Irish version of the name Robin. It means "shining fame." Variants are ROIBIN, ROIBEARD, RAVELIN, RAVELYN, and REVELIN.

**Ronan** (ROH-nawn) Comes from the word *ron,* meaning "seal," and the diminutive *an.* An ogham inscription on a stone cross at Arraglen tells of a Ronan the priest, son of Comgan.

**Rooney** *Red-headed.* A variant is RUANAIDH.

**Rory** Variant of RUAIRI. Another variant is RUAIDHRI.

**Ross** (RAWS) Derived from the word *ros,* meaning "promontory." Kings, heroes, and saints have borne this popular name. It was traditional among the families Coughlin, O'Farrel, and MacMahon.

**Ruadan** (ROO-an) From the word *ruad,* meaning "red-haired." A son of Bress and Brighid, he fought for the Fomorians against the Tuatha De Danann. Variants are RUADHAN and RHODAN.

**Ruaidhri** (RWE-e-ree) The Irish form of the Teutonic name Roderick. It means "famous ruler."

**Ruairi** (ROO-e-ree)   Derived from an Old Irish name Ruaidri, which comes from *ruad,* meaning "red," and *ri,* meaning "king." In 946 Ruaidhri ua Canannain routed the Vikings from Dublin, killing many of them. At one time this name was traditional among the families O'Connor, O'Shaughnessy, MacDonnell, MacCann, McGinley, Mulloy, and O'Donnell. A variant is RUAIDHRI.

**Ruarc** (ROO-ark)   A first name derived from the surname O'Rourke, which comes from *arg,* meaning "champion, hero."

**Ryan**   *Little king.* Variants are RHYAN, RYNE, and RIAN.

**Saoirse**   A male or female name meaning "freedom" or "liberty."

**Scanlon**   *Little trapper.*

**Scully**   Derived from a word meaning "town crier." A variant is SCOLAIGHE.

**Seafra** (SHEE-a-fra or SHE-fra)   This is the Irish spelling and variant of the name Jeffrey, another name brought to Ireland by the Anglo-Normans. Variants are SHEARY, SEAFRAID, and SEATHRUN.

**Seamus** (SHAWM-us or SHEE-a-mus)   Derived from the Norman French name Jehan, this is the Irish version of John. It was a common name among the Anglo-Norman settlers in Ireland. Variants are SEUMAS and SHAMUS.

**Sean** (SHAWN)   An Irish version of the Latin name Joannes, brought to Ireland by the Norman French. Variants are SHAUN, SEAGHAN (SEE-a-gun), SHANE, SION, and SHAWN.

**Seanan** (SHAW-nawn)   Derived from the old word *sen,* meaning "ancient," this name was borne by at least twenty early Irish saints. Variant are SENAN and SHANNON.

**Searbhreathach** (SAR-vra-huhkh)   The Irish version of the name Justin. It means "noble judge."

**Searlas** (SHAHR-las)   The Irish version of the name Charles. It means "full-grown" or "manly." A variant is SEARLUS.

**Semias**   The master of wisdom from Murias, one of the four cities from which the Tuatha De Danann came. He gave the cauldron Undry to the Dagda.

**Seoirse** (SYAHR-sha)   This name means "farmer" and is a form of the name George. A variant is SEORSA.

**Seosamh** (SHOH-sav)   An Irish form of the name Joseph. It means "God will add."

**Setanta**   The birth-name of the legendary warrior Cu Chulainn.

**Shanahan**   *Wise or clever.* An old spelling is SEANACHAN.

**Shanley**   Some sources give the meaning as "small," while others give "ancient." An older spelling is SEANLAOCH.

**Shea**   *Courteous.* Other forms of this name are SEAGHDA, SHAE, and SHAYE.

**Sheehan**   *Peaceful.* Other forms are SHEAN and SIODHACHAN.

**Sheridan**   Derived from a word meaning "wild" or "untamed." An older spelling is SEIREADAN.

**Sierra**   *Black.*

**Siomon** (SHEE-mon)   The Irish version of the name Simon. It means "God is heard."

**Siseal** (SEE-sil)   The Irish form of Cecil that means "blind."

**Sithchean**   A druid who, disguised as a smith, tested all the sons of the King of Tara to see who was fit to be the next king. Only Niall completed the tests satisfactorily.

**Skelly**   *Storyteller.* May come from the Viking influence and their word for bard, which is skald.

**Sleibhin** (SLE-veen)   Comes from the word *sleib,* meaning "mountain," and means "mountain man" or "man of the mountain." A variant is SLEVIN.

**Sloan**   *Warrior.* A variant is SLOANE.

**Somhairle**   The Irish version of the Old Norse-Viking name meaning "summer-farer" or "summer wanderer."

**Strahan**   *Minstrel.* Variants are SRUTHAN and STRACHAN.

**Struthers**   Derived from a word meaning "brook." A variant is SRUTHAIR.

**Sualtam**   The husband of Dechtire and foster-father of Cu Chulainn. His severed head warned the men of Ulster about the attack by Maeve.

**Suibhne** (SHEEV-ne)   The Old Irish name was Suibne, a name borne by several early kings and saints. Anglicized as Sweeney, this was the name of a mad poet, King Suibne Gelt (Mad Sweeney). During the battle of Mag Rath in 637, King Suibne was cursed by a saint he insulted, and this curse drove him insane. For the rest of his life he lived in trees and composed poetry. He died in the church at St. Moling.

**Sullivan**   *Black-eyed.* Other forms are SUILEABHAN and SULLY.

**Sweeney**   A variant of the name SUIBHNE. Another variant is SUIDHNE.

**Tadg** (TAYG)   Some sources say this name means "poet," while others list the meaning as "honors God." Several kings, such as Tadc mac Cathail, king of Connacht, and many saints bore this name. Variants are TADC, TIOMOID, and TIEGE.

**Taggart**   Derived from a word meaning "son of the priest."

**Tairdelbach**   A number of kings bore this name, which means "abettor" or "instigator." One such king was Tairdelbach ua Conchobair, king of Connacht and of Ireland, who died in 1156. A variant is TOIRDHEALBHACH.

**Tarlach** (TAHR-lak)   One who assists or aids. King Tairdelbach of Munster and King Tairdelbach of Ireland both had this name. During the Middle Ages, this was a traditional name in the families O'Connor, O'Brien, O'Donnel, O'Boyle, and MacSweeney. The oldest Irish spelling is TAIRDELBACH.

**Teague**   Another name meaning "bard" or "poet." A variant is TEAGAN.

**Thady**   Some sources list the meaning of this name as "praise." It is an Irish version of Thaddeus.

**Tiaran** (TEER-nawn)   The Old Irish name was Tigernan, which was derived from the word *tigerna,* meaning "lord, superior, chief," and the diminutive *an.* Several kings and saints bore this name in early and medieval Ireland. At one time this was a traditional name among the families O'Rourke, MacGovern, and MacKiernan. Variants are TIER, TIGHEARNACH, and TIERNAN.

**Tiarchnach** (TEER-nakh)   Derived from *tigerna,* meaning "lord, superior, chief." Saint Tigernach of Clones (holy day April 4) and several other Irish saints bore this name.

**Tigernach**   Derived from the word *tigern,* meaning "lord," several saints had this name. The most famous of these was Tigernach of Clones, County Monaghan. In his youth he was captured by Welsh pirates and taken to Britain. He escaped to Scotland where he received his education. Later he went to Rome where it is said he obtained relics of Peter and Paul, which he took back to Ireland. Variants are TIGHEARNACH and TIARNACH.

**Tigernan**   Another name derived from the word *tigern,* meaning "lord." This name was borne by many kings, princes, and chieftains. Variants are TIGHEARNAN and TIAARNAN.

**Tomaisin** (TA-ma-seen)   An Irish version of the name Thomas.

**Tomey** (TA-mahs)   The Irish form of Thomas. A variant is TOMAS.

**Torin**   *Chieftain.* A variant is TORYN.

**Tormey**   The Irish adaptation of the Viking god Thor. It means "thunder spirit." A variant is TORMAIGH.

**Torn**   The Irish version of the name Torrence. A variant is TORAN.

**Torrance**   This name means "knolls" in Ireland. Variants are TOR-RANS and TORY.

**Treasach** (TRAH-sak)   The Old Irish name was TRESSACH, which meant "fierce, warlike."

**Trevor**   *Prudent.* Variants are TREV and TREABHAR.

**Troy**   Derived from a word than means "foot soldier."

**Tully**   In Ireland this name means "at peace with God." An older spelling is TAICLIGH.

**Tynan**   Derived from the word "dark."

**Tyrone** (teer-OHN)   Derived from *tir,* meaning "land," and *eoghain,* a man's name. Tyrone is also the name of a county in Northern Ireland.

**Uaine** (OON-yuh)   A variant form of the names OWAIN and OWEN.

**Uileog** (IH-lig)   A form of the names UILLIAM and LIAM.

**Uilliam**   An Irish version of the Old German name Wilhelm, which was brought to Ireland by Norman invaders. Common among Anglo-Norman families living in Ireland, it was quickly adopted by some Irish families as well. A variant name is LIAM.

**Uinseann** (WIN-shen)   The Irish version of Vincent. Variants are UIS-TEAN and UISDEAN.

**Ultan**   *An ulsterman.* The best known of the many saints to bear this name was Ultan moccu Conchobair of Ardbraccan.

**Uscias**   The master of wisdom who lived in Findias, one of the four cities from which the Tuatha De Danann came. He gave Nuada the sword that killed all enemies.

**Vaughn**   *Small.*

# Scotland

## Female Names

**Agnes**   From a Greek word meaning "pure" or "gentle." Variants are AGGIE, NESTA, NESSA, and NESSIE. The name Segna is also used, which is a form of Agnes spelled backwards, according to an old Scottish custom called backspelling.

**Ailean** (AY-luhn)   From the Old Irish word *ail,* meaning "noble," and the diminutive *an.* Variants are AILEANA, AILA (AY-lah), and ALANA.

**Ailis** (AY-less)   The Scottish form of the name Alice. It means "truthful." Variants of this name are AILI and LISSA.

**Ailsa** (AYL-suh)   This name is taken from Ailsa Craig, which is a rocky island in the Clyde estuary. It may have originated from the Norse-Viking words *alf,* meaning "elf," and *sigi,* meaning "victory."

**Ainsley** (AYN-slee)   *My own meadow.* A variant is AINSLEE.

**Akira**   *Anchor.*

**Alexandra**   The Scottish female form of the name Alexander. It means "defender of humankind." Other variants are ALEXINA, LEXIE, and ALEXIS.

**Alpina**   The Scottish form of the male name Alpin, this name appears in the earliest records in Scotland. It derives from the Latin *albinus,* meaning "white" or "fair."

**Andreana**   The female version of the name Andrew. It means "strong" or "courageous."

**Anice**   The Scottish form of Ann. It means "grace."

**Annot**   *Light.*

**Artis**    A feminine form of the male name Arthur, it means "bear."

**Athdara**    The feminine form of the name Adair, which is probably a Scottish pronunciation of the name Edgar. It means "successful spear-warrior." A variant is ADAIRA.

**Audrey**    *Noble strength.* A variant is AUDRA.

**Barbara**    *Barbarian* or *stranger.*

**Beathag** (BAY-hak)    Derived from the Gaelic *beatha,* meaning "life." In the eleventh century there was a Queen Bethoc, who was the daughter of Malcolm II. A variant is BETHA.

**Beathas**    A Gaelic name that means "wise."

**Blair**    A *dweller on the plains.* A variant is BLAYRE.

**Bonnie**    In Scottish, it means "pretty" or "beautiful."

**Bradana**    A Gaelic name that means "salmon."

**Brenda**    Derived from the Norse *brand,* meaning "sword." This name seems to have originated in the Shetland Islands, an area settled by Vikings.

**Bridget**    The Scottish version of the Irish goddess BRIGHID.

**Cadha**    A Celtic name that means "from the steep place."

**Cailleach** (CAL-yech)    The original name of Scotland was Caledonia, taken from the name of this goddess. The Cailleach Beine Bric, or Veiled One, represented the Crone aspect of the Goddess. She was said to be reborn every Samhain (Halloween) and turned into a stone on Beltane (May 1). A variant is CAILLIC.

**Cairistiona** (ka-rish-CHE-nuh)    The Scottish version of the name Christina.

**Cameron**    *Crooked nose.* A variant is CAMERA.

**Catriona** (ka-TREE-un-nuh)    The Scottish form of the name Catherine. This name means "pure."

**Christel**    A variant of the name CHRISTINA. Another variant is CHRISTAL.

**Ciorstag** (KER-nyuhx)    The Scottish nickname for Catherine. It means "pure."A variant of CATRIONA.

**Coira**    *Seething pool.* A variant is CORA.

**Coleen**    The Gaelic word for "girl." Variants are COLINA and COLLEEN.

**Cullodena, Cullodina**    A personal name derived from the place-name Culloden. It means "from the broken, mossy ground." A variant is CULLODINA.

**Daracha**    *From the oak.*

**Davina**   The Scottish female version of the name David. It means "beloved." Variants are DAVA, VINA, DAVONNA, DAVON, and DAVONDA.

**Deirdre**   An Irish-Gaelic name meaning "sorrow." Deirdre was the tragic heroine in Irish tales who fled to Scotland with her lover Naoise to escape marrying Conchobar the king. Upon their return to Ireland, Naoise was murdered. She died on Naoise's grave.

**Dervorgilla**   Derived from the Old Irish word *der,* meaning "daughter," and the name Forgall, a legendary figure. This name was very popular during the Middle Ages. A modern Irish and Scottish variant is DERVLA.

**Diana**   Although she was a Roman goddess of the moon, Diana was well known in Scotland.

**Dolina**   This Scottish version of the name Donald is compounded of the Old Irish words *domnan,* meaning "world," and *gal,* meaning "valor." Scottish nicknames are DOLLY and DOLLAG (DAW-luhk).

**Ealasaid** (ee-AH-luh-sich)   The Scottish Gaelic form of Elizabeth. It means "consecrated to God." Variants are ELSBETH, ELSPETH, and ELSPET.

**Eara**   *From the east.* A variant is EARIE.

**Edana**   At one time Edinburgh had the name Dunedin, or *dun Edana,* meaning "Edana's castle."

**Edina**   A place name that has been modified into a personal name. It means "from Edinburgh." Variants are EDINE and EDEEN.

**Effie**   The Scottish version of the name Euphemia. The old spelling is OIGHRIG (II-rix). This name was very popular among the nobility until the nineteenth century. It means "good repute."

**Eiric**   The Scottish feminine version of the name Eric, which was taken from the Norse. It means "ever powerful." A variant is EIRICA.

**Erskina**   *From the top of the cliff.*

**Evanna**   *Right-handed.* A variant is EVINA.

**Fearchara**   This Scottish-Gaelic name means "dear one."

**Fenella**   The Scottish version of the Irish name Fionnuala. It is derived from the Old Irish *finn,* meaning "bright or fair," and *guala,* meaning "shoulders."

**Fia**   *Dark of peace.*

**Fiona**   The feminine form of the Irish hero Finn or Fionn, this name means "white" or "fair."

**Floraidh** (FLOH-ree)   The Scottish Gaelic form of the name Flora, which in itself is an anglicized form of Fionnuala. The name Flora means "flower." A variant is FLORAIGH.

**Forba**  Feminine versions of the clan name Forbeis. A variant is FORBIA.

**Fyfa**  A female form of the name Fyfe, which was the name of an ancient kingdom in eastern Scotland. It is believed that the name Fyfe itself came from Fib, the name of one of the seven sons of Cruithne, the ancestor of the Picts.

**Gara**  *Short*. Variants are GARIA and GAIRA.

**Gavina**  *White hawk*. A variant is GAVENIA.

**Gillian** (JILL-ee-an)  A Scottish rendering of the name Jillian. It means "youthful."

**Giorsal** (GI-ruh-shuhl)  This is the Scottish Gaelic version of the name Grace.

**Glenna**  The feminine form of the name Glen, which is derived from the Gaelic *gleann,* meaning "valley."

**Glynis**  A Gaelic name that means "valley."

**Gordania** (GORSH-tuhn-a)  A female version of the name Gordon, which comes from the clan name derived from the British *gor,* meaning "great," and *din,* meaning "hill-fort." A variant is GORDANA.

**Gormla** (gohr-UHM-luh)  A version of the Old Irish name Gormflaith, which comes from *gorm,* meaning "splendid," and *flaith,* meaning "sovereignty."

**Greer**  A male or female name. It comes from the name Gregor and means "vigilant."

**Grizel**  A Scottish adaptation of the Norse name Griselda. It means "gray battle-maid."

**Gunna**  A Scottish version of a Norse-Viking name that means "warrior battle-maid."

**Heather**  A Scottish name derived from the plant heather.

**Ilisa**  The Scottish version of Elisa. It means "truthful." A variant is ILYSA.

**Ina** (EE-na)  Although it began as a nickname for any female names ending in *ina,* it became a Scottish personal name.

**Inghean**  A Scottish feminine form of the Norse-Viking deity Ing. It means "the god's daughter." A variant is INGHINN.

**Innes**  A male or female name. It is the Scottish Gaelic word for "island." It began as a clan name that then became a first name.

**Iona**   Derived from the name of the sacred isle in the Hebrides. Saint Columba is said to have founded the first monastery there in 563.

**Iseabail** (I-shi-bel)   The Scottish version of the name Isabel, this name is also written as ISHBEL. It means "consecrated to God." Variants are BEL, ELLA, IBBIE, ISA, SIB, and TIBBY.

**Isla**   A personal name derived from the Scottish island Islay.

**Jean**   The feminine form of John. It means "God is gracious."

**Jessie**   The modern version of the Gaelic name Seasaidh (SHAY-see). This is the Scottish version of the name Janet. It means "God is gracious."

**Jinny**   The Scottish version of the name Jennifer, which means "white wave."

**Jocelin**   A female or male name. It derives from the Breton Saint Josse, a name brought to Scotland by Norman-French settlers. It has been common since the twelfth century. It means "joyful."

**Keita**   *Woods or an enclosed place.* A variant is KEITI.

**Kelsi**   Scottish versions of the name Chelsea. It means "sea harbor."

**Kenna**   This is the feminine form of the name Kenneth, which itself is derived from the Gaelic name Coinneach and the Pictish name Cinead. It means "handsome."

**Kentigerna**   Derived from the Old Irish *cenn*, meaning "head," and *tigern*, meaning "lord."

**Kenzie**   A personal name adapted from a clan name. It means "light-skinned."

**Kirstie**   A variant of CHRISTINE, which means "Christian."

**Lainie**   *Serves Saint John.* A variant is LEANA.

**Lair**   *Mare.* Variants are LARA, and LARIA.

**Laurie**   The Scottish version of the name Laura. It means "crowned with laurel."

**Lesley**   A female or male name, it probably comes from the Celtic *lis*, meaning "court," and *celyn*, meaning "holy." Some sources give the meaning as "gray fortress." The older spelling is LIOSLAITH.

**Lileas**   This is the Gaelic form of the name Lily, which comes from the Latin *lilium*. It is also written as LILIDH (li-LEE).

**Lorna**   This is the female form of the name Lorne. It means "crowned with laurel." The name was said to have been invented by the Scottish writer R. D. Blackmore for the heroine in his novel *Lorna Doone*, which was written in 1869.

**Machara**   A Gaelic name that means "plain."

**Maili** (MAH-lee)   A Scottish Gaelic version of Mary. It means "bitter."

**Mairead** (MAY-ret)   The Gaelic form of the name Margaret. It means "pearl." It became extremely popular in the Middle Ages after the woman who became Saint Margaret married the King of the Scots, Malcolm III. Three of her sons also became kings. Her feast day is June 10.

**Mairi** (MAH-ree)   The Scottish Gaelic form of Mary. This name means "bitter." Variants are MOIRE and MUIRE.

**Maisie**   The Scottish version of Margaret. It means "pearl."

**Malmuira**   A Gaelic name that means "dark-skinned."

**Malvina**   Some sources say this name was invented by the Scottish writer James MacPherson. Other sources say it is a female version of Melvin and means "armored chief." A variant is MALVI.

**Marcail**   A Scottish version of Margaret or Marjorie, which means "pearl."

**Marion**   A variant of Mary, this name means "bitter."

**Mariota**   A version of the name Mary. Scottish history tells of the Mariota who was the wife of Donald, Lord of the Isles.

**Marsaili** (MAHR-suh-lee)   The Scottish form of the name Margaret, which means "pearl."

**Maureen**   This Celtic name means "great."

**Moibeal**   A female Gaelic name that means "lovable."

**Moira**   This Celtic name means "great one."

**Moireach**   A Gaelic dialect name that means "lady."

**Morag** (MOHR-ahk)   A classic Gaelic name, it is derived from the Old Irish *mor,* meaning "big."

**Morven**   Derived from the Gaelic *mor,* meaning "big," and *bhein,* meaning "peak." This is the name of the mountains in Aberdeenshire and Caithness and has also been used to designate the entire northwest of Scotland. It has lately been used as a personal name. A variant is MORVYN.

**Muira** (MOOR-ah or MOOR-eh)   Derived from the Gaelic word *muir,* meaning "moor." A variant is MUIRE.

**Muireall** (MOOR-uh-yel)   Derived from the Old Irish *muir,* meaning "sea" and *gel,* meaning "bright" or "shining."

**Muirne** (MOOR-nyuh)   Comes from an Old Irish word meaning "beloved."

**Nairne**  A Celtic name that means "lives at the alder tree river." A variant is NAIRNA.

**Nathaira**  *Snake*. A variant is NATHARA.

**Nessa**  This is an Old Irish personal name as well as a Scottish nickname for Agnes.

**Nichneven**  A Samhain (Halloween) witch-goddess also called "divine" and "brilliant." Scottish folk tales say she rides through the night with her followers on Samhain Eve. During the Middle Ages she was known by several names: Dame Habonde, Abundia, Satia, Bensozie, Zobiana, and Herodiana.

**Nighean**  A Gaelic dialect name that means "young woman." A variant is NIGHINN.

**Osla**  Common in the Shetland Islands, this name is the Gaelic version of the Norse Aslaug, and means "god-consecrated."

**Paisley**  A personal name taken from the patterned fabric made in Paisley, Scotland.

**Peigi**  The Scottish version of the name Peggy and a nickname for Margaret.

**Raoghnailt**  A Scottish form of the name Rachel. A variant is RAONAID.

**Rhona**  Some sources say this name is derived from the Scottish name of an island, which itself comes from the Norse *hrauen,* meaning "rough" and *ey,* meaning "island." Other sources say the meaning is "powerful, mighty."

**Robena**  A Gaelic name meaning "robin." A variant is ROBINA.

**Rossalyn**  *A cape or promontory*.

**Saraid** (SAHR-ich)  Derived from the Old Irish word *sar,* meaning "best or noble." SARAIT was the daughter of Conn of the Hundred Battles and is considered to be the ancestress of the Scottish kings.

**Scota**  This Underworld goddess gave her name to Scotland. She was the greatest teacher of martial arts, as well as a warrior woman and prophetess who lived on the Isle of Skye. Variants of her name are SCOTTA, SCOTIA, and SCATHACH.

**Seonag**  The Scottish version of Joan. It means "God is gracious."

**Seonaid**  The Scottish form of Janet. It means "God is gracious."

**Sile** (SHEE-luh)  The Scottish version of the name Cecilia, it is also written as SHEILA and SHEELAGH.

**Sileas**  A Scottish form of the name Julia. It means "youthful one."

**Sima** (SHEE-mah)  *Listener*.

**Sine** (SHEE-nuh)   The Scottish version of the name Jean. Variants are SHEENA and SHEENAGH.

**Siubhan**   *Praised.*

**Siusaidh**   Scottish versions of the name Susan, which means "graceful lily."

**Skena**   A Gaelic name adapted from the place-name Skene.

**Sorcha** (SOHR-uh-xuh)   Derived from the Old Irish word *sorchae,* meaning "bright" or "radiant."

**Struana**   *From the stream.*

**Tavia**   The Scottish version of the name Octavia, which means "eighth." A variant is TEVA.

**Tavie**   A female version of the Scottish name Tavish, which means "twin."

**Tira**   *Land.* A variant is TYRA.

**Torra**   This Gaelic name means "from the castle."

**Una**   From the Old Irish word *uan,* meaning "lamb."

**Vika**   *From the creek.*

**Wynda**   This Gaelic adaptation means "from the narrow or winding passage."

## MALE NAMES

**Abhainn**   *River.* A variant is AIBNE.

**Acair**   A variant of the word that means "anchor." Another variant is ACAISEID.

**Achaius**   *Friend of horses.*

**Adair**   *Oak tree ford.* Variants are ADAIRE and ATHDAR.

**Adhamh**   A Scottish-Gaelic spelling for the name Adam. It means "of the earth."

**Ahearn**   *Lord of the horses.* Variant spellings are AHERIN and HEARN.

**Aidan**   Derived from the Old Irish word *aed,* meaning "fire." This is a very old Scottish name. The ruler of Argyll in the sixth century was King Aidan mac Gabran. He was the first Christian king in the British Isles.

**Ailbert**   *Noble.*

**Ailean**   *Handsome.*

**Ailein**   Derived from a Gaelic word meaning "from the green meadow."

**Aillig**   *From the stony place*. A variant is AIL.

**Aindrea**   The Gaelic form of the name Andrew, which means "strong."

**Ainsley**   *My own meadow or lee*.

**Alan**   From a Gaelic word meaning "handsome."

**Alastair**   This name means "defender of humankind," and is a Scottish version of the name Alexander. Variants are ALAISDAIR and ALASDAIR (AHL-uhs-duhr).

**Alpin**   Probably derived from the Latin *albinus* meaning "white" or "fair." This name has been recorded in Scotland from the earliest times. It is the source of the clan name MacAlpin.

**Amhuinn**   *From the alder tree river*.

**Angus**   The Scottish version of the name of the Irish love-god Aonghus mac Og. It is derived from the Old Irish words *oen*, meaning "one" and *gus*, meaning "vigor." Angus is a traditional name in the clan Donald. Variant spellings are AENGUS and AONGHUS (EUN-eu-uss).

**Anndra** (AH-oon-drah)   This is the Scottish version of the name Andrew and means "manly."

**Aodh** (OOH)   Derived from the Old Irish *aed*, meaning "fire," this is one of the most frequent male names in early Scotland. It is the basis for the surname Mackay. A variant is AOIDH.

**Argyle**   A name taken from the old place-name Arregaithel. It means "from the land of the Gauls."

**Artair** (AHR-shtuhr)   The Gaelic form of the name Arthur. In Scotland this name means "bear." Variants are ARTH and ARTUS.

**Athdar**   A variant of the name ADAIR. It means "from the oak tree ford."

**Aulay**   From the Norse name Olof, adopted by the Scots. The personal name and surname of Macaulay both come from this name.

**Baird**   A clan and personal name, it is derived from the Old Irish *bard*, meaning "poet."

**Balfour**   *Pasture land*.

**Balloch**   From a word meaning "from the pasture."

**Balmoral**   A personal name taken from a place name, it means "from the majestic village."

**Banner**   *Flag bearer*.

**Barclay**   *Birch tree meadow*. A variant is BERKELEY.

**Bean**   Taken from a Celtic word for "spirit" or "fairy," this name means "one who is white-skinned."

**Bearnard**    Derived from the Old German words *Berin-hard,* meaning "brave as a bear."

**Birk**    *Birch tree.*

**Blackburn**    *Black brook.*

**Blair**    Derived from the Gaelic *blar,* meaning "plain, field, battlefield."

**Blane**    Derived from the Gaelic *bla,* meaning "yellow," this was the name of an important Scottish saint who was bishop of Kingarth. He lived in the late sixh century. His feast day is August 11.

**Bothan**    This name comes from a Gaelic word meaning "from the stone house."

**Boyd**    It means "yellow-haired" and comes from the Gaelic *buidhe.*

**Braden**    A modern spelling of the older name BHRADAIN, which means "salmon."

**Braigh**    Derived from a Gaelic word meaning "from the upper part."

**Breac**    Derived from the Celtic word "speckled." A variant is BRYCE.

**Bret**    *From Britain.*

**Brian**    *Strong* or *virtuous.* This name was brought from Ireland, where the famous High King Brian Boru lived. Variants are BRIANT, BRION, and BRYAN.

**Broc**    Derived from an Old English word meaning "badger."

**Brodie**    Derived from the Irish Gaelic word that means "from the ditch."

**Bruce**    Derived from the place-name Braose (now Brieuse) in Normandy. It was brought to Scotland by the Normans. The famous Robert Bruce (or Robert the Bruce), king of the Scots from 1306 to 1329, liberated his country from the English at the Battle of Bannockburn.

**Bryce**    Derived from Saint Bricius of Tours, France, whose cult was brought into Scotland by the Norman invaders.

**Bryson**    *Son of Bryce.*

**Buchanan**    Possibly derived from the Gaelic *bocan,* meaning "young male deer," this surname is used as a personal name. There is also a place of this name in Stirlingshire.

**Busby**    *Village in the thicket.*

**Caelan** (KAH-luhn)    Comes from the Old Irish *cuilen,* meaning "pup, cub, kitten." This has long been a favorite name with the clans Campbell and MacKenzie. Some sources say that this is the Scottish form of the name Nicholas, which means "victorious people." Variants are CAEL, CAILEAN (CAL-lan), CAELIN, and CALLEAN.

**Cairns**   A Gaelic word meaning "a heap of stones traditionally placed on top of a grave." It first became a surname, then a personal name.

**Calum** (KA-luhm)   Derived from the Latin word *columba,* meaning "dove." It is also a shortened form of Malcolm.

**Camden**   *Winding or crooked valley.*

**Cameron**   Derived from the Gaelic *cam,* meaning "crooked," and either *shron,* meaning "nose," or *brun,* meaning "hill." Originally, it was a clan name that was taken from a place in the old kingdom of Fife. Variations are CAMAR and CAMSHRON.

**Campbell**   A Scottish clan name that is used as a personal name. It comes from the Gaelic *cam,* meaning "crooked," and *beul,* meaning "mouth." A variant is CAMBEUL.

**Carlton**   Derived from the Old English words *Carla-tun,* which means "farmers' settlement." An older spelling is CARAIDLAND.

**Carmichael**   *Follower of Michael.*

**Carney**   *Fighter.*

**Carr**   A name that is derived from the Norse word for "marsh." A variant is CATHAIR.

**Cathal**   Derived from the Old Irish word *cath,* meaning "battle." This ancient name is also the source of the surname Macall.

**Cawley**   A name derived from the Gaelic word for "relic." The older spelling is CAMHLAIDH. A variant is CAULEY.

**Ceard**   Derived from the Gaelic word for "smith." A variant is CEARDACH.

**Chalmer**   *Son of the lord.* A variant is CALMER.

**Chattan**   A clan name that comes from the Gaelic word for "cat," it is also used as a personal name. A variant is CHAIT.

**Cinaed**   The legendary King Cinaed Mac Ailpin united the Gaels and Picts into one kingdom, calling it Scotia. A variant is CEANAG (KEN-uhk).

**Clach**   This word comes from the Gaelic word for "stone."

**Cleit**   Derived from the Gaelic word for "rocky promontory."

**Clennan**   Comes from a Celtic word meaning "servant of Finnian."

**Clyde**   The Scottish name of a river that is used as a personal name.

**Coinneach** (KON-yokh or KUH-nyuhx)   Comes from the Old Irish *cain,* meaning "good," "beautiful," and is identical to the Irish name of CAINNECH.

**Collin** (KAW-lin)   The Scottish version of the Irish name COLIN, which means "young cub." Other sources list the meaning as "victory of the people."

**Conan**   The Scottish version of the same Irish name. It means "wise" in Scotland. Variants are CONNOR and CONON.

**Connell**   From a Celtic word meaning "high and mighty."

**Conran**   This name comes from Saint Conran, who was a seventh-century bishop and apostle to the Orkney Islands. His feast day is February 14.

**Corey**   This name comes from a Gaelic word meaning "ravine." It is sometimes translated as "seething pool."

**Craig**   This name comes from the Gaelic place-word *creag,* meaning "crag" or "steep rock." It is used as a surname and personal name. Variants are CRAIGEN and KRAIG.

**Crannog**   *Lake dweller.*

**Criostal** (KREE-uh-stuhl)   This is the Scottish form of the name Christopher.

**Culloden**   A personal name derived from the place-name of Culloden, it means "from the nook of the marsh."

**Dabhaidh** (DA-ee-vee or DAEE-vee)   The Gaelic version of the name David, which means "beloved." A variant spelling is DAIBHIDH.

**Dallas**   The name of a town in Scotland that is used as a personal name. In Scottish Gaelic it means "from the waterfall." Variants are DALLIEASS, DALLIS, and DALYS.

**Dalziel**   *Small field.* Variants are DAZIEL and DALYELL.

**Damh**   *Ox.* A variant is DAIMH.

**Darach**   This name is derived from the Gaelic word for "oak."

**Davis**   *David's son.* Variants are DAVE and DAVIDSON. The old spelling is MACDAIBHIDH.

**Dearg**   From a Gaelic word for "red."

**Denholm**   The name of a town in Scotland that is used as a personal name.

**Diarmad** (DYEER-muht)   This name is based on the Old Irish legendary name of Diarmait, which means "sorrow."

**Doire**   *From the grove.* A variant is DHOIRE.

**Donald**   This modern name is based on the older Gaelic name of Domhnal (DAW-ull), which is itself derived from *domnan,* meaning "world," and *gal,* meaning "valor." The translated meaning would be "proud ruler." The clan Donald, which was the most powerful of the Highland clans, traces its ancestry to a fifteenth-century Donald, grandson of Somerled, Lord of the Isles. Variants of this name are DON, DONN, DONALL, DONALT, DONAUGH, DONEL, DONELL, and DOMHNULL.

**Donnan** This name comes from the Old Irish *donn,* meaning "brown chief."

**Donnchadh** (DON-ah-choo) The old Gaelic spelling of the name Duncan, which means "dark-skinned stranger."

**Dorrell** *King's doorkeeper.*

**Dougal** Derived from the Old Irish *dubh,* meaning "dark," and *glas,* meaning "green." The Gaelic version is Dughall (DOO-ull or DOO-luh). Translated this name means "dark stranger." The clan Mac-Dougal traces its roots to DUGALL, the oldest son of Somerled, a Dane. Variants are DOUGALD (DOO-gald) and DOUGHALL.

**Douglas** The original Gaelic version was DUBHGHLAS (DOOG-lass), which means "dark river or stream" or "dark blue-green." Ireland, Wales, and Scotland all have rivers bearing this name.

**Drummond** Some sources say this name means "druid's mountain," while others say it is a surname and clan name derived from the village of Drymen in Sterlingshire. It means "at the ridge." The name has been popular in Scotland since the thirteenth century.

**Duer** *Heroic.*

**Duff** *Dark.* An older spelling is DUBH.

**Duncan** This name is derived from the Old Irish *dubh,* meaning "dark or brown" and *cath,* meaning "warrior." Older spellings are DONNCHADH and DONNACHADH. It was first a clan name, then a surname, and finally a personal name.

**Dunham** A name that is derived from the Gaelic word for "brown."

**Dunlop** *Muddy hill.*

**Dunmore** A Scottish name that means "fortress on the hill."

**Dunn** A shortened form of the Scottish name Duncan.

**Durell** A name that means "king's doorkeeper." Variants are DOR-RELL, DURIAL, and DURRELL.

**Eachann** (EU-chun) The Scottish version of the name Hector, which means "steadfast."

**Eanruig** *Rules the home.*

**Ear** A name that is derived from the Gaelic meaning "from the east."

**Edan** *Fire.*

**Eideard** (AE-jard)   This is the Gaelic version of the name Edward. The name means "wealthy guardian."

**Eilig**   A name derived from a word meaning "from the deer pass."

**Ennis**   In Scotland, this is an alternate form of Angus.

**Eoghann**   The Gaelic spelling of the name Ewan.

**Eonan** (YOE-wun or YOH-nuhn)   *Youth*. Taken from the Old Irish name Adamnan (little Adam).

**Erskine**   The origin of this name is unknown; however, it means "high cliff" and is based on a place name on the banks of the River Clyde near Glasgow. Variants are ERSKIN and KINNY.

**Evan**   Some sources say this name means "young warrior," while others believe it means "right-handed."

**Ewan**   The Gaelic name is Eoghann, derived from the Old Irish name Eogan, which means "born of the yew tree." A traditonal name among the Campbell and Chattan clans. Variants are EWAN, EUEN, EWEN, EWHEN, and EWEN.

**Fang**   *From the sheep pen*. A variant is FAING.

**Farlan**   Derived from a word meaning "son of the furrows." A variant is FARLANE.

**Farquhar**   The old Gaelic name was Fearchar (FER-uh-xuhr). It was derived from the Old Irish *fir*, meaning "man," and *cara*, meaning "friendly." The ancestor of both Chattan and Farquarson clans was King Ferchar the Long, of the kingdom of Lorne. Variants are FAARQUAR, FARQUHARSON, and FERCHAR.

**Feandan**   *From the narrow glen*.

**Fearchar** (FER-a-char)   A variant spelling of the name FARQUHAR, which means "one especially dear," or "friendly man."

**Fergus**   A form of the name FEARGHUS (FER-ra-ghuss), which comes from the Old Irish *fer*, meaning "man," and *gus*, meaning "strength or vigor." Some sources say the meaning is "first choice."

**Fergusson**   *Son of Fergus*. A variant is FERGUSON.

**Fife**   A personal name derived from Fife, an ancient kingdom in eastern Scotland. Some sources believe this name originated with Fib, one of the seven sons of Cruithne, the legendary ancestor of the Picts. Variants are FYFE and FIBH.

**Fingal**   Derived from the Old Irish *finn*, meaning "bright or fair," and *gall*, meaning "stranger."

**Finlay**   The Gaelic form of this name is FIONNLAGH (FYOON-ee-loo or

FYOHN-lax). It is derived from the Old Irish *finn,* meaning "fair" or "bright" and *laoch,* meaning "warrior."

**Firth**   A personal name derived from a place-name, it means "arm of the sea."

**Forbes**   The Gaelic name was Forbeis (FOR-bish), a clan name derived from the Gaelic word *forba,* meaning "field," and the location suffix *–ais.* Some sources list the meaning as "headstrong."

**Fordyce**   A surname and personal name based on a place in Banffshire.

**Frang** (FRANG-g)   A version of the Teutonic name Frank, which means "free."

**Fraser**   *Strawberry flowers.*

**Gabhran** (GAHV-ruhn)   Derived from a Gaelic word that means "little goat."

**Gare**   Derived from a word meaning "short." A variant is GAIR.

**Gavin**   *White hawk.* This name became very popular in Scotland during the Middle Ages. It is a variant of the name GAWAIN.

**Geordan**   The Scottish version of the name Gordon.

**Geordie**   The Scottish variant of the name GEORGE. It means "farmer."

**Gilchrist**   A modern spelling of the Gaelic name Gille Criosd, which means "servant of Christ." This was very popular in Scotland during the Middle Ages.

**Gillanders**   A modern version of the Gaelic name Gille Anndrais, which means "servant of Saint Andrew."

**Gilleabart**   *Pledge.*

**Gillean** (GIL-yan)   The ancient Gaelic name was Gilla Eoin (gil-yuh-YOWN), or "servant of Saint John."

**Gilleasbuig** (GEEL-yes-pick)   *Genuine or bold.* A variant of the Old German name Archibald.

**Gillecroids**   Derived from the Gaelic word meaning "Christ-bearer" or "servant of Christ."

**Gillespie**   The Gaelic name was Gilleasbuig (gil-yuh-IS-pik). This means "servant of a bishop." The Campbells used this as a traditional first name for centuries.

**Gillis**   The Gaelic name originally was Gille Iosa (gil-yuh-EE-uh-suh). It means "servant of Jesus." This is still a traditional name in the Hebrides.

**Gillivray**   *Servant of judgment.*

**Glen**  A male or female name that comes from the word *gleann*, meaning "valley."

**Glendon**  *Fortress in the glen*. Variants are GLENDEN and GLENN.

**Goraidh**  Derived from a Celtic word that means "peaceful."

**Gordon** (GOR-dan)  The Gaelic name Gordan (GORSH-tuhn) is derived from the words *gor*, meaning "great," and *din*, meaning "hill-fort." Some sources list the meaning as "hero." The clan name might be based on a place-name in Berwickshire.

**Gowan**  A name derived from the Gaelic *gobha*, meaning "a smith." In ancient Celtic society, blacksmiths held great influence because of their magical abilities with metals. Variants are GOW and GOBHA.

**Graeme**  Derived from an Anglo-Saxon word meaning "warlike." It is a Scottish version of the name Graham. A variant is GRAEM.

**Greer**  A male or female name that comes from a Scottish surname. It is possibly a variant of the name GREGOR.

**Gregor**  The ancient Gaelic name is Griogair, which is the Scottish version of the name Gregory. Some sources say this name is related to the name of Saint Gregory of Tours, France, a name brought to Scotland by the Norman French, and that it means "vigilant." Others think it is derived from the Gaelic word *greigh*, meaning "a flock or herd." It has been widely used since the Middle Ages. During most of the seventeenth and eighteenth centuries, all forms of this name were banned because of the misdeeds of some clan members.

**Gunn**  Derived from the Norse-Viking word for "warrior." One source lists the meaning as "white."

**Hamish** (HAY-mish)  The Scottish form of the names James.

**Harailt**  A Scottish version of an Old Norse word meaning "leader."

**Hearn**  The Scottish shortened form of the name AHEARN, which means "lord of the horses."

**Henson**  A surname adopted as a personal name, it means "Henry's son." A variant is HENDERSON.

**Home**  *From the cave*. A variant is HUME.

**Hugh**  Derived from the German *hugi*, meaning "heart" or "mind," this English name has been traditionally used to anglicize such Gaelic names as Eoghann, Uisdeann, and Aodh.

**Ian** (EE-an)  The Scottish form of the name John, which means "God is gracious." Variants are IAIN and IAIAN.

**Innes**　A male or female name derived from the Gaelic word for "island." Originally, it was a clan name and surname, then a personal name.

**Iomhair** (EE-uh-var)　This Gaelic name is borrowed from the Teutonic name Ivor. It means "archer." Variants are IVAR and IVER.

**Ivar**　This name has two sources, the Gaelic name Iomhair (EE-uh-vuhr), and the Old Norse name Ivarr, which means "yew tree army." Some sources list the meaning as "archer." It was a traditional personal name of the Campbell clan of Strachan, as well as the source of the surname MacIver. A variant spelling is IVOR.

**Jamie**　A Scottish variation of the names James and Seumas.

**Jock**　An older Scottish version of the names James and Seumas.

**Joselin**　A male or female name derived from the Breton Saint Josse. This name was brought to Scotland by the Norman French and has been used since the twelfth century.

**Kade**　*Wetlands.*

**Keddy**　The Scottish form of the name Adam.

**Keir**　This was originally a clan name that later became a personal name. It is derived from the Old Irish word *ciar,* meaning "dark."

**Keith**　Based on the place-name Ceiteach in East Lothian, this is either a personal name or a surname. The personal name is interpreted as meaning "battle place."

**Kendrew**　The Scottish version of the name Andrew.

**Kendrick**　*Royal chieftain.*

**Kennan**　*Little Ken.*

**Kennedy**　This name comes from the Old Irish name Cennetig, which itself is derived from *cenn,* meaning "head," and *etig,* meaning "ugly." This has been a consistent personal name and surname in Scotland since the twelfth century.

**Kenneth**　*Handsome face or head.*

**Kentigern**　This name comes from the Old Irish *cenn,* meaning "head," and *tigern,* meaning "lord."

**Kenzie**　*Wise leader.* It is related to the clan name Mackenzie.

**Kermichil**　Derived from a Gaelic word, this name means "from Michael's fortress."

**Kincaid**　*Battle chief.*

**Kinnon**　*Fair-born.*

**Kirk**　The Scottish word for "church." A variant is KERK.

**Kyle**   Derived from the Gaelic word *caol*, meaning "narrow," this is the name of a strait in Ayrshire. It was a surname before it began to be used as a personal name.

**Lachlan**   From the Gaelic word Lachlann (LAKH-lunn or LAX-luhn) based on a Norse word that means "land of the Vikings" or "land of lakes or fjords." An older spelling is LAOCHAILAN.

**Lailoken**   This was the name of a Scottish prophet who was driven partially mad by his prophetic gifts. Some authors claim that Merlin's story was based on his life.

**Laird**   *Wealthy landowner.*

**Leith**   Derived from a word that means "broad river." A variant is LEATHAN.

**Lennox**   *With many elms.*

**Leod**   A Norse-Viking name adopted by the Scots. it means "ugly." The Clan MacLeod claims the Viking chief Leod as their ancestor.

**Leslie**   A male or female name, it is derived from the Celtic *lis*, meaning "court," and *celyn*, meaning "holly." Some sources list the meaning as "gray fortress."

**Logan**   This name comes from the Gaelic place name *lag*, meaning "hollow." It is the name of several places in Scotland, in use as a surname since the twelfth century.

**Lorne**   Based on a place-name in Argyll. According to legend, Loarn was the name of one of the three sons of the first Gael to come to Scotland from Ireland.

**Lulach** (LOO-luhx)   Derived from the Gaelic word for "little calf." It is an ancient royal Scottish name that was borne by the stepson of Macbeth who lived in the eleventh century.

**Lundie**   *Grove by the island.*

**Luthais**   *Famous warrior.*

**Lyall**   In Scotland, this name means "loyal."

**Mac**   In Gaelic this means "son." Also a nickname for names beginning with "Mac" or Mc." Variants are MACK and MAX.

**Machar**   *Plain.* A variant spelling is MACHAIR.

**Malcolm**   Derived from *mael*, meaning "devotee," and the Latin *columba*, meaning "dove." Three Scottish kings of the medieval era bore this name. A variant is MEALCOLUIM.

**Manius**   The Scottish version of the Norse-Viking name Magnus, which means "great." A variant is MANUS.

**Maolmuire**    *Servant of Mary.* Some sources list the meaning as "dark-skinned."

**Martainn** (MAHRSH-teen or MAHR-shtan)    The Scottish version of the name Martin. This name means "warlike."

**Micheil** (MEECH-yell or MEE-hyel)    The Scottish form of the name Michael, which means "who is like God."

**Mirren**    The modern version of the sixth-century Meadhran.

**Moncreiffe**    *From the hill of the sacred bough.*

**Montgomery**    This is a French name based on a German one. The name is actually derived from the French word *mont,* meaning "hill," and the German words *guma,* meaning "man," and *ric,* meaning "power."

**Morgan**    *Sea warrior.*

**Morven**    From a Gaelic word meaning "mariner." A variant is MORVIN.

**Muir** (MYOOR)    It is either a surname or personal name, both based on the Gaelic place-word *muir,* that means "moor" or "marshland."

**Muirfinn**    *Dweller by the shining sea.*

**Mungo**    This is a nickname of Kentigern. It may be derived from the Old Irish *mo,* meaning "my," and *cu,* meaning "hound." Other sources list the meaning as "amiable."

**Munro**    This personal name comes from the clan name Mac An Rothaich, which is itself derived from the Gaelic name Rothach (a person from Ro). The family Munro originally came from a place near the River Roe in Derry, Ireland.

**Murchadh** (MOOR-uh-choo or MOOR-uhx)    This name comes from the Old Irish *muir,* meaning "sea," and *cath,* meaning "warrior." Other sources say it means "wealthy sailor." Variants are MURDO, MURDOCH, and MURTAGH.

**Murray**    This personal name, which was taken from a clan name, means "sailor" or "man of the sea." Variants are MACMURRAY, MORAY, MURRY, and MOROGH.

**Nab**    Derived from a Gaelic word for "abbot."

**Nairn**    *River with alder trees.*

**Naomhin** (NUH-veen)    Derived from the word *naomh,* meaning "saint," this traditional personal name originated in Galloway and Ayrshire. A variant is NEVIN.

**Nathair**    This name is derived from the Celtic word *nathdrack,* meaning "snake."

**Naughton** *Pure*. Variants are NACHTON and NECHTAN.

**Nealcail** This name comes from Gaelic words meaning "victorious people."

**Niall** (NYEE-all or NEEL) This Old Irish name may be derived from *nel*, meaning "cloud." Other sources say the meaning is "champion."

**Niels** A form of the Celtic name Niall. It means "champion."

**Oidhche** Derived from a word meaning "night."

**Ossian** (UH-sheen) This is a Scottish version of the Old Irish name Oisin, which means "little deer or fawn."

**Padruig** (PA-trik) This is the Scottish version of the name Padraig (PAH-dreek). This name means "noble." Variants are PADYN, PATON, and PADAN.

**Parlan** A Gaelic version of the Old Irish name Partholon. The surnames MacFarland and MacFarlane come from this name.

**Peadair** (PED-dur or PAY-tuhr) The Scottish Gaelic version of the name Peter. This name means "stone."

**Perth** A personal name taken from a county in Scotland. It means "thornbush" or "thicket."

**Pol** (PAHL) A Gaelic form of Paul. The name means "little."

**Pony** *Small horse*.

**Rae** This name comes from an Old French word meaning "king." It was brought to Scotland by the Norman French.

**Raghnall** (REU-ull) A Scottish version of the Teutonic name Ronald. It means "wise power."

**Raibeart** (RAB-burt or RAH-bercht) The Scottish version of the name Robert, which means "shining fame."

**Ranald, Ronald** This name comes from the Gaelic name Raghnall (RUHLL) and the Norse-Viking name Rognvaldr, meaning "power" or "might." The MacDonald clan traditionally use this name.

**Rob Roy** The anglicized version of Rob Ruadh, which means "red Rob." History tells of Rob Roy MacGregor, who was born in Balquiddher, Scotland, and who harried the English overlords and English sympathizers at every opportunity.

**Ronald** The modern version of the name Ranald. Some sources list the meaning as "king's advisor." Variants are RONAL and RONNOLD.

**Ronan** This name is derived from the Old Irish *ron*, meaning "seal." Variants are RENAN and RONAT.

**Ronson** *Son of Ronald*. A variant is RONALDSON.

**Rory**   The Gaelic name was Ruairidh (ROO-uh-ree). It was derived from the Gaelic word *ruadh,* meaning "red."

**Ross**   This name comes from the Gaelic place name *ros,* which means "upland" or "promontory." It has been a Scottish personal name since the twelfh century.

**Roy**   This personal name comes from the Gaelic word for "red."

**Ruairdh** (RO-urree)   The Scottish version of the Teutonic name Roderick. This name means "famous ruler."

**Ryan**   Derived from a Gaelic word meaning "little king."

**Sandy**   *Defender of man.*

**Scot**   *A Scotsman* or *from Scotland.*

**Scrymgeour**   *Fighter.*

**Seoras** (SHAW-russ)   Another Scottish version of the German name George, which means "farmer."

**Seumas** (SHAY-muhs)   The Scottish version of the name James. It means "supplanter" or "substitute." A variant of this name is HAMISH.

**Sheiling**   *From the summer pasture.*

**Sholto**   Derived from the Gaelic *sioltaich,* meaning "propagator," this was a traditonal name among the Douglas families.

**Sim**   A nickname of the name Simon, this name means "listener." Associated particularly with the clan of Fraser, this has been a popular name in Scotland for centuries. Variants are SYM, SYME, SIMEON, and SYMON.

**Somerled**   The ancient Gaelic name was Somairle (SOH-uhr-lyuh), and came from the Old Norse *summarliethi,* meaning "one who goes forth in the summer" or "a Viking raider." According to history, the Vikings spent the autumn and winter on the islands around Scotland, including the Shetlands, Orkneys, and the Isle of Man. Then they raided the coasts of Ireland and mainland Scotland during the spring and summer. Somerled, Lord of the Isles, was an eleventh-century chieftain who was half-Gaelic, half-Norse. Born about 1100 and killed in 1164, he ruled over the Isle of Man, the southern Hebrides, and Argyll. His planning and fighting ability finally drove out the Norse from the Western Isles. He is considered to be the primary ancestor of the clan MacDonald.

**Stewart**   *Caretaker or steward.* The original Gaelic name was Stiubhart. At first this was a name given to the keepers of the royal Scottish households; later it became a hereditary surname. When the House of Stuart began ruling Scotland in 1371, and England from 1603–1714, it became associated with royalty. A variant spelling is STUART.

**Stratton**  *River valley town.*

**Struan** (STROO-uhn)  This name possibly comes from the Gaelic word *struan,* meaning "stream." At one time it was a common male name of the clan Donnchaidh (the Robertsons) who owned the lands of Struan in Perthshire.

**Sutherland**  A Norse-Viking name used by the Scots. It means "southern land."

**Tavish**  The Scottish version of the name Thomas. It means "twin." Variants are TAVIS, TAVEY, TEVIS, and TAMNAIS.

**Tearlach** (TCHAR-lokh or CHAR-luhx)  Derived from a Gaelic word meaning "well-shaped," it was popular among the Stewarts. Some sources say this name came from the Old French name Charles, which means "strong and manly."

**Tevis**  Another Scottish form of the name Thomas. A variant is TEVISH.

**Todd**  *Fox.*

**Tomas** (TO-mass or TAW-muhs)  This is another Scottish Gaelic version of the name Thomas. It means "twin." A variant is TAMHAS.

**Tormod** (TOR-ro-mot)  The Scottish Gaelic form of the Teutonic name Norman. This name means "from the north."

**Torquil**  The original Gaelic name was Torcaill. It was a name adopted by the Scots from the Norse-Viking, meaning "Thor's kettle." A variant is TORKILL. It has been a popular name in the clan of MacLeod, as they claim that as the name of their founder.

**Tremaine**  *House of stone.*

**Tyree**  This name is derived from a Gaelic word meaning "island dweller." Variants are TYRAE, TYRAI, and TYREA.

**Uilleam** (OOL-yam or OOL-yuhm)  This is the Gaelic version of the Teutonic name William, a name that was brought to Scotland in the Middle Ages by the Norman French. The name means "resolute soldier."

**Uisdean** (OOSH-jan or OOS-juhn)  This is a Gaelic form of the Teutonic name Hugh, which means "intelligent." Other sources list the source-names as Austin and Augustine.

**Urquhart**    A Scottish version of an Old English name meaning "from the fount on the knoll."

**Wallace**    This name comes from the Anglo-Saxon word *walas* or *wealas,* which means "a Celt." It is also the source for the words Wales and Welsh. It was first used as a surname in the Lowlands of Scotland. After the great warrior and patriot William Wallace was executed by the British in 1305, it began to be used as a personal name. William Wallace (1273–1305) was known as the Hammer and Scourge of England because of his exploits against the invading British. A variant spelling is WALLIS.

**Walter**    The Gaelic version was BHATAR (VAH-tuhr), which came from the German words *wald,* meaning "rule," and *harja,* meaning "folk."

**Wyndham**    *Village near the winding road.*

# Wales

Names from the Arthurian legends are also included here, as they are a vital part of Welsh history and tradition.

**Aberfa**  *From the mouth of the river.*
**Abertha**  Derived from a word meaning "sacrifice."
**Adain**  This name comes from a Welsh word meaning "winged."
**Adara**  *Catches birds.*
**Addfwyn**  Derived from a word meaning "meek."
**Addiena**  *Beautiful.* A variant is ADDIEN.
**Adyna**  *Wretched.*
**Aelwyd**  Derived from words meaning "from the hearth."
**Amser**  *Time.*
**Angharad**  (AHN-hahr-ahd or ahng-HAHR-ahd)  Derived from the Welsh *an* and *car*, meaning "love," this name means "greatly loved one." A variant is ANGHARD.
**Anna**  According to Geoffrey of Monmouth, this was the name of one of Arthur's sisters.
**Argel**  *Refuge.*
**Arglwyddes**  Derived from a word meaning "lady."
**Argoel**  *Omen.*
**Argraff**  Derived from a word meaning "impression."
**Arial**  *Vigorous.*
**Ariana**  *Silvery.* It is a variant of ARIONRHOD. Another variant is ARIAN.

**Arianell** (ah-ree-AHN-elh)  This name is derived from the Welsh *arian*, meaning "silver."

**Arianrhod** (ah-ree-AHN-rhod)  In ancient legends, the goddess Arianrhod verch Don was the mother of Dylan eil Ton and Llew Llaw Gyffes. She lived in Caer Sidi, an Otherworld castle of inspiration and an abode for humans between incarnations. In Welsh, the Corona Borealis is called Caer Arianrhod. A variant is ARANRHOD (ah-RAHN-rhod).

**Arianwen** (ah-ree-AHN-wen)  Derived from the Old Welsh *arian*, meaning "silver," and *gwen*, meaning "shining" or "holy." A variant is ARANWEN (ah-RAHN-wen).

**Arlais**  *From the temple.* A variant is ARTAITH.

**Armes**  Derived from a word meaning "prophetess."

**Arthes**  The feminine form of the male name Artur. It means "she-bear."

**Arwydd**  *Sign.*

**Asgre**  Derived from a word meaning "heart."

**Auron** (AYR-on)  It comes from *aur*, meaning "gold." A variant is EURON.

**Avenable**  In one of the Merlin legends, a girl with this name took the covering name of Grisandole and, disguised as a squire, found work in the court of the Emperor of Rome. The Emperor sent her to a wild man (Merlin) who lived in the woods to discover the meaning of a powerful dream he had. Merlin interpreted the dream and also revealed that the squire was a woman. She married the emperor.

**Banon**  Derived from a word that means "queen."

**Berth**  *Beautiful.*

**Berthog**  *Wealthy.*

**Bethan** (BETH-ahn)  A Welsh version of Elizabeth, this name means "consecrated to God." Variants are BET, BETI, BETSAN, and BETSI.

**Blanchfleur**  The name of Perceval's sister, who was a healer.

**Blodeuwedd** (BLOD-eh-weth or blod-AY-weth)  Derived from the Old Welsh *blodau*, meaning "flowers," and *gwedd*, meaning "appearance." A variant is BLANCHEFLOR.

**Blodwin** (BLOD-wen)  Derived from *blodyn*, meaning "flower," and *gwen*, meaning "shining" or "holy," this is a classic female name in Wales. Variants are BLODWEN and BLODWYN.

**Braith**  Related to the Celtic Irish word *brec,* this name means "freckled."

**Brandgaine**  She was the maid to Isolde, sometimes called Iseult. She administered the love potion that bound Isolde and Tristan together forever.

**Branwen** (BRAN-oo-wen or BRAN-wen)  Derived from the Old Welsh *bran,* meaning "crow," and *gwen,* meaning "holy" or "shining," this name means "white bosomed," or "a girl with black hair and white skin." Variants are BRANGWEN and BRONWEN (BRON-oo-wen or BRON-wen).

**Bregus**  *Frail.*

**Briallen** (bree-ALH-en)  This name comes from the Welsh word *bri-allu,* meaning "primrose."

**Brisen**  According to Malory, she was the greatest enchantress who ever lived. In order to bring about the birth of Galahad, she drugged Lancelot, then told him that the woman Elaine was actually Guinevere.

**Buddug**  The Welsh version of the name Victoria. It means "victory."

**Cadwyn**  *Bright chain.*

**Caethes**  Derived from a word meaning "slave."

**Cafell**  *Oracle.*

**Caniad**  Comes from a word that means "song."

**Cari** (KAHR-ee)  This name is derived from the Welsh *caru,* meaning "to love." Some sources list the meaning as "friend," while others think this is the Welsh form of the name Caroline. Variants are CARYL (KAHR-il) and CARYS (KAHR-ees).

**Caron**  *Loving or kind-hearted.*

**Carys**  A variant of the name CARI. Other variants are CARIS and CERYS.

**Cath**  *Cat.*

**Catrin** (KAHT-reen)  A Welsh version of the name Catherine, this name means "pure." Variants are CATI (KAHT-ee) and CADI (KAHD-ee).

**Ceri** (KER-ee)  This personal name is taken from the names of two rivers in Wales, one in Dyfed and one in Glamorgan. It may be derived from *caru,* meaning "to love."

**Cerridwen** (ker-ID-wen)  It may be derived from the Old Welsh *cerdd,* meaning "song," and *gwen,* meaning "holy," "shining." The

Crone aspect of the Goddess, she was married to the giant Tegid and had a daughter Creirwy and a son Avagdu. *Greal,* the potion she brewed in her cauldron, was considered to be the source of inspiration, wisdom, and initiation for all true bards and magicians. Variants are CARIDWEN and CERIDWEN.

**Cigfa**   She was the daughter of Gwyn Gohoyw and of the royal line of Casnar Wledig. Her husband was Pryderi.

**Clarisant**   This name is mentioned in only one of the Arthurian legends as the name of the sister of Gawain. A variant is CLARISSE.

**Cordelia**   A variant of CREIDDYLAD.

**Corsen**   *Reed.*

**Cragen**   Derived from a word meaning "shell."

**Creiddylad**   She was the daughter of Lludd Llaw Ereint. She eloped with Gwythyr ap Greidawl, but was kidnapped by Gwynn ap Nudd and taken to the Underworld. According to one Welsh tradition, the two gods must fight for her every May Day. Variants are CREUDYLAD and CORDELIA.

**Creirwy**   The daughter of the goddess Cerridwen. The Welsh Triads call her one of the three beautiful maids of Britain.

**Cymreiges**   *A woman of Wales.*

**Daron** (DAHR-on)   Derived from the Welsh word *dar,* meaning "oak," this was the name of a minor oak goddess and the name of a river in Caernarvonshire.

**Dee**   *Dark or black sorrow.* Variants are DEA, DEEA, DU, and DELIA.

**Dierdre**   The Welsh spelling of the Irish name Deirdre, which means "sorrow."

**Del**   From the word *del,* meaning "pretty." A variant is DELYTH (DEL-ith).

**Dera**   Derived from words meaning "wild spirit" or "fiend." A variant is DAERE.

**Derwen**   *From the oak tree.* May be related to the Celtic word *druid.*

**Deryn**   *Bird.* Variants are DERRINE, DERREN, and DERYNE.

**Dicra**   From a word that means "slow."

**Difyr**   *Amusing.*

**Dilys** (DIL-ees)   Derived from the Welsh word *dily,* meaning "genuine" or "true," this was a popular name that came into being in the nineteenth century.

**Don** (DOHN)   In Welsh legends, this was the name of the primary Mother Goddess, who corresponds to the Irish goddess Danu. As the Celtic Magna Mater, she was considered to be the ancestress of the Welsh people. Variant spellings are DONN and DONA (DOHN-an).

**Druantia**   A Celtic goddess known as Mother of the Tree Calendar and Queen of the Druids.

**Drysi**   *Thorn.*

**Dwyn** (DWIN)   It is taken from the words *dwyn*, meaning "pleasant" or "agreeable" and *gwen*, meaning "shining" or "holy." A variant is DWYNWEN (DWIN-wen).

**Dyllis**   Derived from a word meaning "sincere."

**Ebrill**   *April or one born in April.*

**Efa**   The Welsh version of the name Eve, which means "life."

**Eheubryd**   A legendary name that belonged to the daughter of Kyvwich.

**Eira** (AY-rah)   This name is derived from the word *eira*, meaning "snow." A variant is EIRY (AY-ree).

**Eirianwen** (ayr-YAHN-wen)   Comes from the Welsh words *eirian*, meaning "splendid," "bright," or "fair," and *gwen*, meaning "shining" or "holy."

**Eiriol** (AYR-yol)   Taken from the Welsh word *eira*, meaning "snow," these names both refer to the snowdrop flower. A variant is EIRLYS (AYR-lees).

**Elaine**   In the Arthurian tales, Elaine of Corbenic and Elaine de Astolat. Elaine de Astolat, sometimes called The White, fell in love with Lancelot and died when he did not return her love. In literature she is known as the Lady of Shallot.

**Elen**   The Welsh form of the name Helen, which means "light."

**Eleri** (el-AYR-ee)   The name of a river in Ceredigion and also of a fifth-century saint, this name may be derived from the words *el*, meaning "greatly" or "much," and *geri*, meaning "bitter."

**Ellylw**   A legendary name that belonged to the daughter of Neol Hang Cock.

**Eluned** (el-EEN-ed)   Derived from the words *el*, meaning "greatly" or "much," and *iuned*, meaning "wish" or "desire." A variant is LUNED (LEEN-ed).

**Eneuawy**   A legendary name, this was the name of the daughter of Bedwyr.

**Enfys** (EN-vees)    Taken from the Welsh word for "rainbow."

**Enit**    May be derived from a word meaning "soul," "life," or "spirit." Originally, this name may have been connected to a minor Celtic goddess of sovereignty. A variant is ENID (EE-nid).

**Enrhydreg**    The daughter of Tuduathar of the Welsh legends.

**Epona**    Known to all the Celts as the Divine Horse and Great Mare, this goddess was associated with horses, their breeding, and all warriors who used horses.

**Erdudvyl**    The daughter of Tryffin of Welsh tales.

**Eres**    *Wonderful.*

**Essyllt** (ES-ilht)    Possibly derived from the British word *adsiltia*, meaning "she who is gazed upon." This is the Welsh version of the name Isolde, who was a tragic heroine in the Tristan story. A variant spelling is ESYLLT.

**Eurneid**    The daughter of Clydno in Welsh tales.

**Eurolwyn**    In Welsh legends, this was the daughter of Gwydolwyn.

**Eyslk**    *Fair.*

**Ffanci**    The Welsh version of the name Fancy.

**Ffion** (FEE-on)    This is a popular name derived from *ffion*, meaning "foxglove." A variant is FFIONA (fee-OH-nah).

**Fflur** (FLEER)    This name comes from the Welsh word for "flower."

**Ffraid** (FRAYD)    This is the Welsh name for the Irish goddess Brighid. The feast day of the Saint Brigid is February 1.

**Gaenor** (GAY-nor)    Variants of the Welsh name GWENHWYFAR or GUINEVERE, this name was very popular during the nineteenth century.

**Ganieda**    The *Vita Merlini* calls her the sister of Merlin. Sometimes called Gwenddydd, she was said to live in the forest and give prophecies.

**Garan**    *Stork.*

**Glenna**    *From the valley or glen.*

**Glenys** (GLEN-is)    This name comes from the Old Welsh word *glan*, meaning "riverbank" or "shore." A variant is GLAN. The Irish Gaelic form was GHLEANNA.

**Glynis** (GLIN-is)    Derived from the Welsh word *glyn*, meaning "valley," it means "one who lives in the glen or valley."

**Goewin**    This was the fabled name of the daughter of Pebin. She was the virgin foot-holder for King Math until she was raped by Gilfaethwy. To erase her disgrace, Math married her.

**Goleuddydd** *Bright day.* In Welsh stories she is listed as the mother of Culhwch.

**Gorawen** *Joy.*

**Guinevere** In the Arthurian sagas, she is the daughter of Leodegrance of Cameliard, and the wife of King Arthur. In Malory's story, she was found guilty of adultery and banished to the monastery of Amesbury. This spelling is a variant of the Welsh name GWENHWYFAR.

**Gwaeddan** The name of the daughter of Kynvelyn in Welsh tales.

**Gwanwyn** *Spring.*

**Gwawr** (GWOWR) This name comes from the Welsh word for "dawn."

**Gwen** (GWEN) Derived from the Old Welsh words *gwen,* meaning "shining" or "holy," and *gwyn,* meaning "white." This name means "perception or discovery of the meaning of the light of the Otherworld." A shortened form of the name Guinevere. A variant is GWYN (GWIN).

**Gwenda** (GWEN-dah) Derived from the Welsh words *gwen,* meaning "holy" or "shining," and *da,* meaning "good."

**Gwendolyn** This name is a variant of Guinevere and means "white brow." In Old Welsh legends Gwendolyn is listed as the wife of Merlin the magician. At least one source lists the second half of the name as coming from *dolen,* meaning "link."

**Gwener** The Welsh version of the name Venus, goddess of love.

**Gweneth** This name comes from the Welsh words meaning "white, blessed one." One source lists the meaning as "wheat." Variants are GWYNEDD, GWENITH (GWEN-ith), and GWYNETH.

**Gwenhwyfar** (gwen-HWIV-ahr) This Welsh name is the origin of the name Guinevere. The name is derived from the words *gwen,* meaning "holy" or "shining," and *hwyfar,* meaning "spirit," "fairy," or "phantom." Gwenhwyfar was one of the most common names in Wales during the Middle Ages.

**Gwenledyr** The legendary name of the daughter of Gwawrddur Hunchback.

**Gwenllian** (gwen-LHEE-ahn) A popular name since the Middle Ages, it is derived from *gwen,* meaning "shining" or "holy," and *lliant,* meaning "stream." A variant is GWENLLIANT (gwen-LHEE-ahnt).

**Gwenn Alarch** The legendary name of the daughter of Kynwal.

**Gwerfyl** Among the very few Welsh female poets was Gwerful

Machain, a poet of the fifteenth century. A variant is GWERFUL (GWAYR-vil).

**Gwladys** (goo-LAH-dis)    Derived from the Welsh word *gwlad,* that means "land, nation, or sovereignty." Some sources think this name means "a small sword," while others believe it is derived from the gladiolus flower. A variant is GLADYS.

**Gwyneth** (GWIN-eth)    This name comes from the Welsh words *gwen,* meaning "shining" or "holy," and *geneth,* meaning "girl." Other sources believe it is derived from *gwynaeth,* meaning "happiness, bliss."

**Hafgan** (HAHV-gahn)    A male or female name, it is derived from *haf,* meaning "summer," and *can,* meaning "song."

**Hafren** (HAHV-ren)    This is the Welsh name for Sabrina, goddess of the Severn River.

**Heledd** (HEL-eth)    This name comes from the words *hy,* meaning "goodness," and *ledd,* meaning "wound."

**Hellawes**    An enchantress who was said to live in the Castle Nigramours (Necromancy). When she failed to win Lancelot's love, she died.

**Heulwen** (HIL-wen)    It is derived from *heul,* meaning "sun," and *gwen,* meaning "shining," or "holy." A variant is HEULYN (HIL-een), meaning "ray of sunshine," which can be either a male or female name.

**Hywela** (huh-WEL-ah)    The feminine version of the male name Hywel, which comes from *hywel,* meaning "eminent."

**Idelle**    The Welsh version of the name Ida.

**Igerna**    The wife of Gorlois of Cornwall who was loved by Uther Pendragon. She became the mother of Arthur through a shapeshifting deception of Merlin's making.

**Indeg**    The legendary name of the daughter of Garwy.

**Iola** (YOH-lah)    The feminine version of the male name Iolo, which itself comes from the name Iorwerth. All three names are derived from the Norse word *ior,* meaning "lord," and the Welsh word *gwerth,* meaning "worth," or "value."

**Isolde**    *Fair.* This was the name of the tragic heroine in the Tristan saga and also the name of a princess in the Arthurian sagas. Variants are ISOLDA and ISOLT.

**Jennifer**    A variant of Guinevere.

**Kelemon**   In Welsh tales, the name of the daughter of Kei.

**Kigva**   The legendary name of the wife of Partholon's son.

**Lilybet**   *God's promise.*

**Linette**   This name is derived from a Welsh word meaning "idol."

**Llinos** (LHEE-nos)   This is the Welsh word for the bird "linnet."

**Llio** (LHEE-oh)   This is a nickname for the name GWENLLIAN.

**Lowri** (LOW-ree)   The Welsh version of the name Laurel or Laura, this name means "crown of laurels."

**Lysanor**   The mother of one of Arthur's illegitimate sons.

**Mab**   It means "baby" in Welsh. In Welsh tales, Mab was the queen of Faery.

**Mabli**   The Welsh version of the name Mabel, which means "lovable."

**Mair** (MIR)   The Welsh form of the name Mary, which means "bitter." Variants are MEIRA (MAYR-ah), or MAIRWEN (MIR-wen), which is derived from the combination of Air (Mary) and *gwen*, meaning "holy" or "shining."

**Maledisant**   The wife of the knight Bruno le Noir. The name means "ill speech."

**Mali**   The Welsh form of the name Molly, which is itself a form of Mary and means "bitter."

**Marged** (MAHR-ged)   This is the Welsh version of the name Margaret. Variants are MARGIAD (MAHR-gyahd) and MARARED (mahr-AHR-ed).

**Megan**   A nickname and form of the name Margaret. Some sources list the meaning as "pearl," while others say it means "mighty one."

**Melangell** (mel-AHNG-elh)   A female saint by this name is the Welsh patron saint of animals because legend says she rescued a hare from hounds. In the area where she had her Welsh convent, the hare is known as Melangell's little lamb, and was not hunted until recently.

**Meleri** (mel-AYR-ee)   This name is a combination of the word *my*, meaning "my" and Eleri, who was a fifth century saint.

**Meredith**   Some sources say this name means "magnificent," while others believe it means "protector of the sea."

**Meriel** (MER-yel)   The Welsh adaptation of a name derived from the Old Irish words *muir*, meaning "sea," and *gel*, meaning "bright." A variant is MERYL (MER-eel).

**Modlen**   The Welsh version of the name Magdalene, which means "tower."

**Modron**   This name simply means "mother." Modron was the mother of Mabon, a son whose father came from the Otherworld.

**Mona** (MOH-nah)   This name comes from Mon, the Welsh name for the Isle of Anglesey, off the north coast of Wales. This island was once a druid stronghold, but the inhabitants were wiped out by Roman legions during the occupation.

**Morfudd**   It is possible that this name derives from *mawr,* meaning "great" and *gwyd,* meaning "sight" or "knowledge." A variant is MORFYDD (MOHR-vith).

**Morgan** (MOHR-gahn)   Either a male or female name in Wales. There is confusion as to the source-words for this name. Some authors think it is derived from *mor,* meaning "sea," and *can,* meaning "bright," while others believe its variant, MORGANT, comes from *mawr,* meaning "great," and *cant,* meaning "circle." In the Arthurian legends, Morgan le Fay was King Arthur's sister and a skilled sorceress. She was the mother of Owain by Uriens of Gore. A variant is MORGANA and MORGANT (MOHR-gant). The Welsh also knew of the Irish goddess by this name.

**Morgause**   The daughter of Gorlois of Cornwall and Igerna, she was the half-sister of Arthur by whom she bore Modred. A variant is MARGAWSE.

**Morvudd**   The legendary name of the daughter of Uryen.

**Morwen** (MOHR-wen)   This name is derived from the Welsh word *morwyn,* meaning "maiden." A variant form is MORWENNA (mohr-WEN-ah).

**Myfanawy** (muh-VAHN-wee or mih-FAN-uh-wee)   In Old Welsh this means "my fine one." A variant spelling is MYFANWY.

**Nerys** (NER-ees)   The feminine version of the Welsh word *ner,* meaning "lord." The medieval version of this name was GENERYS.

**Nesta** (NEST-ah)   A popular Welsh form of the name Agnes. Variants are ANNEST (AHN-nest).

**Neued**   The legendary name of the daughter of Kyvwich.

**Nia** (NEE-ah)   This name is a Welsh version of the Irish goddess Niamh. It is derived from the Old Irish *niam,* meaning "luster" or "brilliance."

**Nimue**   A moon goddess who was sometimes called Viviene, Niniane, or Lady of the Lake.

**Nona** (NOH-nah)   A woman with this name is listed in legend as the mother of Saint David, who is the patron saint of Wales. She was thought to be the cousin of King Arthur. Her feast day is March 2.

**Olwen** (OHL-ween)  Derived from the Old Welsh words *ol,* and *gwen,* which together mean "white footprint" or "shining track."

**Owena**  This name means "born to nobility," and is the feminine form of the male name Owen.

**Penarddun**  The legendary name of the daughter of Beli.

**Petra** (PET-rah)  The Welsh female version of the name Peter.

**Ragnell**  Enchanted into the ugly form of the Loathly Lady, she aided Gawain in finding the answer to the riddle, "What do women desire?" He married her in her ugly form not knowing that with the first kiss she would become beautiful.

**Rathtyen**  In Welsh tales, the name of the daughter of Clememyl.

**Rhan**  *Fate.*

**Rhawn**  Derived from words meaning "coarse or long hair."

**Rhedyn**  Derived from a word that means "fern."

**Rhian** (RHEE-an)  Derived from the Welsh word *rhiain,* meaning "maiden," this name is very similar to that of the goddess Rhiannon. A variant is RHIAIN (RHEE-in).

**Rhiannon** (rhee-AHN-on)  This name may come from the ancient Celtic *rigantona* or "divine queen." The Welsh goddess Rhiannon was the daughter of Hefaidd Hen, Lord of the Underworld. She eventually married Pwyll and bore the son Pryderi. She had Otherworld birds that sang more sweetly than any other bird.

**Rhianwen** (rhee-AHN-wen)  It is derived from *rhiain,* meaning "maiden," and *gwen,* meaning "shining" or "holy."

**Rhonda**  Derived from a word meaning "grand."

**Rhonwen** (RHON-wen)  This name possibly is derived from the Welsh words *rhon,* meaning "spear," and *gwen,* meaning "shining" or "holy." Other sources say it means "white hair" and is related to the name Rowena.

**Rhosyn**  Derived from the Welsh word meaning "rose."

**Rowena**  This name means "white- or fair-haired."

**Saeth**  *Arrow.*

**Saffir**  The Welsh word for "sapphire."

**Sarff**  Some sources say this name means "snake."

**Seren**  *Star.*

**Sian** (SHAN)  This name means "God's gracious gift," and is a version of the name Jane or Jean. Variants are SIANI (SHAN-ee) and SIONED (SHON-ed).

**Siwan** (SHOO-ahn)   The Welsh form of the name Joan.

**Sulwen**   Derived from the words *sul,* meaning "sun," and *gwen,* meaning "shining" or "holy," this name means "bright as the sun."

**Taffy**   A Welsh name meaning "beloved." Variants are TAFFIA and TAFFINE.

**Talaith**   *Diadem.*

**Talar**   Derived from the Welsh words meaning "from the headland in the field."

**Tangwen**   The legendary name of the daughter of Gweir.

**Tanwen** (TAHN-wen)   It is derived from the Welsh words *tan,* meaning "fire," and *gwen,* meaning "shining" or "holy."

**Tarian**   *Shield.*

**Tarren**   *From the knoll.*

**Tegan** (TEG-ahn)   This name, of both an early Welsh saint and a river in Ceredigion, comes from the word *teg,* meaning "pretty" or "fine."

**Tegau** (TEG-ay)   From the word *teg,* meaning "pretty" or "fine."

**Tegeirian** (teg-AYR-yahn)   This is the Welsh word for "orchid."

**Tegwen** (TEG-wen)   A name compounded of the words *teg,* meaning "pretty" or "fine," and *gwen,* meaning "shining" or "holy."

**Teleri** (tel-AYR-ee)   This is derived from Eleri, the name of a saint and a river in Dyfed, and *ty,* meaning "your." The story of *Kulhwch and Olwen* mentions a maiden in Arthur's court whose name was Teleri verch Peul, or daughter of Peul.

**Telyn**   *Harp.*

**Terrwyn**   Derived from the word meaning "brave."

**Toreth**   *Abundant.*

**Torlan**   Derived from words meaning "from the river bank."

**Torri**   *Break.*

**Trevina**   A name meaning "homestead," it is the feminine version of the male name Trevor.

**Una**   Derived from the Irish Gaelic word that means "white wave."

**Vala**   *Chosen.*

**Vanora**   A variant of GUINEVERE that means "white wave."

**Vivian**   A legendary name from the tales of King Arthur.

**Wenda**   A variant of the name GWENDOLYN.

**Winnifred**   A variant of GUINEVERE that means "white wave."

**Wynne**    A variant of the name GWEN that is derived from the Welsh word *gwyn,* meaning "fair" or "white."

**Ysbail**    The Welsh version of the name Isabel. It means "consecrated to God."

**Yseult**    An alternate form of the name ISOLDE.

## MALE NAMES

**Aberthol**    *Sacrifice.*

**Accalon**    A champion from Gaul who was the lover of Morgan le Fay in the Arthurian sagas. He and Morgan le Fay plotted to steal Excalibur, but Merlin helped Arthur to overcome Accalon in combat.

**Adda**    This is the Welsh version of the name Adam, which means "of the red earth."

**Addolgar**    *Devout.*

**Adwr**    *Coward.*

**Aedd**    A name derived from the Irish *aedh,* meaning "fire." It was the name of a king of Ireland.

**Aglovale**    This was the son of King Pellinore, who was accidentally killed by Lancelot when Lancelot rescued Guinevere.

**Alawn**    *Harmony.*

**Albanwr**    A Welsh name that means "one from Scotland."

**Alwyn**    A Welsh version of the Anglo-Saxon name Alvin, which means "friend of all." There is also a River Alwyn in Wales.

**Amaethon**    In Welsh legends, this was the name of the son of the goddess Donn.

**Amerawdwr**    Derived from a word that means "emperor."

**Amhar**    In obscure Welsh legends, this was given as the name of a son of Arthur.

**Amlawdd**    Welsh tales say this was the name of the father of Goleuddydd.

**Amren**    In the Welsh Arthurian sagas, this was the name of the son of Bedwyr.

**Amynedd**    This name means "patient." A variant is AMYNEDDGAR.

**Andreas**    The Welsh version of the name Andrew.

**Aneurin**    *Honorable* or *golden.* It is a name that appears in Welsh mythology. A variant is ANEIRIN.

**Anfri**  *Disgrace.*

**Angawdd**  In legends this is the name of the son of Caw.

**Angor**  This comes from the Welsh word for "anchor."

**Anir**  Listed in the sagas as a son of Arthur. It is vaguely hinted in the stories that he was killed by his father and buried in Wales at Licat Amir. A variant is AMR.

**Anwar**  *Wild.*

**Anwas**  This is the name of the father of Twrch in ancient legends.

**Anwell**  This comes from the word "beloved." A variant is ANWIL.

**Anwir**  *Liar.*

**Anynnawg**  This is a legendary name of the son of Menw.

**Anyon**  This name comes from the Welsh word for "anvil."

**Ap-**  One of the Welsh prefixes used to denote "son of," as is "O" and "mac" in Ireland, and "mac" in Scotland.

**Arawn** (AR-awn)  In Welsh mythology, he was the god of Annwn. In the beginning, Annwn (an-OON) was the Underworld but not associated with terror or eternal punishment. Later, it became the underground kingdom of the dead.

**Ardwyad**  *Protector.*

**Arglwydd**  Derived from the word meaning "lord."

**Arian**  This name means "silver" and is the male version of the name of the goddess Arianrhod.

**Arthur** (AHR-thir)  Comes from the Celtic word *artos,* meaning "bear." Wales, Brittany, and Cornwall all have legends of King Arthur. In the Grail sagas, Arthur was the son of Uther Pendragon and Igerna and taken at birth by Merlin to be raised by Ector. He became King of Britain, married Guinevere, and founded the Round Table. He was killed at the Battle of Camlan by his son Mordred. Three otherworldly queens took him away to Avalon to heal his wounds and let him sleep in a hidden cave until he was needed again to save Britain. Variants are ARTHWR and ARTHVAWR.

**Arvel**  *Wept over.*

**Avagdu**  The son of the goddess Cerridwen and the obscure god Tegid Foel, his name means "utter darkness." To compensate for Avagdu's ugliness, Cerridwen brewed the *greal,* a potion of great knowledge in her cauldron. Before the boy could drink it, however, Gwion Bach (who later took the name of Taliesin) swallowed the last three drops. Variants of this name are AFAGDDU and MORFRAN (great crow).

**Avaon**  In Welsh tradition, this was the name of the son of Taliesin.

**Awstin**  A name derived from the Welsh word for "august."

**Baddon**  *One from Baddon.*

**Baeddan**  From the word meaning "boar."

**Barri** (BAHR-ee)  Possibly taken from the Welsh word *bar,* which means "mound," "summit," or "dune."

**Barris**  *Son of Harry.* A variant is BARRYS.

**Baudwin**  One of the later knights of the Round Table, he came from Brittany. He was very skilled as a surgeon. He survived the Battle of Camlan to become a hermit.

**Beda**  This is the Welsh version of the name BEDE (673-735), who was a famous monk and historian.

**Bedwyr**  In the earliest Arthurian sagas, this was also the name of one of Arthur's companions to whom the king sometimes entrusted Excalibur.

**Bedyw**  In legends, this was the name of the son of Seithved.

**Beli**  This was the name of the Irish sun god, who was also known in Wales. According to later tales, Beli was the brother-in-law of the Virgin Mary. The original Beli was closely connected with the druids and their rituals. His festival was May 1, or Beltane, on which day both the Welsh and Irish drove their cattle between bonfires to ensure fertility. Variants are BELI MAWR, BELENUS, and BELINUS.

**Bellieus**  A knight of the Round Table who fought Lancelot over an incident with his wife.

**Benedigeidfran**  This name means "blessed" and was applied to the god Bran. Bran the Blessed, a giant in Welsh mythology, was the brother to the goddess Branwen.

**Bercelak**  Known as the Green Knight in the Arthurian stories.

**Berth**  In legends, this was the name of the son of Cadwy.

**Berwyn**  In ancient tales, this was the son of Kerenhyr.

**Beven**  *Son of Evan* or *youthful.*

**Blair**  *Place.* A variant is BLAYRE.

**Blaise**  Merlin's mysterious teacher who lived in Northumberland.

**Blathaon**  This is the legendary name of the son of Mwrheth.

**Bleddyn** (BLETH-in)  This name is derived from the Welsh word *blaidd,* meaning "wolf." The slang name Wolf was applied to both warriors and outlaws in Wales.

**Bledri** (BLED-ree)  This name comes from the Welsh *blaidd,* meaning "wolf," and *rhi,* meaning "king." Translated, this means "leader of the warriors or outlaws."

**Bleidd** (BLAYTH)    *Wolf.*

**Bleiddian** (BLAYTH-yahn)    Derived from the Welsh words *blaidd,* meaning "wolf," and -*ian,* this name means "one who goes out looting and raiding."

**Bogart**    In both Ireland and Wales, this name means "bog" or "marshland."

**Bors**    He was the son of the king of Benoic and cousin to Lancelot. Along with Perceval and Galahad, he was one of the best knights of the Round Table.

**Bowen**    *Son of Owen.* Variants are BOWIE and BOWE.

**Brac**    *Free.*

**Brad**    Derived from the word for "treason."

**Bradwen**    In ancient legends this name belonged to the son of Moren.

**Bradwr**    A variant of BRAD, this name means "traitor."

**Braen**    *Corrupt.*

**Bran**    Derived from the Welsh word for "raven" or "crow." In ancient legends, Bran the Blessed (Bran Bendigeidfran) was the brother of the goddess Branwen.

**Brastias**    Originally a knight in Cornwall, he became one of Arthur's captains, and later Warden of the North.

**Brathach**    In old tales, this was the name of the son of Gwawrddur.

**Brian**    The legendary name of the son of Turenn.

**Brice**    *Alert.*

**Broderick**    *Son of the famous ruler.* In Welsh, the name ap-Roderick often appears, signifying "son of Roderick."

**Bryn** (BRIN)    Derived from the Welsh word for "hill," this is a popular name for boys in Wales. Variants are BRYNN, BRYNLEY, and BRINLEY.

**Brys**    A legendary name of the son of Brysethach.

**Bwlch**    In old tales this was the name of the son of Cleddyv Kyvwlch.

**Cadarn**    *Strong.*

**Caddoc**    *Battle-sharp* or *eager for war.*

**Cadell**    Derived from a word meaning "spirit of the battle."

**Cadellin**    In legends, this was the name of the son of Gweir.

**Cadeyrn** (KAHD-ayrn)    This name comes from the Welsh words *cad,* meaning "battle," and *teyrn,* meaning "prince."

**Cadfael** (KAHD-file)   Authorities disagree on whether this name is derived from the words *cad,* meaning "battle," and *ban,* meaning "summit," or *cad,* meaning "battle," and *mael,* meaning "prince." A variant of both CADFAN and CADOC.

**Cadfan** (KAHD-vahn)   Derived from the Welsh *cad,* meaning "battle," and *ban,* meaning "summit."

**Cadman**   *Warrior.* A variant is CADMON.

**Cadoc** (KAHD-ok)   This name comes from the word *cad,* meaning "battle." In the beginning, it was a nickname for Cadfael (KAHD-file or KAHD-vil).

**Cadwaladr** (kahd-WAHL-ah-der)   From *cad,* meaning "battle," and *gwaladr,* meaning "ruler" or "leader."

**Cadwallen**   *Battle dissolver.*

**Cadwgawn**   The legendary name of the son of Iddon.

**Cadwr**   In old tales, the name of the son of Gwryon.

**Cadyryeith**   *Well-spoken.*

**Caer Llion**   *One from Caerleon (Castle of the Lion).*

**Caerwyn** (KIR-win or KAYR-win)   Derived from the Welsh words *caer,* meaning "fort," and *gwyn,* meaning "holy" or "shining."

**Cai** (KAY)   This name comes from the Irish *cai (coi),* which means "path" or "way." Other sources say the meaning is "rejoicer." In Arthurian legends, Cai was a close companion of the King. He was also said to have rid the Isle of Anglesey of the Palug Cat. Variants are CAIUS, CAW, and CEI.

**Cain**   *Clear water.*

**Cairn**   In Welsh, this is the word for a pile of stones used as a landmark. A variant is CARNE.

**Calcas**   In legends this was the name of the son of Caw.

**Calder**   *Brook or stream.*

**Caledvwich**   In Welsh legends this was the name of Excalibur.

**Cant**   *White.*

**Caradawg**   In old tales, this name belonged to the father of Eudav.

**Caradoc**   *Beloved.* Variants are CRADDOCK and CRADOC.

**Carey**   *From the castle.* Variants are CARY and CAERAU.

**Carnedyr**   The legendary name of the son of Govynyon.

**Cas**   This was the name of the son of Seidi in legends.

**Casnar**   This was the name of a nobleman in old tales.

**Casswallawn**   Legend says this name belonged to the son of Beli.

**Caw**   A name out of old legends.

**Cedric**   *Bountiful.*

**Ceithin**   In old tales, this was the name of the uncle of Lugh.

**Celyn** (KEL-in)   From the Welsh word for "holly." In the medieval tale *Kulhwch and Olwen,* Celyn ap Caw belonged to King Arthur's court.

**Cerdic**   *Beloved.* A variant is CEREDIG.

**Ceri** (KER-ee)   Either a male or female name, it is derived from *caru,* meaning "to love." A river in Dyfed and one in Glamorgan both have this name.

**Cian** (KEE-an)   From the Welsh *ci (cwn),* meaning "hound" or "wolf." The Old Irish word cu means the same thing. One of the founding poets of the Welsh tradition was named Cian.

**Clud**   *Lame.*

**Clust**   In legends this was the name of the son of Clustveinydd.

**Clyde**   One source says this name means "loud-voiced," another says it means "warm." A variant is CLYWD.

**Cnychwr**   This name belonged to the son of Nes in old tales.

**Coed**   *Dwells in the woods.*

**Colgrevance**   A knight of the Round Table who was slain when the knights tried to capture Lancelot while he was in Guinevere's chamber.

**Collen** (KOLH-en)   This name comes from the Welsh word for "hazel tree."

**Colwyn**   This is the name of a river in Wales.

**Conwy** (CON-oo-ee)   This personal name is the same as that of a river in northern Wales. It is derived from the Irish Gaelic name Connmhaighe, which means "hound of the plain."

**Corryn**   *Spider.*

**Cradelmass**   A king of North Wales whom Arthur defeated at the beginning of his reign.

**Crist**   Derived from the word "Christian."

**Cubert**   The legendary name of the son of Daere.

**Culhwch** (COOL-oo)   The son of Kilydd in old tales.

**Culvanawd**   The name of the son of Gwryon in ancient legends.

**Custenhin**   The legendary name of the father of Erbin.

**Cymry** (KIM-ree)   The Welsh people's name for themselves, meaning "from Wales."

**Cynan** (KUHN-ahn)  Derived from the Celtic word *kuno*, meaning "great" or "high." During medieval times in Wales, this was a very popular name.

**Cynbel**  *Warrior chief.* A variant is CYNBAL.

**Cystennin**  Derived from the word "constant."

**Dadweir**  An obscure name from old legends.

**Dafydd** (DAH-vith)  This is the Welsh form of the name David, and means "dearly loved." Since Saint David is the patron saint of Wales, this is a very popular name.

**Dagonet**  King Arthur's jester who was made a knight and who excelled in bravery during many tournaments.

**Dalldav**  In old legends, this was the son of Cunyn Cov.

**Daned**  The son of Oth in old tales.

**Davis**  Variant of the name DAFYDD. It means "David's son."

**Deiniol** (DAYN-yol)  This is the Welsh version of the name Daniel.

**Deverell**  *From the river bank.*

**Digon**  The son of Alar in old tales.

**Dillus**  The legendary name of the son of Eurei.

**Dilwyn**  *Shady place.* A variant is DILLWYN.

**Dinadan**  A knight of the Round Table who had quite a sense of humor. He loved to play jokes on the other knights. Later, he was killed by Mordred.

**Dirmyg**  The legendary name of one of the sons of Caw.

**Drem**  *Sight.*

**Dremidydd**  In old Welsh tales, this was the father of Drem.

**Drew**  *Wise.* Variants are DRU and DRYW.

**Druce**  In Welsh this means "son of Dryw." A variant is DRYWSONE.

**Drudwas**  In old Welsh tales, this was the name of the son of Tryffin.

**Drwst**  An obscure name out of Welsh tales.

**Drych**  The legendary name of the son of Kibddar.

**Drystan**  The Welsh version of the name Tristan, which means "full of sorrow."

**Duach**  In old legends, this was the name of the son of Gwawrddur.

**Dylan** (DIL-un or DUHL-an)  Derived from a Welsh word for "ocean" or "sea." In legends, Dylan eil Ton (Sea Like a Wave) was a son of the goddess Arianrhod.

**Dyvynarth**  The legendary name of the son of Gwrgwst.

**Dyvyr**  In ancient stories this was the name of the son of Alun.

**Dywel**  The legendary name of the son of Erbin.

**Earwine**  *White river.* A variant is ERWYN.

**Ector**  In the Arthurian sagas, one man with this name—Ector of the Forest Sauvage—was Arthur's foster-father.

**Edern**  In legends, this was the son of Nudd.

**Edmyg**  *Honor.*

**Ehangwen**  A name out of old legends.

**Eiddoel**  In old tales, this was the name of the son of Ner.

**Eiddyl**  A name of unknown meaning out of legends.

**Eiladar**  The legendary name of the son of Penn Llarcan.

**Einion**  *Anvil.* A variant is EINIAN.

**Eiryn**  In old stories, the name of the son of Peibyn.

**Eivyonydd**  A name out of old tales.

**Elis** (EL-is)  This name is the Welsh version of the name Elijah.

**Elphin**  In old legends, this was the name of the son of Gwyddno. In the Taliesin stories, Elphin rescued the infant Gwion Bach, who was later named Taliesin, from a salmon weir.

**Emhyr**  *Ruler.* A variant is EMYR.

**Emlyn** (EM-lin)  A Welsh name derived from the Latin word *aemilianus*, which means "flattering" or "charming." Another source says the meaning is "waterfall."

**Emrys** (EM-rees)  The Welsh form of the Latin name *Ambrosius* or Ambrose. It means "immortal." This was one of the names of the magician Myrddin, or Merlin.

**Ennissyen**  A giant Welshman who was related to Bran the Blessed and who started the war with the Irish, which led to the death of Branwen and her son.

**Eoin**  A variant of the name Evan.

**Erbin**  The legendary name of the son of Custenhin.

**Ergyryad**  In old tales this was the name of one of the sons of Caw.

**Ermid**  The name of the son of Erbin in legends.

**Eryi**  *From Snowdon.*

**Eudav**  In ancient stories, the son of Caradawg.

**Eurosswydd**  A name out of old Welsh tales.

**Eus**  In legends, the name of the son of Erim.

**Evan** (EV-ahn)  This is the Welsh version of the name John. Variants are IOAN (YOH-ahn), IANTO (YANH-toh). IWAN (YEW-ahn), and IEUAN (YAY-ahn).

**Evnissyen** (ev-NESS-yen)   *Lover of strife.* In ancient legends, Ennissyen was the half-brother of the giant-god Bran. In the Welsh battle with the Irish over the poor treatment of Branwen, who had married the Irish king, he caused the death of Branwen's infant son and many of his companions. His behavior was much like that of the Norse trickster god Loki.

**Evrawg**   *From York.*

**Evrei**   A name out of old stories.

**Fercos**   In old Welsh legends, the name of the son of Poch.

**Fflam**   The legendary name of the son of Nwyvre.

**Fflergant**   The legendary name of one of the kings of Brittany.

**Fflewdwr**   The name of the son of Naw in old Welsh stories.

**Ffodor**   The son of Ervyll in old tales.

**Ffowc**   *Of all the people.*

**Ffransis** (FRAWN-sis)   This is the Welsh form of the name Francis. The nickname Ffranc is the equivalent of Frank.

**Fychan**   *Small.*

**Fyrsil**   The Welsh version of the name Virgil, which means "bears the staff." A variant is FFERYLL.

**Galahad**   The illegitimate son of Lancelot and Elaine, he was a pure knight who surpassed his father's deeds of valor and died when he saw the Grail.

**Galehodin**   The brother of Lancelot. He became the duke of Saintongue.

**Gamon**   A name from old stories.

**Gandwy**   A name that appears in ancient legends.

**Garanhon**   The legendary name of the son of Glythvyr.

**Gareth** (GAHR-eth)   Some sources say this name is derived from the Welsh word *gwaraidd,* meaning "civilized" or "gentle." Other sources, however, believe it comes from an Anglo-Saxon word meaning "powerful with the spear." A variant is GARTH.

**Garnock**   *Dwells by the alder tree river.*

**Garselid**   A name from old legends.

**Garwyli**   In old legends, this was the name of the son of Gwyddawg Gwyr.

**Garym**   A name from old stories.

**Gavin**   *Hawk of the battle* or *white hawk.*

**Gawain**   A knight of the Round Table and one of the sons of Lot and Morgause of Orkney. Early versions of the Arthurian tales call him a Knight of the Goddess. In Wales, he was known as Gwalch-mai (Hawk of May).

**Geraint** (GER-iint)   Derived from the Celtic word *gerontios,* which means "old."

**Gerallt** (GER-alht)   This is the Welsh version of the name Gerald.

**Gerwin**   *Fair love.*

**Gethin** (GETH-in)   Derived from the Welsh word *cethin,* which means "dark" or "dusky." A variant is GETH.

**Gilbert**   The legendary name of the son of Cadgyffro.

**Gildas** (GIL-dahs)   In the sixth century, a monk named Saint Gildas wrote *De excidio Britanniae (The Destruction of Britain),* in which he blamed the Welsh for the fall of Britain to the Anglo-Saxons. His feast day is January 29.

**Gilvaethwy**   The name of one of the sons of the goddess Donn. He lusted after his uncle Math's virgin foot-holder and, in order to get her, caused a war between Gwynedd and Dyfed. As punishment, he was forced to undergo shapeshifts into various animals, and to bear young.

**Gleis**   The legendary name of the son of Merin.

**Glendower**   *One from Glyndwr.* A variant is GLYNDWER.

**Glew**   The son of Ysgawd in old stories.

**Glewlwyd**   Arthur's gatekeeper in the old myth *Culhwch and Olwen.*

**Glinyeu**   The name of the son of Taran in legends.

**Glyn** (GLIN)   Derived from the Welsh word *glyn,* meaning "valley," it means "one who lives in the glen or valley."

**Glythvyr**   A name from ancient tales.

**Gobrwy**   The son of Echel Pierced Thighs in old stories.

**Gofannon**   One of the sons of the goddess Donn. He was a god of blacksmiths and the equivalent of the Irish Goibniu.

**Gogyvwlch**   A legendary name.

**Goreu**   The legendary name of one of the sons of Custenhin or Custennin and an unnamed woman who was sister to Igraine. As told in *Culhwch and Olwen,* he joined the knight Cei.

**Gorlois**   The Duke of Cornwall and husband to Igerna, the woman whom Uther Pendragon coveted. He was the father of Morgan, Morgause, and Elaine.

**Gormant**   In old tales, this was the name of the son of Rica.

**Goronwy** (gohr-ON-wee)   Comes from the Welsh *gwr,* meaning "man."

**Gorsedd**   *From the mound.*

**Govan**   In old legends, this was the name of one of the sons of Caw.

**Govannon**   The son of the goddess Donn in old legends, Govannon was a smith-god.

**Govynyon**   A name from old legends.

**Gowerr**   *Pure.*

**Gowther**   A hero from the Arthurian tales who tames his savage disposition by penances.

**Granwen**   In Welsh legends, this was the name of one of the sons of the god Llyr.

**Greid**   The legendary name of the son of Eri.

**Greidyawl**   An obscure name from old tales.

**Griffin** (GRIFF-in)   This name comes from the Welsh *cryf,* meaning "strong" and *udd,* meaning "lord." Several medieval Welsh rulers bore the variant name of GRUFFUDD.

**Griffith** (GRIF-ith)   *Red-haired.*

**Griflet**   King Arthur accepted him as one of the first knights although he was very young.

**Gromer**   In the story of *Gawain and Dame Ragnell,* this powerful shapeshifter and magician captured Arthur.

**Gronw Pebr**   The lover of Blodeuwedd and a rival of Llew.

**Gruddyeu**   The name of the son of Muryel in Welsh legends.

**Gruffen**   *Fierce lord.* A variant is GRUFFYN.

**Guinglain**   The only legitimate son of Gawain and the Lady Ragnall. A knight of the Round Table, he was killed by Lancelot.

**Gusg**   The legendary name of the son of Achen.

**Gwalchmei**   *Hawk of May* or *hawk of the battle.* The legendary name of the son of Gwyar. Variants are GAVIN, GAVAN, and GAVEN.

**Gwalhaved**   In old legends this was the name of one of the sons of Gwyar.

**Gwallawg**   This was the name of the son of Llenawg in old tales.

**Gwallter**   The Welsh version of the name Walter, which means "strong fighter."

**Gwarthegydd**   The name of one of Caw's sons in old legends.

**Gwawl**   The legendary name of the son of Clud and at one time betrothed to the goddess Rhiannon before her marriage to Pwyll.

**Gwern**   *Old.* In the story of the goddess Branwen, this was the name of her son by the Irish king Matholwch. The infant boy was thrown into a fire and killed by Branwen's half-brother Ennissyen.

**Gwevyl**    The name of the son of Gwastad in Welsh legends.

**Gwilym** (GWIL-im)    This is the Welsh version of the name William.

**Gwion Bach**    The original name of Taliesin.

**Gwitart**    The name of the son of Aedd in ancient stories.

**Gwrddywal**    The legendary name of the son of Evrei.

**Gwres**    In old tales, this was the name of the son of Rheged.

**Gwyddawg**    Menestyr's son in old legends.

**Gwyddno** (GWITH-noh)    Derived from the Welsh words *gwyd,* meaning "knowledge," and *gno,* meaning "fame."

**Gwydion** (GWID-yon)    This name comes from *gwyd,* meaning "knowledge." In ancient Welsh myths, Gwydion ap Don was a powerful magician and sorcerer and the son of the goddess Donn. *The Caer Gwydion* (Gwydion's Castle) is the Milky Way.

**Gwydre**    In old Welsh legends, this was the name of one of Arthur's sons.

**Gwyglet**    This was the name of a hero in the epic *The Goddoddin.* He fought and died at the battle of Catreath (Catterick).

**Gwyn** (GWIN)    Derived from the Welsh word *gwyd,* meaning "white" or "shining," this name refers to the brilliant light of the Otherworld. In legends and myths, the leader of the Wild Hunt was Gwyn ap Nudd.

**Gwyneira** (gwin-AYR-ah)    This name comes from the words *gwyn,* meaning "shining" or "holy," and *eira,* meaning "snow."

**Gwynn ap Nudd**    At first this deity was Lord of the Underworld and leader of the Wild Hunt. He abducted Creiddylad, thus causing a perpetual battle with Gwythyr ap Greidawl, her intended husband. He later became known as the king of the Fairies and the Plant Annwn, or subterranean fairies. Medieval tales say the entrance to his kingdom lies in Galstonbury Tor.

**Gwyr**    *From Gower.*

**Gwythyr**    In old legends the son of Greidyawl. This was also the name of the lord of the Upperworld.

**Hafgan** (HAHV-gahn)    A male or female name, it is derived from *haf,* meaning "summer," and *can,* meaning "song." In ancient legends this is the name of an Otherworld deity who must annually fight Arawn for rulership of the Underworld.

**Heddwyn** (HETH-win)  This name comes from the Welsh words *hedd,* meaning "peace," and *gwyn,* meaning "shining."

**Hefaidd Hen**  In ancient legends this was the name of Rhiannon's father, who ruled part of the Underworld.

**Heilyn**  In old legends this was the name of the son of Gwynn.

**Hen Beddestyr**  The legendary name of the son of Erim.

**Hen Was**  *Old servant.*

**Hen Wyneb**  *Old face.*

**Howel**  *Remarkable* or *attentive.*

**Huw** (HYOO)  The Welsh form of the name Hugh, which itself comes from the Old German word *hugi,* meaning "intelligence." Variants are HEW, HEWE, HU, and HUW.

**Hydd**  *Deer.*

**Hywel** (HUH-wel)  Derived from the Welsh word *hywel,* meaning "eminent."

**Iago**  The Welsh version of the name James, which means "God's gift."

**Iau**  The Welsh form of the name Zeus.

**Iddawg**  In old legends, the name of the son of Mynyo.

**Idris**  *Eager lord.* Variants are IDRISS and IDRIYS.

**Iestyn**  The Welsh version of the name Justin, which means "one who is just."

**Ieuan** (YAY-an)  The Welsh version of the name John, which means "God is gracious." Variants are IOAN and IWAN.

**Ifor**  The Welsh version of the Teutonic name that means "archer."

**Inek**  The Welsh form of the name Irvin.

**Iolo** (YOH-loh)  Although this is a nickname for Iorwerth, it is a popular name in its own right.

**Iona**  In old legends, the name of a French king. Also the Celtic name for the Isle of Anglesey off the coast of northern Wales.

**Iorwerth** (YOHR-wayrth)  Derived from the Norse word *ior,* meaning "lord," and the Welsh word *gwerth,* meaning "worth" or "value."

**Irvin**  *White river.* Variants are IRV, INEK, and IRVING.

**Ithel**  *Generous lord.*

**Iustig**  The name of one of Caw's sons in old legends.

**Jestin**  The Welsh version of the name Justin.

**Jones**  *Son of John.* A variant is JOENNS.

**Kai**  A variant of the name CEI. Other variants are KAY, KAI, and KEI.

Some authors say it is derived from a word meaning "fiery," while others believe it means "keeper of the keys."

**Kane**   Derived from a Welsh word meaning "beautiful."

**Keith**   *Dwells in the woods.* Variants are KEATH and KEITHON.

**Kelli**   In Welsh this name means "from the wood."

**Kelyn**   The name of one of Caw's sons in old tales.

**Kenn**   *Clear water.*

**Kent**   *White.*

**Kenyon**   *From Ennion's mound.*

**Kevyn**   Some sources say this name means "from the ridge." Others, however, say it comes from the Irish Gaelic Caoimhin, and means "gentle" or "lovable."

**Kian**   May be the Welsh version of the Irish name Cian, which means "ancient." In old Welsh legends, this was the name of the father of Lugh.

**Kilydd**   The legendary name of the son of Kelyddon.

**Kim**   *Leader.*

**Kynan**   *Chief.*

**Kyndrwyn**   The legendary name of the son of Ermid.

**Kynedyr**   In Welsh legends this was the name of the son of Hetwn.

**Kynlas**   The name of Kynan's son in old stories.

**Kynon**   The name of the son of Clydno in ancient tales. May be a variant of KYNAN.

**Kynwal**   The name of one of Caw's sons.

**Kynwyl**   The name of a very early Welsh saint.

**Lancelot du Lac**   He was the son of King Ban of Benoic in France and the father of Galahad, as well as being a knight of the Round Table. Although he was an unbeatable warrior, he had an affair with Queen Guinevere, thus causing the death of many knights, and the destruction of Arthur's kingdom.

**Lavaine**   Old Arthurian legends say this young knight was the son of Sir Bernard of Astolat. He was knighted by Lancelot and became one of the greatest knights of the Round Table.

**Leodegrance**   This is the name given in old tales to the King of Cameliard, who was the father of Guinevere.

**Lionel**   A knight of the Round Table, he was a cousin to Lancelot and a brother to Bors.

**Llacheu**   In ancient Welsh legends, this was the name of one of

Arthur's illigitimate sons by Lysanor. Some versions call him BORRE, BOARE, or LOHOT.

**Llara**   Derived from a word meaning "meek."

**Lleu**   The Welsh sun god was Llew Llaw Gyffes. He was born to Arianrhod and an unnamed father and raised by his uncle Gwydion. Because of a curse to have no earthly wife, his uncles made him one out of flowers and called her Blodeuwedd. She and her lover Gronw Pebr plotted his death, but because of Lleu's divine origins the death simply became an annual duel between the two men. His Welsh symbol was the white stag, and he was celebrated on August 1 in the Celtic ceremony of Lunasa.

**Llevelys**   The legendary name of the son of Beli.

**Lloyd**   *One with gray hair.* Variants are LOY, LLWYD, and LOYDE.

**Lludd**   Some sources say this name means "from London." However, there was a Welsh god whose name was Llud Llaw Ereint, who was very similar to the Irish deity Nuada and the Greek God Neptune. He was a god of waters, healing, smiths, harpers and poets, and sorcerers. A variant is LLUNDEIN.

**Llwch Llawwyanawc**   When the great cauldron was stolen and taken into Annwn, this Welsh warrior went with Arthur to get it back.

**Llwybyr**   The legendary name of one of the sons of Caw.

**Llwyd** (LHOO-eed)   The Welsh form of the name Lloyd, it is derived from *llwyd,* meaning "gray" or "holy."

**Llwydeu**   The name of the son of Nwython in old stories.

**Llwyr**   The legendary name of the son of Llwyryon.

**Llyn**   *From the lake.*

**Llyr**   A Welsh sea and water god, similar to the Irish god Lir. In ancient legends, he is listed as the father of the goddess Branwen and the god Bran. His name means "of the sea." The modern version of this name is Lear.

**Llywelyn** (lhu-WEL-een)   A popular patriotic name, it comes from the words *llyw,* meaning "leader," and *eilun,* meaning "image."

**Lot**   The king of Orkney and Lothian and the husband of Morgause. A variant is LOTHA.

**Lovel**   One of Gawain's illegitimate sons who was killed by Lancelot.

**Lug**   The Welsh version of the name Luke, which means "the bringer of light." A variant spelling is LUC.

**Mabon**   The name of a mysterious child in the Welsh Arthurian sagas. He was stolen from his mother when he was only three nights old and kept in a prison at Gloucester. The name means "the son." His story is told in *Culhwch and Olwen.*

**Mabsant**   The legendary name of one of the sons of Caw.

**Macsen** (MAK-sen)   A Welsh name derived from the Latin name Maximus. A variant is MAXEN.

**Madawg**   In old legends, the son of Teithyon. A variant of the name MADOC.

**Maddox**   *The benefactor's son.*

**Madoc** (MAH-dog)   Derived from the ancient British word *mad,* meaning "fortunate" or "lucky." Legends say that Madoc or Madog ap Owain Gwynedd sailed to North America in the late twelfth century.

**Mael**   The legendary name of the son of Roycol.

**Maelgwn** (MAYL-goon)   This name comes from the Welsh words *mael,* meaning "prince," and *ci* or *cwn,* meaning "hound" or "wolf," or "prince of the hounds."

**Maelogan** (may-LOH-gahn)   Derived from *mael,* this name means "divine prince." A variant is MAELON.

**Maelwys**   In old Welsh tales, the name of the son of Baeddan.

**Mallolwch**   The name of the legendary king of Ireland who married Branwen.

**Malvern**   *Bare hill.*

**Manawydan**   The name of the son of the sea god Llyr. He is the same as the Irish god Manannan mac Lir. A skilled shapeshifter, he kept the Isle of Man and the Isle of Arran in the Firth of Clyde under his protection. He broke the enchantment on Dyfed.

**March** (MAHRX)   Taken from the Welsh word *march,* meaning "horse." In Celtic cultures the horse was a symbol of the king. A common variant is MARK.

**Marrok**   A knight who was secretly a werewolf, a man who became a wolf at night.

**Math** (MAHTH)   Derived from the Celtic word *math,* meaning "bear."

**Math Mathonwy** (MAHTH mahth-ON-oo-ee)   The Welsh god of sorcery, magic, and enchantment. He was the uncle of Gwydion, Gilfaethwy, and Arianrhod. He helped created a flower-wife for Llew, his great-grandson.

**Mawrth**   The Welsh version of the name Mars, who was the Roman god of war.

**Maxen** A variant of the name MACSEN.

**Medyr** The legendary name of the son of Medyredydd.

**Meical** (MAYK-al) The modern Welsh version of the name Michael. The more ancient form is Mihangel (mi-HAHNG-el). A variant is MEIC (MAYK).

**Melkin** This pre-Merlin prophet and poet is mentioned in the Annals of Glastonbury Abbey.

**Menw** In old tales, the name of the son of Teirwaedd.

**Mercher** The Welsh form of the name Mercury, the Roman messenger of the gods.

**Meredith** (me-RED-ith) Derived from *mawr,* meaning "great" or "big," and *udd,* meaning "lord." Some sources give the meaning of this name as "guardian of the sea." This was the name of many of the medieval Welsh princes.

**Merlin** The great sorcerer in the Arthurian sagas. His father was from the Otherworld, but his mother was earthly. The legends say he learned all his magic from the Goddess under her names of Morgan, Viviane, Nimue, Lady of the Lake, and Queen of the Fairies. Old legends say he is the guardian of the Thirteen Treasures of Britain that he locked away in a glass tower on Bardsey Island. Welsh tradition says Myrddin still sleeps in a hidden crystal cave. The Welsh name Myrddin means "hawk."

**Meurig** The Welsh version of the name Morris or Maurice, which means "dark-skinned."

**Mil** In old legends, this was the name of the son of Dugum.

**Modred** The name of King Arthur's son by his half-sister Morgause in the Arthurian sagas. He was raised with his half-brothers, the other children of Morgause by Lot. He was killed by Arthur at the Battle of Camlan. A variant is MORDRED.

**Moesen** The Welsh version of the name Moses, meaning "from the water."

**Mordwywr** *Sailor.*

**Morgan** (MOHR-gahn) A male or female name. Possibly derived from the Welsh words *mor,* meaning "sea," and *can,* meaning "bright," or *cant,* meaning "circle." It could mean "sea-born," "bright sea," or "bright circle." Some sources believe it means "dwells near the sea." Variants are MORCAN and MORGANT (MOHR-gahnt).

**Morgannwg**   *From Glamorgan.*

**Morthwyl**   This name is derived from a word meaning "hammer."

**Morvran**   The name of the son of Tegid.

**Mostyn**   *Fortress in a field.*

**Myrddin** (MUHR-din or MUHR-thin)   Derived from the ancient British word *moridunon,* meaning "sea fortress." The name of the sorcerer Merlin was taken from Welsh sources.

**Naw**   In legends, the name of Seithved's son.

**Neb**   The name of one of the sons of Caw.

**Nentres**   He was one of the eleven kings who revolted against Arthur. He later married Elaine and became the king's ally.

**Nerth**   The name of the son of Cadarn in old tales.

**Nerthach**   The son of Gwawrddur in Welsh legend.

**Neued**   The legendary name of the father of Tringad.

**Newlin**   *Dwells near the new pool.*

**Nissyen** (NESS-yen)   *Lover of peace.* The brother of Evnissyen and the total opposite in morals and temperament. He was a half-brother of the god Bran.

**Nodens**   A variant name of the sea god Llud Llaw Ereint.

**Nynnyaw**   The legendary name of one of the sons of Beli.

**Odgar**   The name of one of the sons of Aedd.

**Ofydd**   The Welsh version of the name Ovid, who was a Roman poet.

**Ol**   The legendary name of the son of Olwydd.

**Olwydd**   *Tracker.*

**Oswallt**   The Welsh form of the name Oswald, which means "strength from God."

**Owein**   The Welsh version of the name Eugene, which means "noble born." Some sources list the meaning as "young warrior."

**Padrig** (PAHD-rig)   The Welsh form of the name Patrick, which means "noble." Saint Patrick was the patron saint of Ireland, who was also known in Wales. His feast day is March 17.

**Parry** (PAHR-ee)   This name comes from the Welsh *ap Harri,* which means "son of Henry (or Harry)."

**Pasgen** (PAHS-gen)   Derived from the word *Pasg,* meaning "Easter."

**Pawl** (POWL)   The Welsh version of the name Paul, which means "little."

**Pedr** (PEDR)   The Welsh form of the name Peter, which means "rock." Variants are PEDRAN (PED-rahn) and PETRAN (PET-rahn).

**Peissawg**    In legends, the name of a king of Brittany.

**Pelles**    He became known as the Wounded King of the Grail Castle after he was wounded through both thighs. His daughter Elaine bore Lancelot's child Galahad.

**Pellinore**    He was the brother of Pelles, King of the Isles, and one of the greatest knights of the Round Table.

**Pellyn**    *From the lake's headland.*

**Pembroke**    *Headland.*

**Penn**    *From the peak.*

**Pennar** (PENahr)    Derived from the Welsh words *pen,* meaning "head," and *ardd,* meaning "hill" or "height."

**Penvro**    *From Pembroke.*

**Perceval**    The earliest records of this knight of the Round Table are in the Welsh *Peredur* and the French *Le Conte du Graal.* A variant is PARZIVAL.

**Peredur** (per-ED-eer)    Possibly comes from the Welsh words *peri,* meaning "spears," and *dur,* meaning "hard." One of the Welsh grail romances mentions a Peredur mab Efrawc as a hero. This is also the legendary name of the son of Evrawg.

**Powell**    *Son of Howell.* One of the Welsh kings was named Howell.

**Price**    *Son of Rhys.* It also means "son of the ardent one."

**Pryderi** (pra-DAYR-ee)    In Welsh mythology, Pryderi is the son of Pwyll and Rhiannon. He was stolen on the night he was born and left by mysterious forces in the stable of Teyrnon Twrf Fliant, who raised him. He later married Cigfa and became lord of Dyfed.

**Prydwen**    *Handsome.*

**Prys**    Taken from *ap Rhys* or "son of Rhys."

**Puw**    The Welsh version of the name Pugh, which means "son of Hugh."

**Pwyll**    *Son of Howell.* In ancient legends, Pwyll was the lord of Dyfed when he met Arawn, lord of Annwn, and took his place for a year in the Otherworld.

**Pyrs**    This is the Welsh form of the name Pierce, which means "stone" or "rock."

**Ren**    *Ruler.* A variant is RYN.

**Renfrew**    Some authors give the meaning as "dwells near the still river," while others say it means "raven wood." A variant is RHINF-FREW.

**Rhain** (RHIIN)    Derived from the Welsh word *rhain,* meaning "spear" or "lance." A similar name is RHAINALLT, from *rhain,* and the word *allt,* meaning "hill."

**Rheged**    The legendary name of the father of Gwres.

**Rhioganedd**    In old legends, this was the name of a prince of Ireland.

**Rhisiart** (RHISH-art)    The Welsh version of the name Richard, which means "strong ruler."

**Rhobert**    The Welsh form of the name Robert, which means "brilliant" or "renowned."

**Rhodri** (RHOD-ree)    Derived from the Welsh words *rhod,* meaning "circle," and *rhi,* meaning "ruler."

**Rhun**    The name of one of the sons of Beli.

**Rhuvawn**    In legends, the name of the son of Deorthach.

**Rhyawdd**    The name of the son of Morgant in old tales.

**Rhychdir**    *From the plow land.*

**Rhyd**    *From the ford.*

**Rhydderch** (RHUHTH-erx)    This name comes from *rhi,* meaning "king," and *derchafu,* meaning "ascending."

**Rhys**    Derived from the Welsh word *rhys,* meaning "ardor" or "passion." This has been a popular male name throughout Welsh history. Variants are REECE, RICE, REIS, RIESS, and RHETT.

**Robat** (ROB-at)    This name is the Welsh version of the name Robert. A nickname is Robyn (ROB-een). A variant is ROBET.

**Romney**    *Dwells near the curving river.* A variant is RUMENEA.

**Sadwrn**    The Welsh version of the name Saturn, Roman god of the harvest.

**Sayer**    Derived from the word for "carpenter."

**Seith**    *Seven.* A variant is SAITH.

**Sel**    The legendary name of Selgi's son.

**Selwyn** (SEL-ween)    Derived from the Welsh words *sel,* meaning "ardor," and *gwyn,* meaning "shining" or "holy."

**Selyf**    The Welsh version of the name Solomon, which means "peace."

**Selyv**    A name in old legends of the son of Kynan.

**Seren** (SER-en)    A male or female name. It is derived from the Welsh word for "star."

**Siam** (SHAM)    The Welsh version of the name James.

**Siarl** (SHARL)   The Welsh form of the name Charles, which means "manly."

**Siawn**   In old tales, this was the name of the son of Iaen.

**Siencyn**   The Welsh form of the name Jenkin, which means "God is gracious."

**Sinnoch**   The name of one of the sons of Seithved in Welsh tales.

**Sion** (SHON)   This is the Welsh version of John. Nicknames are Sionyn (SHON-een) and Sioni (SHON-ee).

**Sior** (SHOR)   This name is the Welsh form of George, which means "farmer."

**Steffan**   The Welsh version of the name Stephen, which means "crowned with laurels."

**Sugyn**   The legendary name of the son of Sugynedydd.

**Sulien** (SIL-yen)   Derived from the Welsh words *sul*, meaning "sun," and *geni*, meaning "born," this was originally the name of a Celtic sun deity.

**Sulyen**   A variant of SULIEN. Also the name of one of the sons of Iaen in old tales.

**Syvwlch**   The legendary name of the son of Cleddyv Kyvwich.

**Tad**   *Father.* A variant is TADD.

**Taliesin** (tahl-YES-in)   Derived from the words *tal*, meaning "forehead" or "brow," and *iesin*, meaning "radiant, shining." The most famous man with this name was Taliesin, the archetypal bard and poet, who, according to ancient legend, gained his magic and wisdom from drinking Cerridwen's magic potion.

**Tarrant**   A variant of the name TARANIS, a thunder and storm god, similar to Jupiter. Other variants are TARRAN, TARYN, TAREN, and TERRANT.

**Tegid Foel**   The husband of the goddess Cerridwen, whose home lay under Lake Tegid.

**Tegvan**   The name of the goddess Cerridwen's son.

**Teilo** (TAY-loh)   Welsh folklore tells of a Saint Teilo who founded a church at Llandeilo Fawr in Dyfed. It was said that when he died, his body became three bodies so he could be buried in Llandeilo, Llandaf, and Penally. His celebration day is February 9.

**Teithi**   In old tales, this was the name of one of the sons of Gwynnan.

**Teregud**   The name of one of the sons of Iaen in old stories.

**Teryrnon** (TAYR-non)   This name comes from the Celtic word *tigernonos,* meaning "divine prince."

**Timotheus**   The Welsh version of the name Timothy, which means "honors God."

**Tomos** (TOHM-os)   The Welsh version of the name Thomas, which means "twin." A nickname is Twm (TOOM).

**Tor**   The natural son of King Pellinore, who was raised as a cowherd. The truth of his ancestry came out when he asked to be made a knight of the Round Table.

**Trahern**   *Incredibly strong* or *strong as iron.*

**Trefor** (TREV-ohr)   This name comes from the Welsh words *tref,* meaning "home" or "town," and *mor,* meaning "great." It has been in use as a personal name since the tenth century.

**Tremayne**   *Lives in the house by the rock.* A variant is TREMEN.

**Trent**   *Dwells near the rapid stream.* A variant is TRYNT.

**Trevelyan**   *From Elian's home.*

**Tringad**   The legendary name of the son of Neued.

**Tristan**   From the Old Welsh word for "noisy one." This name is often confused with another Welsh name, Tristram. Tristan is mentioned in the Arthurian sagas as a knight of the Round Table.

**Tristram**   This name means "sorrowful." A Welsh tale of tragic love is about Tristram (Tristan in Arthurian legend) and Isolde. The son of King Meliodas and Queen Elizabeth of Lyonnesse, he went to his uncle King Mark in Cornwall after his country sank under the ocean. He fell in love with Isolde, his uncle's bride, causing a great scandal. For a time he served King Arthur, but later went to Brittany where he was mortally wounded.

**Tudur** (TID-ir)   Derived from the Celtic word *teutorigos,* meaning "king of the tribe," this name may be related to Teutates, a god of the Celts in Gaul. This is a common name in Welsh history. A variant is TUDOR.

**Twm**   The Welsh version of the name Tom, which means "gift from God."

**Twrgadarn**   *Tower of strength.*

**Tywysog**   *Prince.*

**Uchdryd**   In ancient Welsh tales, this was the name of the son of Erim.

**Urien**   This was the traditional name of the king of the land of Gorre who was associated with the Round Table. He married Morgan le Fay. Their son's name was Owain.

**Vaddon** *From Bath.*

**Vaughn** *Small one.* A variant is VYCHAN.

**Wadu** In legends, this is the name of one of the sons of Seithved.

**Waljan** *Chosen.*

**Weyland** A god of smiths, tradition says he made Excalibur. His name is still associated with several sites throughout Wales and Britain.

**Wmffre** (OOM-free) This name is the Welsh version of the name Humphrey, which means "friend of the Huns." A variant is WMMFFRE.

**Wren** *Ruler.*

**Wyn** *Handsome* or *fair, white one.*

**Yale** *Fertile upland.*

**Yestin** A Welsh version of the name Justin.

**Ysberin** In old tales this is the name of the son of Fflergant.

**Ysgawyn** The name of the son of Panon in old Welsh tales.

**Yspadaden Pencawr** In the story *Culhwch and Ol,* he is called the father of Olwen.

# Part 11

# Surnames

# Ireland

The areas of Ireland listed for each family describe the points of origin for the main family and its most numerous branches. When the Scots were brought into northern Ireland, there was a blending of Scottish and Irish surnames in many cases. Many Irish surnames were affected by invasions from the Vikings, French Normans, Welsh, Anglo-Saxons, and English. Obviously, all clan names are not listed here. That would take an entire book alone.

**Ahearne**   Originally this name was spelled O'hEachtighearna, which means "lord of the horse." This family counts the High King Brian Boru as its ancestor. Much of the change in spelling occurred when Irish families emigrated to France, the United States, Canada, and Australia in the seventeenth and eighteenth centuries. The surname Hearne, without an Irish background or lineage, is very common in England also. Many Ahernes fled from Ireland to France during the seventeenth century to escape religious persecution. James Ahern (A. Hearn) came to New York in the late 1800s and became an actor and very popular playwright. Variant spellings are HERNE, HERON, and AHERON.

**Barrett**   A family whose ancestors came in with the Norman invasion around 1169. their original name was Baroid. They settled primarily in Cork, Mayo, and Galway.

**Barry**   Irish people with the name Barry trace their ancestry back to Wales. Two brothers with this name came to Ireland with the Anglo-Norman invasion in 1170 and soon held vast tracts of land in County Cork. They began the entire family with the name Barry.

Eventually, there were so many in Ireland with the surname Barry that they had to be distinguished by such names as Barry Mor (the Senior), Barry Og (the Young), or Barry Roe (the Red). Members of this family have been prominent in the arts, medicine, on stage, and in the military. Actors from this family have been on stage from the sixteenth century to the present day. Commander Tom Barry served courageously in the Irish war of independence. John, Ethel, Lionel, and Drew Barrymore were all American actors of the same family. Variants are DE BARRA and BARRYMORE.

**Beirne**   Although this surname sounds like the name Byrne, it is a distinctly different family. The original form of this name was O'Beirne, meaning "son of Beirne." It is thought to come from the Norse-Viking name Bjorn. The family settled primarily around County Roscommon and aren't in the records until the eighteenth century, when two Beirne brothers from County Meath joined the priesthood in Rome. The surname Beirne is more prominent, however, in the military roles of France, Spain, and the United States. A variant is O'BIRN.

**Blake**   This family came to Ireland with the French Norman invaders by way of Wales, where their surname was actually Caddell. The present surname came from an ancestor who had particularly dark hair and darker skin coloring. He was nicknamed Le Blaca (the Black). For hundreds of years members of this family were powerful landowners and merchants in the city and county of Galway. In fact, they were among the famous Fourteen Tribes of Galway. A few of the castles they built in Connacht still survive. Other family members went into the military, taking part in the crusades and later the Irish rebellions, such as the Battle of Kinsale. In the western part of Ireland there are Blake families whose names are written as O'BLATHMHAIC or BLOWICK.

**Boland**   This family started with a Norwegian who came to Ireland centuries ago. In Ireland the name is primarily written as O'Beollain, but in England it became O'Bolan. The branch of the family that lived around Lough Derg claimed that their ancestor was Mahon, a brother of the High King Brian Boru. A town there is named Ballybolan (Bolans' town). Another branch of the family settled in Sligo near Doonalton. In the twentieth century the Boland family took part in raising money for Irish independence. In the

1950s, Frederick Boland was the Irish ambassador in London, and then president of the United Nations. His daughter, Eavan Boland, is a leading Irish poet.

**Boyle**    The Irish spelling of this surname is O'BAOIGHILL or O'BAOILL, which may mean "having profitable pledges." The chieftains of this family were inaugurated in Donegal where the family was influential. Quite a bit of land in County Derry was owned at one time by the O'Boyles of Boylagh; they had a castle at Desart in County Armagh also. However, the Boyle family began with an English adventurer named Richard Boyle (1566-1643), who came to Ireland in the sixteenth century. He was the first Earl of Cork, had fifteen children, and was a millionaire by today's standards. This Richard Boyle managed to buy most of the lands belonging to the leading Irish families in Munster, even purchasing Waterford estate when Sir Walter Raleigh was executed. By the nineteenth century, the Boyle descendants went abroad to live: Richard Vicars Boyle built railroads in Japan and India, and John J. Boyle became a sculptor in New York. One of the earliest playwrights for the Abbey Theatre in Dublin was William Boyle.

**Brady**    The original Irish spelling of this surname was MacBradaigh, which means "spirited." They settled mainly in Ulster, Leinster, and Cavan. Sometimes this clan is confused with the O'Gradys of Limerick who changed their name to Brady. One of the first war photographers during the American Civil War was Matthew Brady (1823-1896).

**Breen**    The original Irish spelling is O'Braoin, which means "sadness" or "sorrow." They are primarily found in Kilkenny, Wexford, and Westmeath. From 1303-1324 Donal O'Breen was Bishop of Clonmacnoise. Elizabeth Breen was with a group of Irish nuns who were imprisoned during the French Revolution. Variants are MACBREEN and BRAWNEY.

**Brennan**    Primarily residents of Kilkenny, Kerry, and Westmeath, the original Irish Gaelic spelling of this surname was O'Braonain. There is some discussion whether this name means "little drop" or "sorrow." Louis Brennan invented the torpedo used during World War I. Maire Ni Bhraonain and her twin brothers are musicians with the group Clannad, and her sister Enya is a best-selling singer.

**Browne**    The le Brun family came to Ireland with the Norman invaders in the twelfth century. They put down roots in Galway and joined the Fourteen Tribes of Galway through marriage with the leading families. Historical records show that Elizabeth I gave a Browne from England a very large piece of property in Kerry. The last Browne to live in their Ross Castle by the lakes of Killarney was Lord Castlerosse. A great many of the men of this family became soldiers of fortune for foreign governments. Unfortunately, many of the Browne men fought for the ill-fated Stuart monarchy in Scotland and either died on the fields of battle or clung blindly to the exiled monarch. Alexander Browne, who left Ireland in 1800, opened stores in Philadelphia and New York, becoming one of America's first millionaires. Valentine Browne (1891-1943) turned his estate of Kenmare into the famous Killarney golf course. Christy Brown (1932-1981) wrote his autobiography *My Left Foot*, from which the movie was made. Variants are BROWN and BROUN.

**Buckley**   The Irish Gaelic spelling was O'Buachalla, which means "boy." Members of this family come primarily from Cork and Kerry. Many of this family were outlawed after the defeat of King James II. There are several Buckleys listed as having fought in America's Meagher's Irish Brigade.

**Burke**   This French Norman family, descended from William the Conqueror, came to Ireland with the Norman invasion in the twelfth century. Their original name was de Burca, which means "of the borough." Beginning with a grant of vast amounts of O'Conor land in Connacht, they rapidly grew into several large families (called *septs* in Ireland). They were never accepted into the Fourteen Tribes of Galway, although a Burke was a major contributor in the building of the city of Galway. Exchanging their chieftaincy of Clanricarde for the titles of Earl and Marquess of Claricarde, they became prominent in Anglo-Irish politics. The Tipperary branch of the Burke family became known for their book *Burke's Peerage* (later known as *Burke's Landed Gentry*), a great contribution to genealogy. Variants are BOURKE and DE BURGH.

**Butler**   Another family who came to Ireland with the Norman invasion. The ancestor of this clan was Theobald Fitzwalter (d.1205). The family changed the surname from Fitzwalter to de Buitleir, or Butler, when Theobald was created Chief Butler of Ireland by Henry II in 1177. Later, the title of earl of Ormond was conferred upon them along with other important titles. The Butlers had fortresses at Gowran and Kilkenny Castle that they used in their constant battles with the FitzGeralds. Anne Boleyn (mother of Elizabeth I) and William Butler Yeats were both descended from this family.

**Byrne**   The name Byrne, with or without an O, is one of the most widely found Irish names. The original name was O'Broin, which is derived from Branach (raven), who was a son of Maolmordha, the eleventh-century king of Leinster. The O'Broins held Kildare until they were driven into the mountains by the Anglo-Normans. Later they went to Crioch Bhranach where they established Ballinacor as their headquarters. Led by Fiach MacHugh O'Byrne, their chief, they waged guerrilla warfare against the English. When Fiach was caught, he was killed and his head impaled outside Dublin Castle. During the exodus of 1691, many of this family went to France. However, a number of them were imprisoned and executed during the French Revolution. One O'Byrne family had a successful vineyard at Bordeaux. Of those who emigrated to the United States, several were prominent bishops and surgeons. This family is completely separate from and not related to the O'Beirnes. A variant is O'BYRNE.

**Cahill**   One of the earliest recorded Irish surnames, it was originally Cathail, which is derived from the Irish word for Charles and means "manly" or "valor." A southern Galway family was the first to bear this name, but soon there were branches in other areas with slightly changed surnames. For example, there are families with the surname Ballycahill in both County Tipperary and County Clare. During World War I, three sons of the Ballyragget family of County Kilkenny died in France.

**Callaghan**   The original Gaelic name was O'Ceallachain. The name may be derived from the personal name of a tenth-century king of Munster, Ceallachan, whose name means "strife." He led his men often in raids on neighboring counties and killed Cinneide, the father of Brian Boru. During the period immediately before Cromwell's forces wreaked havoc on Ireland, a Colonel Donogh O'Callaghan was outlawed for his participation in the Irish Confederation of Kilkenny. He fled to France. One branch of the family who fled with the Wild Geese (Irishmen who had to flee) to Spain produced Don Juan O'Callaghan, a Barcelona lawyer. Variants are CALLAHAN and O'CALLAGHAN.

**Carey**   This family settled mostly in Kildare and Kerry. The original Gaelic spelling was O'Ciardha. Matthew Carey (1760-1839) founded the *Pennsylvania Herald.* Hugh Carey was a governor of New York State. Variants are O'KERRY, KERRY, and CAREW.

**Carroll**   The Carroll or (O'Carroll) family traces its ancestry to two important historical figures: a third-century king of Munster with the name of Oilioll Olum, and a leading swordsman of Brian Boru's army named MacCearbhaill, which means "son of the warlike champion." This swordsman became famous during the Battle of Clontarf in 1014. When the Normans invaded in 1170, there were six different, but important, O'Carroll families headed by O'Carroll Ely of Tipperary and Offaly, and O'Carroll Oriel of Monaghan and Louth. When the powerful Norman family with the name Butler took most of their lands, the O'Carroll families left for other parts of Ireland, particularly County Offaly. Leap Castle, their Offaly castle, is considered to be one of the most haunted in Ireland. Members of this vast family founded monasteries, married Irish and British royalty, and hired out their swords in the armies of France. The family has a legendary guardian spirit named Queen Una. In Ireland there is a separate, but related, family called MacCarroll. An anglicized variant is MACCARVILL.

**Casey**   The Gaelic spelling of this surname is O'Cathasaigh, which means "vigilant" or "watchful." The family lived in Munster. Thomas Lincoln Casey built the Washington Monument in the United States. A variant is O'CASEY.

**Cassidy**   Originally, this family lived in Fermanagh, but has become quite widespread. The Gaelic spelling was O'Caiside. The name originated from a personal name of the head of a family who were teachers and physicians to the Maguire chieftains of Fermanagh for 300 years.

**Clancy**   The Irish Gaelic MacFhlannchaidh means "ruddy warrior." Most of this family lives in Clare and Leitrim. Willie Clancy (1921-1973) was a well-loved traditional musician who gave concerts in the United States. Variants are CLANCHY, GLANCHY, and MACCLANCY.

**Clarke**   The anglicized version of the name Clery. This family dates its line back to a nineth century Cleireach, whose name means "clerk," who was related to King Guaire of Connacht. During medieval times, Cleireach gave grand banquets at his Dunguaire

Castle on Galway Bay. Later, the Clerys were driven out of their homes in Connacht and reestablished themselves in Ulster. There, they became churchmen, poets, and lawgivers. When Gaelic Irish names were outlawed by the English conquerors, the Clerys changed their name to Clarke, which is an English name. Variants are O'CLEIRIGH, O'CLERY, MACALARY, and MACCLERY.

Coghlan  Originating in Offaly and Cork, this family's surname was once spelled MacCochalin or O'Cochlain. It means "cape" or "hood." The wife of Jeremiah Coughlan was a smuggler who used her income to build Ardo Castle on the County Waterford coast. She also arranged marriages for her daughters with wealthy dukes and earls. Variants are O'COUGHLAN, COUGHLAN, COHALAN, and MAC-COUGHLAN.

Collins  When Irish Gaelic names were outlawed, the family surname O'Coileain, meaning "young dog," was changed to Collins, thus making it difficult to separate the Irish branch from the large English family with this same name. The Irish name O'Coileain means "whelp" or "young animal." The O'Coileain family were lords of Connello in County Limerick until they were driven out by the Anglo-Norman invaders. They then moved farther south, settling in West Cork. Many of the Collins family went into the church, but remained of a militant nature. A Jesuit Collins was hung for inciting riots in 1602, and a Dominican Collins led an attack on Bunratty Castle in 1647. The most famous Collins politician was Michael (1890-1922), known as The Big Fellow, who was killed in the Irish civil war of 1922.

Connolly  O'Conghaile was the Gaelic spelling. It means "valorous." An ancient family who once held influence in Connacht, they eventually separated into three branches and dispersed to live mostly in Connacht, Ulster, Monaghan, and Cork. At one time they were one of the Four Tribes of Tara. The records of 1591 show that a Tirlogh O'Connola was chief of his clan and lived in Monaghan. In the early eighteenth century, William Connolley, a lawyer in Donegal, made his fortune by buying and selling the lands of the old Irish families who were exiled after the Battle of the Boyne. He became speaker in the Irish House of Commons and built Castletown Mansion in County Kildare. Possibly the most famous member of this family, however, was Maureen Connolly (1934-1969), known as

Little Mo, the United States tennis star of the 1950s. Variants are CONNELY and CONNOLLEY.

**Conroy**   The original Irish spelling was O'Conratha, which means "hound of prosperity." The family lived in Roscommon and Clare. For generations they were hereditary poets and chroniclers to the kings of Connacht. A few of these were Tanaidhe O'Maolchonaire (c. 1100), Torna O'Mulconry (c. 1250-1310), John O'Mulconry (c. 1440), and Fearfeasa O'Mulconry (c. 1636). Variants are O'MULCONRY, MULCONRY, CONARY, CONREE, and CONRY.

**Conway**   In Irish Gaelic this surname is MacConnmhaigh, which means either "hound or wolf of the plains" or "head-smashing." Another branch of the family came from Wales in the fourteenth century. This Welsh branch began with Jenkin Conway and his three brothers, who were granted 5,260 acres at Killorglin, County Kerry. During the Famine this family was outstanding as progressive landlords who cared for their people. This family primarily lived in Clare, Kerry, and County Dublin. Richard Conway (d. 1623) was a Jesuit priest who helped carry out church reforms during the Reformation. Thomas Count Conway (d. 1800) was a major-general in the French army and later a governor of French territory in India. He also served as a general in the American War of Independence. A variant is O'CONWAY.

**Cooney**   This family of Galway, Clare, and West Cork originally spelled their surname as O'Cuanachain, which means "handsome" or "elegant." Mary Cooney was famous in both Ireland and the United States for poetry in the 1880s. Variants are CONAN, COONAN, O'CUANA, and COUNIHAN.

**Corcoran**   The original Gaelic name was O'Corcrain, which means "ruddy." The family mainly lived in the areas of Fermanagh, Offaly, Mayo, and Kerry. Brigadier General Michael Corcoran took part in the Battle of Bull Run in the United States. A variant is O'CORCORAN.

**Costello**   A Norman name that began in Connacht as de Angulos, it changed to the Gaelic spelling of MacOisdealbh, which means "son of Oistealb." Paul Costello (b. 1945) is a top dress designer whose clientele included Diana, Princess of Wales. Variants are NANGLE and COSTELLOE.

**Crowley**   The Gaelic spelling was O'Cruadhlaoich. Some sources say this name means "hunchbacked," while others say it means "strong hero." The family primarily lived in Roscommon and Cork. Thady Crawley was chaplain to King James II, one of the many members of this family who served the Stuarts. Presently, Niall Crowley is chairman of the Allied Irish Bank and president of the Dublin Chamber of Commerce. A variant is CRAWLEY.

**Cuif**  The French version of the surname O'Keeffe. Georgia O'Keeffe was a famous painter in the United States.

**Cullen**  The original Gaelic spelling of this name was O'Cuillin, which means "holly tree." This vast family began in Wicklow, but were driven out by the O'Byrnes and O'Tooles. They later settled in County Kildare, giving their name to the town of Kilcullen. By the sixteenth century, they had also moved into Wexford and founded Cullenstown. Many male members of this family became clergymen and bishops. Paul Cullen (1803-1878) was Ireland's first Cardinal. Variants are CULLION, CULHOUN, MACCULLEN, and CULLINANE.

**Cummins**  The Gaelic versions of this surname were O'Comain and O'Cuimin, which mean "a hurley." They mainly lived in Mayo, Kerry, and Limerick. Geraldine Cummins (1890-1969) was a novelist and biographer. Her sister Ashley was an international hockey player. Variants are COMMONS, COMYNS, and HURLEY.

**Curran**  A family scattered through Ulster, Galway, Waterford, and Kerry, they once used the Gaelic spelling O'Corrain, which means "a descendant of O'Corrain." John Philpot Curran (1750-1817), an attorney who, although he was Protestant, defended the Catholic clergy who were unjustly treated, as well as many of the United Irishmen. His son Henry Grattan Curran (1800-1870) was a barrister and writer.

**Curtin**  Originally, the Irish name of this family was Cruitin, which means "hunchback." There are several variants of this name, even in Ireland: MACCUIRTIN, MACCURTIN, and CURTAYNE, as well as MACCRUITIN. At one time the MacCruitin family held territory on the coast between Ennistymon and Corcomroe Abbey in County Clare. Many of this family became medieval scholars, poets, and bards. However, internal battles for control split the families apart, and they scattered around Ireland, particularly settling in Limerick, Cork, and Dublin.

**Cusack**  When the Anglo-Normans invaded Ireland in 1211, a family called Cusak moved from Guienne in France to take over a large area of Kildare and Meath. Although they integrated with their Irish neighbors with few problems, they used aggression to acquire more land in Mayo, where they became known as MacIosog or Ciomhsog. Because so many of this family fought with James II at the Battle of the Boyne, most of them had to emigrate to France, where they fought in several European armies. At least one member of the Cusack family turned to privateering. The family members who had remained in Ireland produced some widely varied personalities, such as Dr. James Cusack, a distinguished Dublin surgeon, and Margaret Cusack, called "the nun of Kenmare," who frequently changed her religion.

**Daly**    The original Irish Gaelic name for this family was O'Dalaigh, which means "a meeting place." The Daly family traces their ancestry back to Niall of the Nine Hostages in the fourth century. Niall, a High King with a castle at Tara, is also claimed as an ancestor by the families O'Neill and O'Donnell. From the eleventh to the eighteenth century, the Daly clan produced many extraordinary men who excelled in bardic literature, poetry, and music. These talented men often served the leading families. However, the Daly family also excelled in other fields. Daniel, who was a Dominican friar, fled religious persecution in Ireland and established colleges in Louvain and Lisbon. Six mayors of the city of Galway were members of the Daly clan. Several of those who emigrated to the British colonies, the United States, and Australia became administrators or prominent members of the military in their new homes. A variant is DAWLEY.

**Delany**    Originally, this Gaelic surname was spelled O'Dubhshlaine, which comes from *dubh,* meaning "black," and *Slaine,* meaning "the river Slaney." They lived in Leix and Dublin. Felix O'Dulany, Bishop of Ossory in 1202, built the cathedral in Kilkenny. Ronny Delany (b. 1935) won a gold medal in the Melbourne Olympic Games in 1956. Variants are DELANE and DELANEY.

**Dempsey**    This family of Leix and Offaly originally spelled their Gaelic name as O'Diomasaigh, which means "proud." They claim descent from Ros Failghe, the eldest son of Cathaoir Mor, the second-century king of Ireland. Jack Dempsey was a famous boxer in the United States.

**Devine**    The Gaelic spelling is O'Daimhin, which means "bard" or "poet." The family lived in Fermanagh, Tyrone, Dublin, Cavan, and Louth. Edward Thomas Devine (1867-1948) was a professor at Columbia University in the United States. Variants are DAVIN, DEVANE, DEVIN, and DOWNES.

**Devlin** Originally spelled O'Doibhlin, this family lived in Sligo and Tyrone.

**Dillon** Eight hundred years ago, when the Dillon family arrived from Brittany, their name was de Leon. The Irish version was Diolun. They owned so much land and prospered so much that part of the area of Longford, Westmeath, and Kilkenny was once known as Dillon's Country. A few branches of the family moved to Mayo and Sligo, where the family head was Viscount Dillon of Costello-Gallen. During the seventeenth-century unrest of Anglo-Irish politics, they were rewarded with several peerages for their political part. However, they later lost their castles and land because they were staunch Catholics. When Cromwell invaded Ireland, much of the family fled to France where they organized a Regiment of Dillon. One of their remaining castles is Portlick Castle in Glasson, County Meath. Clonbrock House in Ballinasloe, Galway, was occupied by a Daly from 1575 until a few years ago, when the house was given to the nation of Ireland.

**Doherty** In Irish Gaelic this surname was O'Dochartaigh, which means "obstructive." There are also many variants of the anglicized form of the name. They claim descent from the High King Niall of the Nine Hostages and had a very early stronghold on the Inishowen Peninsula in Donegal. One of their chiefs, Cahir O'Doherty, attacked Derry in rebellion but only managed to get himself and most of his men massacred. This turmoil was used to bring in Scottish settlers to Ulster, thus laying the foundation for much of the present unrest. As a result of this, many of the family O'Doherty fled to Scotland and England, then emigrated to Australia and North America. Variants are DOUGHARTY, MACDEVITT, and O'DOGHERTY.

**Dolan** Originally of Galway and Roscommon, this family once used the Gaelic spelling of O'Dobhailen, which means "black defiance" or "challenge." In California there is the Dolan Winery in Redwood Valley. Variants are DOOLAN, DOWLING, DOELAN, and O'DOELAN.

**Donaghue** In Irish Gaelic this surname was O'Donnchadha or

O'Donnchu. There are many variations of the anglicized form of this name, including Dunphy and Donju (the Spanish version). This family claims as an ancestor a king of Munster who fought at Clontarf in 1014. Ross Castle was their fortress in early history when most of the family lived in Cork and Kerry. Their chieftain at this castle was O'Donoghue Mor. Another chieftain, O'Donoghue of the Glens, also lived in the same region. Other branches of this family eventually moved to Galway, Kilkenny, and Cavan, where they changed the spelling of their surname to Donohue. Juan O'Donju was the last Spaniard to rule in Mexico. Variants are DONOHOE, DONOHUE, and DUNPHY.

**Doran** The Gaelic spelling of this surname is O'Deoradhain or O'Deorain, which means "exile" or "stranger." The family primarily lived in Down, Armagh, Leix, Wexford, and Kerry. John Doran (1807-1878) was a journalist and stage historian.

**Dowling** This family once lived in Leix, Kilkenny, Carlow, Wicklow, and Dublin, and used the Gaelic spelling of O'Dunlaing. Reverend Thadeus O'Dunlaing was abbot at Trinity College during the Middle Ages. Donncha O'Dulaing is a popular broadcaster for Irish radio today.

**Doyle** The Gaelic form of this surname was O'Dubhghaill, MacDubhghaill, and O'Duill, which means "dark foreigner." The name very likely came from the Irish description of the Norse-Viking invaders. This family name is more prevalent around Wexford and the southeast coast, an area of Viking settlement, than anywhere else in Ireland. The ancient genealogies do not mention this family name. However, from the seventeenth century onward, this name appears in the army lists of Britain and several Europe countries. Sir Arthur Conan Doyle came from a Dublin branch of this family. Variants are DOYELLE, DOYLEY, and MACDOWELL.

**Driscoll** This family predominantly lived in Cork. In Gaelic their surname is spelled O'hEidersceoil and means "interpreter" or "intermediary." They claim descent from the Milesians who came from Spain. Because of their allegiance to the doomed Stuarts, they had to flee to France where they became prominent in the Irish brigades there. John O'Driscoll (d. 1828), a barrister from Cork, was appointed chief justice in the West Indies. His son William was also a barrister in Dublin. A variant is O'DRISCOLL.

**Duffy**   The Gaelic form of this name was O'Dubthaigh, which is derived from *dubh,* meaning "black." There is very little known about this family until the seventh century when they became active in the church in Monaghan. The Ulster version of this name is Dowey. During the twelfth century, many of this family were highly skilled craftsmen and worked on monasteries and churches for the High King, Turlough O'Conor. In Roscommon, where a branch of this family lives, there is a town called Lissyduffy. Duffy's is one of the oldest circuses performing in Ireland. Variants are DOOHEY, DOWEY, DUHIG, and O'DUFFY.

**Duggan**   The Gaelic form of this surname is O'Dubhagain, which means "black head." The family resided in Cork, Galway, Donegal, and Tipperary. Sean Mor O'Dubhagain (d.1372) was chief poet to the O'Kellys of Galway. Variants are DOOGAN and DOUGAN.

**Dunne**   Although there are Dunnes in England, they are a different family from the one in Ireland. This widespread Irish name in Gaelic is O'Duinn and is derived from a word meaning "brown." The usual version of this surname in Ulster is Dunn. At one time the family was one of the most important in Ireland and were lords of Iregan. After their participation in the Jacobite wars, many in this family emigrated to the United States. There they became active as church officials, lawyers, and military personnel. Sir Patrick Dun's Hospital in Dublin is a memorial to a Scottish family member who was President of the Royal College of Physicians in Ireland five times.

**Egan**   The original Gaelic form of this name was MacAodhagain and means "son of Aodh." The name Aodh is anglicized as Hugh. Although this family originated in Galway, Roscommon, and Leitrim, they scattered into Tipperary, Kilkenny, and Offaly. Many generations of them held the post of *ollav* (lawyer) for the ruling Irish families. Some of them also held high church offices. When Irish names were forbidden, this family changed to the surname Egan. However, in Dublin and Wicklow the name was more often written as Keegan. Many of them are now known as MacEgan. Their Redwood Castle in Lorrha, Tipperary, has been restored.

**Fagan**   The Gaelic original of this surname was O'Faodhagain, which means "little Hugh." The family is possibly of Norman ancestry with their name coming from the Latin *paganus.* They primarily lived in

Kerry and Dublin. James Bernard Fagan (1873-1933) was a Belfast playwright who founded the Oxford Playhouse. Variants are O'HAGAN, FEGAN, and O'HOGAN.

**Fahy**  The Gaelic spelling of this surname was O'Fathaigh and means "field green." The family lived mostly in Falway and Tipperary. One of the quartermasters of the 1864 Irish-American brigades in New York was Captain John Fahy. Variants are FAHEY, FAGHY, and GREEN.

**Fallon**  This family lived in Galway, Donegal, Cork, Kerry, and Wexford, and at one time used the Gaelic spelling of O'Fallamhain, which means "ruler." James O'Fallon was an officer in the American War of Independence; his brother, Colonel John O'Fallon, was a philanthropist. A variant is FALLOON.

**FitzGerald**  Maurice FitzGerald came to Ireland with the Norman invaders in 1170 and settled there after the war. The Gaelic name MacGearailt means "son of Gerald." His descendants became very powerful, among them the earls of Kildare, the dukes of Leinster, and the earls of Desmond (Kerry and Cork). During the sixteenth century, the eighth earl of Kildare, Garret Mor FitzGerald, was regarded as king of Ireland for forty years, although he actually did not have the title. Of the other branches of the Fitzgerald family, many of them were imprisoned or executed in the Tower of London for opposing English rule. The entire family clan seems to have always been influential in politics in one form or another. James FitzGerald, twentieth earl of Kildare and first duke of Leinster, had twenty-two children. One of his sons, Lord Edward FitzGerald, had a military career in America and France. The American writer F. Scott Fitzgerald wrote novels, including *The Great Gatsby.*

**Fitzpatrick**  Although this family began in Leix, they spread throughout Ireland. The Gaelic original of their surname was MacGiolla Padraig, which means "servant of Saint Patrick." This is the only Fitz surname that is Irish and not Norman in origin. Variants are KILPATRICK and MACGILLAPATRICK.

**Flanagan**  The original Gaelic spelling was O'Flannagain, which means "red." The family basically lived in Roscommon, Offaly, and Fermanagh. A Flannagain was a hereditary poet at the court of the O'Conor kings of Connacht. Variant is O'FLANNAGAN.

**Flynn**  The majority of this family lived in Cork, Roscommon, and Antrim. This surname, which means "red" or "ruddy," was once spelled as O'Floinn. Errol Flynn (1909-1964) was a romantic Hollywood film star. Variants are FLINN, O'LOINN, and O'LYNN.

**Fogarty**   A family mainly from Tipperary, they once used the Gaelic name of O'Fogartaigh, which means "exiled" or "banished." J. Fogarty and Sons built St. Mary's Catholic church in Limerick and the Wesley College in Belfast. A variant is GOGARTY.

**Foley**   O'Foghladha, which means "plunderer," was the Gaelic spelling of this surname. They lived mostly in Munster, although a few families with this name were found in Waterford. May Foley was the mother of Arthur Conan Doyle, who created Sherlock Holmes.

**Gaffney**   This family lived primarily in Connacht. The Gaelic version is O'Gamhna, which means "calf." It could also be O'Caibheanaigh, MacConghamhna, MacCarrghamhna, or Mag Fhachtna. Austin Gaffney is one of Ireland's most popular singers. A variant is CAULFIELD.

**Gallagher**   One of the principal family clans in Donegal, they claimed to be older than the Cineal Connail, the royal family descended from Connal Gulban, who was the son of King Niall of the Nine Hostages. In Gaelic, this surname O'Gallchobhair probably means "foreign help." The name may have been acquired from three centuries of service to the O'Donnells as army marshalls. Most of their notable members made their mark in the church. The position of bishop of Raphoe in Donegal was held by six different O'Gallaghers. Frank Gallagher (1898-1962) was editor of the *Irish Press* and fought in the Irish War of Independence.

**Galvin**   The Gaelic form of this surname is O'Gealbhain. The family lived in Kerry and Roscommon.

**Garvey**   A family of Armagh, Down, and Donegal, they originally used the Gaelic spelling of O'Gairbith or MacGairbhith, which means "rough." They were lords of Morrish and Tully, as well as having castles in County Down and Kilkenny. John Garvey (1527-1605) was archbishop of Armagh, while Callagh Garvan (1644-1735) was a physician to the royal Stuarts.

**Geraghty**   The original Gaelic version of this surname was O'Roduibh, which later became Mag Oireachtaigh, which means "a court" or "assembly." The family lived in Roscommon and Galway. There are more than seventeen variants of this name, two of which are GARRITY and GERITY.

**Guinness**    The original Irish Gaelic version of this surname was MacAonghusa, which means "son of Aonghus." By 1894, however, records show sixteen different variations of this Ulster name. They trace their ancestry back to the fifth century and a chief of Dal Araidhe. By the twelfth century they had managed to become lords of Iveagh in County Down and had a fortress at Rathfriland. Although they pretended sympathy with the Elizabethan English, they fought alongside Hugh O'Neill in 1598 at the Battle of the Yellow Ford. Even after the defeat at Kinsale, they managed to get back their 22,000 acres and have Magennis of Iveagh created Viscount. Although their politics were strictly for Ireland, they were divided in the matter of religion. Several of this family were bishops, for both the Catholics and Protestants. After the Battle of the Boyne, many of this family emigrated to Austria, France, Spain, and the United States, where they often served in the military. This surname has become famous through Arthur Guinness, who set up his brewery on the River Liffey in Dublin in 1759. Variants are MCGENIS, MACGINNIS, MAGENNIS, MACGUINNESS, and MACINNES.

**Hagan**    This family from Tyrone originally used the Gaelic spelling O'hAodhagain or O'hAgain. This family had the hereditary right to perform the inauguration ceremony for the O'Neills of Ulster. Mary O'Hagan (1823-1876) founded the order of the Poor Clares. Variants are AIKEN, O'HAGAN, and HOGG.

**Healy**    The original of this surname was O'hEildhe or O'hEalaighthe. Two different families, O'hEildhe (claimant) of Lough Arrow in County Sligo, and O'hEilaighthe (ingenious) of Donoughmore in County Cork, combined. They both had been deprived of their lands by the followers of Cromwell. A John Hely of Cork married a Hutchinson heiress and combined their names; thus began a line of Hely Hutchinsons who were the earls of Donoughmore, with an ancestral home Knocklofty in County Tipperary. The first son to bear this joined name was John Hely Hutchinson, who was a provost of Trinity College Dublin. Variants are O'HEALY, HELY, and O'HEALIHY.

**Hennessy**    The original Gaelic of this surname was O'hAonghusa, which is derived from the personal name Aonghus or Angus. The branches of the family that live in Connacht and Munster gradually anglicized their name to Hennessy, Hensey, and Henchy. There are also many places in these areas with the name Ballyhennessy. The leading branch of the family lived in Offaly near Kilbeggan, while another branch lived on the borders between Meath and Dublin. After the Normans invaded in 1170, the greater part of this clan moved to Limerick, Tipperary, and Cork. At one time they held the stronghold of Ballymacmoy near Mallow, County Cork. Many men of this family served with great honor in the French court and army, where they gained titles of nobility. Richard Hennessy (1720-1800), a member of the Irish family in France, discovered the secret for making Cognac brandy. They also had a passion for horses; one of their thoroughbreds won the Triple Crown and the Hennessy Gold Cup.

**Hickey**   This family lived in Clare, Limerick, and Tipperary. The Gaelic form of this name is O'hIcidhe, which means "healer." Generations of this family were physicians to the royal O'Briens of Thomond.

**Higgins**   The original Gaelic surname of this family was O'hUigin, which means "knowledge." The Higgins of Britain are not related to this ancient family, who were once a branch of the O'Neills in Westmeath. Between the thirteenth and seventeenth centuries, eight O'hUigins were poetic bards, with one also being a bishop. When the position of bard died out, members of this family went into medicine and the sciences where they again gained honor. A member of the Meath branch of the family immigrated to Peru. His son was Bernardo O'Higgins, known as the Liberator of Chile and that country's first president.

**Hogan**   The original Gaelic name was O'hOgain, which is derived from *og*, meaning "young." They were part of the Dalcassian people and lived in Thomond, Clare, and Limerick, until they began to spread out. Later they moved into Tipperary where they had a fortress at Nenagh. This family claims the tenth century Brian Boru as its ancestor. Although they lost their land under Cromwell's rule, they regained most of it when Charles II took the throne. In 1690 a man called Galloping Hogan helped to destroy the Williamite seige train at Ballyneety. Like other Irish families, many Hogan members went abroad. Austin Hogan established the Transport Workers Union of America.

**Jennings**   One source says that the Gaelic version of this surname,

MacSheoinin, means "son of little John." The family primarily lived in Connacht. Sir William Jennings fought at the battle of the Boyne, while Sir Patrick A. Jennings (1830-1877) was a governor of New South Wales.

Joyce   This surname probably came into Connacht, Ireland with the Norman invaders and was derived from the French personal name Joie, or Joy. The Gaelic version was Seoigh. They intermarried with the strong local families, such as the O'Briens, and were permitted to join the Fourteen Tribes of Galway. At one time this large family owned great portions of land in the barony of Ross, County Galway, an area that is still known as Joyce's Country. Joyce bishops and crusaders went to the Holy Land during the Crusades. One such man, captured en route, discovered a buried treasure. Upon escaping from his captors, he returned with the treasure and built the walls of Galway city. Another captured Joyce learned the art of gold and silver smithing during his Middle East confinement; he designed the Claddagh ring. James Joyce (1882-1941), the famous playwright, poet, musician, and author, was a member of this family.

Kavanagh   This ancient Irish family is directly descended from Diarmuid MacMurrough, who was king of Leinster in the twelfth century. His son Donal was educated at Cill Caomhan, St. Kevin's Church, Wexford. To distinguish him from others with the name Donal, this young man took the name Caomhanach, which was later anglicized to Kavanagh. After this, many of the family took the name Caomhanach or Kavanagh instead of MacMurrough. Since Donal/Caomhanach was not chosen to be the next king, he was compensated with large areas of land in Wexford and Carlow. Art MacMurrough, who took the name Kavanagh, was king of Leinster for forty-two years. He, and a succession of McMurrough Kavanagh kings, fought to expel foreign invaders until the time of Henry VIII. Variants are CAVANAGH and MACMURROUGH.

Keane   The original Gaelic spellings of this family name were MacCathain in West Clare, O'Cathain in Ulster, and O'Cein in Munster. All these Gaelic Irish names are derived from the personal name of Cian. Variants of the anglicized name are Kane and O'Keane. The Keanes are mostly grouped in Munster and Connacht, while the Kanes are primarily found in Ulster. In the twelfth century, Blosky O'Kane, the ancestor of the MacCloskeys, killed the heir to the throne. The McEvinneys trace their ancestry back to Aibhne O'Cathain. An active military family for centuries, historical records show that fourteen O'Keane brothers served in Europe during the eighteenth century. However, during the nineteenth century the family members turned to more productive pursuits. A number of men bearing the name of Kane or Keane were in the sciences, architecture, and the arts. Variants are KANE, O'CAHAN, and MACCLOSKEY.

**Kelleher**    O'Ceileachair is the original Gaelic form of this surname, and means "companion." The family lived in Claire, Cork, and Kerry. Edward Kelliher (b.1920) took part in the 1964 Tokyo Olympics. A variant is KELLER.

**Kelly**    The Gaelic form of this surname was O'Ceallaigh, which came from Ceallach, who was a renowned chieftain in the ninth century. Ceallach means "war" or "contention." At one time this clan held most of Galway and Roscommon, but became so large that it divided into eight separate families. Tadgh Mor O'Ceallaigh was killed during the battle of Clontarf in 1014. One Archbishop of Tuam was Murtough O'Kelly, who wrote the famous history of his family. In 1499 when the Irish clans were involved in a bloody inter-tribal massacre at Knocktoe of each other, Malachy O'Kelly led his family's warriors. When many Irish families had to flee their homeland, the O'Kellys fought in the Irish regiments in France. Jack Kelly was the first American oarsman to win an Olympic gold medal in 1920. His daughter was the American, Grace Kelly, who married the Prince of Monaco.

**Kennedy**    The Gaelic original of this surname was O'Cinneide. The Scottish clan with the name Kennedy may be related to those of the same name in Ireland as both clans claim descent from King Brian Boru. The name actually comes from Cean Eidig, meaning ("ugly head") who was the father of King Brian and his brother Dunchad. The O'Kennedys lived in Clare near Killaloe until the O'Briens and the MacNamaras drove them down to Tipperary and Kilkenny (Ormond). There, for 400 years, they were known as the Lords of Ormond. The clan became so large that it finally divided into several new branches. Although they managed to hold their own against the Normans for a time, eventually the Normans and then Cromwell took away their lands, forcing many of them to flee to France. Their name was translated into Quenedy in Spain. The most famous members of this family were John Fitzgerald Kennedy (1917-1963) who was a president of the United States, and his brother Robert (1925-1968). Both were assassinated.

**Keogh**  Descended from the early kings of Ulster, the Irish Gaelic name of this family—MacEochaidh—was anglicized to Keogh (pronounced KEE-oh). At one time there were three separate branches of this family in Ireland: the first lived in Limerick and Ballymackeogh, the second were lords of Moyfinn at Athone and Roscommon, the third were the MacKeoghs of Leinster. They were hereditary bards for the O'Byrnes. After the Norman invasion, the MacKeoghs moved south to Wexford. A Limerick branch of the family spelled their name K'EOGH, and others changed it to O'HOEY or HOY. Other variants are HAUGHEY and MACKEHOE.

**Kinsella**  This family of Wexford and Wicklow once used the Gaelic name O'Cinnsealach. The name originated with Enna Cinsealach, one of the illegitimate sons of Dermot MacMurrough, king of Leinster in the twelfth century. Another Thomas Kinsella (b.1928) is a professor of English at Temple University at Philadelphia and has won many prizes for literature.

**Kirwan**  The Irish Gaelic name of this family was O'Ciardubhain, which means "black." They trace their ancestry back to Heremon of the Milesians, one of the invading tribes that settled ancient Ireland. One of the Fourteen Tribes of Galway, they originally settled in Louth. The family has a long history of churchmen, both Catholic and Protestants, as well as those engaged in the military. One branch of this family had a French chateau where Medoc wine was made. By 1803, the Kirwans were into politics. The Cregg Castle, Ireland, branch of the family produced Richard Kirwan, a one-time Jesuit, who was the first president of the Royal Irish Academy.

**Lacy**  The original French Norman name was Lascy. The family settled in Ireland after the Norman invasion. Their founder was Hugh de Lacy, who was given 800,000 acres of Irish land, thus deposing the royal O'Melaghins (MacLaughlin). Hugh, who built Trim Castle on the River Boyne, married the daughter of O'Conor, king of Connacht. His son Walter, who was made earl of Ulster by the English, settled on land in County Down. The English King John, who feared the power of the de Lacy family, exiled them to Scotland for a time. In retaliation, this family joined with the native Irish in the sixteenth century in an attempt to drive the English from Ireland. Because of their military attitude, they had to leave Ireland and join the Irish brigades in France. After the Battle of the Boyne, Peter Lacy went to Russia where he was hired by Peter the Great to train his elite forces. Peter Lacy was made a count and, after fifty years of service, retired on his Russian estates. There is still a branch of the Lacy family in Russia.

**Lalor**   The Gaelic surname of this family from Leix was O'Leathlobhair, which means "half-leper." A variant spelling is LAWLOR.

**Lee**   The Gaelic spelling of this surname is MacLaoidhigh or Mac an Leagha, which means "son of the physician." The family lived in Tipperary, Galway, Cork, and Limerick. Several Lees served in the American War of Independence.

**Lynch**   One ancestor of this family was a de Lynch who came to Ireland with the French Norman invaders, while another was Labradh Longseach, meaning "mariner," who was a sixth century B.C.E. king of Ireland. The Gaelic version of this name was O'Loingsigh. Most of the Lynch family settled in Clare, Sligo, and Limerick, with one branch in Donegal. The Norman branch of the Lynch family was a member of the Fourteen Tribes of Galway. Between 1484 and 1654, the city of Galway had eighty-four mayors with the surname Lynch. They built strong castles in Connemara and Galway city. Part of the Lynch family later emigrated to Argentina, Australia, and Chile. Thomas Lynch, whose family settled in the United States, signed the Declaration of Independence.

**Lyons**   The original Gaelic surname of this family from Galway was O'Laighin or O'Liathain. They are quite distinct from the English and Scottish families with this surname. Matthew Lyon (1746-1822) became a colonel in the American War of Independence and a member of Congress. Variants are LEHANE, LEYNE, O'LYNE, LYNE, and LANE.

**MacAuley**   Although this surname originated with the Norse invasion and the name Olaf, the Gaelic spelling is MacAmhlaoibh. The family lived in Fermanagh, Westmeath, and Cork. Catherine McAuley (1778-1842) founded the Sisters of Mercy. Variants are MACAWLEY, CAWLEY, and MAGAWLEY.

**MacAuliffe**   This surname also comes from the Norse name Olaf and in Gaelic is MacAmhlaoibh. The family lived primarily in Cork. Originally this family was a branch of the powerful McCarthy clan. Michael MacAuliffe was a colonel in the Spanish army and died in Spain in 1720.

**MacBride**   This Donegal family took their Gaelic name MacGiolla Bhrighde from the meaning "devotee of Saint Brigid." An Ulster name, in medieval times this family administered the lands around Raymunterdoney and Tory Island. David MacBride (1726-1778) was a physician and inventor.

**MacCabe**   During the Middle Ages, many Irish chieftains imported Scottish mercenaries, known as *gallowglasses,* to help them in their fights. The MacCabe family came from Inis Gall, or Isles of the Norsemen, in the Hebrides. The meaning of their surname is unclear, but it has been suggested that it may come from *caba,* meaning "hat" or "cap." The Gaelic version of this name was MacCaba. They fought for the O'Reillys and O'Rourkes of Leitrim and Cavan. Some of them remained in Ireland when their mercenary terms were over. Cardinal Edward MacCabe (1816-1885) became archbishop of Dublin in 1879. A Monaghan farmer named Eugene MacCabe wrote many plays that were performed at Dublin's Abbey Theatre.

**MacCann**   This family from Armagh originally spelled their name as McCana. Ambhlaith MacCanna claimed descent from the O'Neills of Ulster. John McCann, once Lord Mayor of Dublin, and Donal McCann were both playwrights. Variants are CANNY, MCCANN, MACANNA, and MACCANNA.

**MacCarthy**   This surname is very ancient and goes back to a third century king of Munster. The Gaelic version was MacCarthaigh, which means "loving one." Cormac, a MacCarthy king and bishop, built the chapel on Rock of Cashel. The family had many fine castles all over Munster, of which Blarney is the most famous. The name "blarney" came from the correspondence between Cormac MacCarthy and Elizabeth I in which Cormac used his silver tongue to avoid submission to the English crown. This irritated the queen, who called it "blarney." This family had a number of eloquent poets and writers. Lord Carberry (Florence MacCarthy), another member, irritated the queen again by marrying his cousin, Lady Ellen Carthy. He was imprisoned in the Tower of London, where he spent the next thirty-seven years. MacCartney is the Scottish form of this name. The musician Paul McCartney of the Beatles was born in Liverpool in 1942.

**MacCormack**   The Gaelic spelling is MacCormaic, meaning "son of Cormac." The family was found living all over Ireland. Wright McCormick started the movement in 1920 for an annual St. Patrick's Day celebration in Boston. A variant is MACCORMICK.

**MacDermot**   The Gaelic form of this surname is MacDiarmada, which means "free man." The family can trace their ancestry back to Muiredach Mullethan, brother of the eighth-century king of Connacht, and Dermot, king of Moylurg in the twelfth century. Three families actually sprang from Muiredach Mullethan:   the O'Conors of Connacht; the MacDermottroes of Alderford, Roscommon; and the MacDermotts of Airtech. For a long time the MacDermot lands in Roscommon and Sligo were called MacDermot's Country. Their fortress was on the legendary island of Lough Ce. Because this family supported the ill-fated Stuarts, they lost much of their land and had to move their chief seat to Coolavin in Sligo. Although many of the MacDermot family emigrated abroad, the princes of Coolavin stayed behind, and many of them held high office. The present head of the clan, Sir Dermot MacDermot, was at one time an ambassador in the British Diplomatic Service. There are several spelling variants of this surname; the most rare is KERMODE.

**MacElroy**   The Gaelic spelling is MacGiolla Rua, which means "red-haired youth." The family lived in Fermanagh and Leitrim.

**MacEvoy**   Spelled MacFhiodhbhuidhe, meaning "woodsman" in Gaelic. The family lived in Louth and Leix. Another Gaelic version of this name is Mac a Buidhe meaning "yellow." A variant is MACAVOY.

**MacGee**   The Gaelic spelling of this name was Mag Aodha, meaning "son of Hugh." The family primarily lived in Antrim, Down, and Armagh. Many of this family were Ulster Protestant archbishops. Martha Maria Magee (d.1846) founded the Magee College in Derry city, later part of the University of Ulster. Variants of this surname are MAGEE and MACKEE.

**MacGovern**   Spelled Mag Samhrain, meaning "summer" in Gaelic, this family lived in Cavan, Leitrim, and Fermanagh. The surname is derived from Samhradh who lived around 1000. They were allies of the powerful Maguires and O'Rourkes. Hugh Magauran was a popular Gaelic poet, and John McGovern (1850-1917) was an American writer. Variants are MAGAURAN and MACGOWRAN.

**MacGrath** Originally this surname was MacRaith or Mag Raith, which means "son of Raith (prosperity)." One family with this surname lived in Donegal and Fermanagh where they were hereditary guardians of Saint Daveog's monastery at Lough Derg. Their Termon Castle was near Pettigo. Another family lived in Clare and Limerick where they were the poets and patrons of the royal O Briens of Thomond. They also headed the prestigious school for bards at Cahir in Tipperary. Myler Magrath was a notorious member of this family, who began as a Franciscan friar and then became Anglican bishop of Cashel, under Elizabeth I's reign, in Ireland. He switched with the political wind whenever he thought he could gain, as when he held four bishoprics at the same time in both the Catholic and Anglican churches. Married twice, Myler lived to be one hundred years old. His son Joseph was just as scandalous; he acted as a spy against his own family for the Cromwell forces, receiving much MacGrath land as payment, and burning the castle outside Waterford. Later, however, Joseph served during the Irish Rising, was a government minister, helped found the Irish Hospitals Sweepstakes, and revived the Waterford crystal industry. Variants are MACGRAW, MAGRATH, and MAGRAW.

**MacHugh** This surname was spelled MacAoda meaning "son of Hugh" in Gaelic. The family lived in Galway, Mayo, Leitrim, Donegal, and Fermanagh. Roger McHugh (1908-1987) was a professor of English and Anglo-Irish literature at University College Dublin. Variants are EASON, HEWSON, MACCOY, MCKEE, HUGHES, and MACKAY.

**MacInerney** This family originated in Connacht. In Gaelic their surname was spelled Mac an Airchinnigh, which means "steward of church lands." Some of the family now living in the United States have changed the spelling to MACNAIRNEY and MCNERNEY.

**MacKenna** The original Gaelic name was MacCionaoith, which means "son of Cionaoid." Little was recorded of the MacKenna family until fairly recently. In Ulster they were lords of Truagh in County Monaghan. The MacKennas are noted for their literary pursuits. John MacKenna was killed in a spectacular duel in Buenos Aires. Siobhan McKenna was a well-known Irish actress. T. P. McKenna worked on stage, screen, and television.

**MacLoughlin** O'Maoilsheachlainn, meaning "follower of St. Secundinas," or MacLochlainn, are the Gaelic spellings of this surname. The family lived in Donegal, Derry, Meath, and Clare. They claim descent from Niall of the Nine Hostages. John MacLoughlin (1784-1857) became a prominent member of the Hudson Bay Company and trapped for furs in Oregon in the United States where he built Fort Vancouver. Variants are O'LOGHLEN, MACLAUGHLIN, and O'MELAGHLIN.

**MacMahon** The Gaelic name is MacMathuna meaning "son of the bear." There are two separate Irish families with this surname. One family is descended from the royal O'Briens and lived in Corcabaskin, Clare. The other family became the lords of Oriel in Louth and Monaghan. Irish folklore says that Maire Rua (Red) MacMahon had an amorous nature and a quick mind that enabled her to save herself and her family on more than one occasion. After her first husband died, she married Conor O'Brien; they built the castle of Lemaneagh in Clare. When her second husband was killed, she married a Cromwellian to save her family and property. Variants are MAHON, MOHAN, and VAUGHAN.

**MacManus** This Gaelic adaptation of the Norse-Viking name Magnus was originally spelled MacMaghnuis. The family claims descent from Turlough O'Conor who was High King of Ireland in 1119. The family lived primarily in Fermanagh and Connacht.

**MacNally** Spelled Mac an Fhailghigh in Gaelic, this surname means "poor man." The family lived in Mayo, Armagh, and Monaghan. Leonard MacNally was both a traitor to the United Irishmen and a writer of verse plays. Variants are MACANALLY and NALLY.

**MacNamara** This Irish surname means "son of the hound of the sea." In early times their territory was on the west coast of Clare. Their ancestor Cas was the first chief of the Dalcassians. This clan built fifty-seven castles, fortresses, and abbeys in Clare, including Quin Abbey, Bunratty Castle, and Knappogue Castle. There were actually two separate families bearing this surname: MacNamara Fion (fair) was of Clancullen West, and MacNamara Reagh (swarthy) was of Clancullen East. Both families lost all their titles and possessions in the Cromwell invasion, after which they fled to Europe and the new world. Another name used by some members of the MacNamara clan was MacConmara. Robert MacNamara of the United States was president of the World Bank, general manager of the Ford Motor Company, and secretary of defense.

**MacNulty**   In Gaelic this surname was Mac an Ultaigh, which means "of Ulster." The family lived in Ulster and Mayo. Owen McNulty served in the 69th New York Volunteers in the American Civil War. His oldest son Frank (1872-1926) was a labor leader. A variant is NULTY.

**MacQuaid**   Spelled Mac Uaid in Gaelic, this surname means "son of Walter." The family originated in Ulster. Harry McQuade served in the 69th New York Volunteers during the American Civil War. Variants are MACQUAIDE, MACQUOID, and MACWADE.

**MacQuillan**   This surname, spelled MacUighilin, meaning "son of little Hugh" in Gaelic, came from the Welsh-Norman Hugeli de Mandeville in the twelfth century. The family lived in Ulster. John Hugh MacQuillan (1826-1879) was a dentist in Philadelphia who helped to organize the American Dental Association, and founded the Philadelphia Dental College.

**MacSweeney**   In Gaelic this name was spelled MacSuibhne, which some sources say means "pleasant." The family lived in Donegal and Cork. The MacSweeneys in Donegal were descendants of Suibhne O'Neill, a chieftain of Scotland. Variants are MACSWINEY, SWEENEY, and SWEENY.

**Madden**   In Gaelic this surname was spelled O'Madain, which means "little dog." The family lived in Limerick, Longford, Galway, and Offaly. Richard Robert Madden (1798-1886) was a surgeon who worked internationally to abolish slavery.

**Maguire**   The first record of this surname occurred in 956. However, it was not until the fourteenth century that they became a prominent family in Fermanagh. The original Gaelic name was MagUidhir, *mag* being the same as *mac,* meaning "son of." The name means "pale colored." They were related to the royal O'Neills and the princely O'Connells of Ulster. Their stronghold was on Lough Erne, where they were known as the barons of Enniskillen. The Battle of the Yellow Ford was led by their greatest chief, Hugh Maguire. In this battle the Irish defeated the British. When the English captured Ireland, many of the Maguires went to France where their lineage was recognized. Many Maguires who went to the United States became distinguished in their chosen careers.

One was the chief surgeon to Stonewall Jackson and a professor at Virginia Medical College. The ancestors of those who spell their surname as MacGuire or McGuire originated in Connacht.

**Maher**   This surname was spelled O'Meachair in Gaelic and means "hospitable." The family primarily lived in Tipperary and Kilkenny. Thomas Francis Meagher (1823-1867) was sentenced to penal servitude in Australia for his revolutionary activities, however, he escaped to the United States and became a journalist. A variant is MEAGHER.

**Mahony**   The ancient form of this surname was O'Mahuna or O'Mathghamhna. It came from Mathghamhan, meaning "bear," the son of Cian Mac Mael Muda who was a 10th century prince. He married Sadbh, the daughter of the High King Brian Boru. They had vast lands in Munster and fourteen castles on the Cork coast. Their descendants held distinguished appointments in the military and diplomatic circles of Europe, even marrying into nobility. Variants are O'MAHONY and MAHONEY.

**Malone**   The original Irish Gaelic name of this family was O'Maoileoin, which means "one who serves Saint John." Their early history centers around their estate at Ballynahown in Offaly. They were related to the nearby royal O'Conors in Connacht. Several Malones acted as abbots or bishops at Clonmacnoise, an ecclesiastical seat of learning. Some members of this family supported James II; they fled to Europe after he lost his bid for the kingship and served in French and Spanish armies. One Malone priest became a church historian and an enthusiast on saving the Irish language. Sylvester Malone went to Brooklyn, New York, to help Irish immigrants fleeing from the famine.

**Martin**   There were several variations of the name of this family. One of the original Irish names was MacGiolla Martain or Mac-Martain, which was anglicized to Gilmartin, while another was O'Martain. They were related to the family O'Neill of Tyrone. Records show that a Giolla Earnain O'Martain, an important bard, died in 1218. The branch of the family that live in Connacht trace their ancestry to a Norman crusader, whose name was Olyver Martin. They were listed as one of the Fourteen Tribes of Galway, and at one time owned as many as 200,000 acres in Connemara. Richard Martin, whose father changed his religion to Protestant so his son could sit in parliament, was called Hair Trigger Dick in his younger days because of his constant dueling. Variants of this name are MARTYN, KILMARTIN, and GILMARTIN.

**Molloy**   Spelled O'Maolmhudaidh in Gaelic, this surname means "noble chief." The family began in Offaly and became widespread in Ireland. They claim descent from Niall of the Nine Hostages. Albin O'Molloy (d. 1223) officiated at the coronation of Richard I at Westminster Abbey. Francis Molloy, a Franciscan monk, compiled the first printed Irish grammar in the seventeenth century. Variants are MALOY, MILEY, MILLEA, and MULLOY.

**Moloney**   This name was spelled O'Maoldhomhnaigh, meaning "descendant of a church servant" in Gaelic. The family lived in Clare and Tipperary. Paddy Moloney is a musician and part of the group called The Chieftains. Variants are MALONEY, MALONY, and MOLONY.

**Monaghan**   This family from Roscommon originally spelled their name as O'Manachain, which means "monk." This family is listed as the lords of Roscommon in 1287. Variants are MINOGUE, MONAHAN, and MONK.

**Mooney**   The Gaelic spelling of this name was O'Maonaigh, which means either "wealthy" or "dumb." The family lived in Ulster, Offaly, and Sligo. Ria Mooney (1904-1973) was an actress and the first woman director at the Abbey Theatre Company. Variants are MAINEY, MEANEY, MEENEY, and MOONY.

**Moore**   Originally known as O'Mordha, which means "noble," this family is descended from Conal Cearnach, a chieftain of the Knights of the Red Branch. The Cistercian Abbey in Leix was built as the tomb of the last chief, Malachi O'More. There is some confusion over the descendants of this family as there is the Irish name O'Mordha and the English-Norman name Moore. The O'Moores, an anglicized version of the name of one of the branches, were basically warriors who successfully defended their territories from all invaders for some time. When Elizabeth I sent the earl of Essex to bring the Irish to heel, Conor O'More gave him a resounding defeat. The English Moores trace their ancestry to a soldier who had lands at Mellifont in Meath. The best known member of the Moore family was Thomas Moore, a poet and musician, whose songs were sung by the famous tenor John McCormack.

**Moran**   Spelled O'Muireain in Gaelic, this name means "big" or "great." The family lived in Connacht. David Patrick Moran (1870-1936) founded *The Leader*, a patriotic review. A variant is MURRIN.

**Moriarty**  The Gaelic spelling of this surname was O'Muircheartaigh. It means "expert navigator." The family originated in the Dingle peninsula along the coast. Patrick Moriary went to Philadelphia where he founded Villanova College in 1842. Variants are MURDOCH and MURTAGH.

**Morrissey**  O'Muirgheasa was the original Gaelic spelling of this surname. It means "sea choice." The family lived in Sligo, Waterford, Limerick, and Cork. Enri (Feargus Mac Roigh) O'Muirgheasa (1874-1945) was a poet and compiled volumes of folklore.

**Mulcahy**  Spelled O'Maolchathaigh in Gaelic, this surname means "battle chief." The family originated in Munster. His son, Dr. Risteard Mulcahy, is a leading Dublin heart surgeon.

**Mulligan**  This family lived in Donegal, Monaghan, and Mayo. They originally spelled their name O'MAOLAGAIN.

**Mulrooney**  The anglicized version of the Gaelic name Maelruanaidh, an ancestor of the MacDermot clan.

**Murphy**  The original Gaelic name was O'Murchu, which means "sea warrior." At one time there were several branches of this family in Tyrone, Sligo, and Wexford. They were kings of Leinster. The Norman invasion of Ireland can be laid at the feet of Dermot MacMurrough, a Murphy, who invited them. Daibhi O'Murchu, who was a blind harper, often played for the famous Irish pirate queen, Grace O'Malley. The Murphy clan has produced many artists, sculptors, and writers, including Arthur Murphy, the actor and playwright. The branch of the family living in Cork went into brewing. They later merged with Powers and Jamesons, a whiskey distillery. Variants are MACCAMORE, MACMURROUGH, O'MORCHOE, and O'MURCHADHA.

**Nolan**  This surname was spelled O'Nuaillain in Gaelic and means "noble" or "famous." The family lived in Carlow and West Cork. Don Diego Nolan was a captain in the Spanish Netherlands in 1660. A variant is NOWLAN.

**Nugent**  The Gaelic version of this name is Nuinseann. This family originated in Nogent, France and emigrated to Ireland in the twelfth century, settling in Westmeath. There they were created barons of Delvin. A branch of the family lived at Aghavarton Castle in Cork. There was a division of sympathies within the Nugent family, some of them supporting the Irish, the others serving as lord deputies for the English. Christopher Nugent of Meath, however, excelled in medicine and helped find the cure for rabies (hydrophobia). Ballinlough Castle in Westmeath is still owned by the Nugent family. A variant is GILSENAN.

**O'Brien**   The royal O'Briens trace their ancestry to the tenth-century High King Brian Boru. They primarily lived in Clare, Limerick, and Munster. Historical records show that this family opposed the Normans and the Tudors, but had many titles, such as earls of Thomond, viscounts Clare, and earls of Inchiquin. However, the sixth earl of Thomond helped the Cromwell forces when they ravaged Ireland. The family fought on both sides during the Battle of the Boyne, and those of the viscounts Clare had to flee to France afterwards.

**O'Connell**   The Gaelic spelling of this name is O'Conaill. They trace their Irish ancestry back to the High King Eremonium Aengus Tuirneach who ruled about 280 B.C.E. There were several branches of this family living in Derry, Galway, and Munster, with their main castle at Ballycarberry near Cahirciveen. The invasion of Cromwell forces drove many of the O'Connells to France and Austria where they tended to serve in the military. Muircheartach O'Connell (1738-1830) changed his name to Moritz when he was appointed imperial chamberlain by Empress Maria Theresa. This change was necessary because a kinsman, Count Daniel O'Connell, had fought in the Prussian army against the empress.

**O'Connor**   This family traces its name back to the tenth-century king of Connacht, Conchobhair. However, there were six O'Conor families, all of whom were not necessarily related to this king. The predominant line was the royal O'Conors of Connacht, who had Turlough Mor O'Conor as High King of Ireland in the twelfth century. The family mansion, Clonalis near Roscommon, still exists and is filled with Irish relics and archives. When other Irish families were forced to flee, the O'Conors retreated to their isolated Belanagare holdings. The Royal Irish Academy holds many ancient and translated manuscripts, thanks to the eighteenth-century efforts of O'Conor scholars and antiquarians. Charles O'Connor of New York turned down the presidency of the United States in the nineteenth century.

**O'Dea** This surname was spelled O'Deaghaidh in Gaelic. The family lived in Limerick, Tipperary, Cork, and Dublin.

**O'Donnell** This family is descended from Niall of the Nine Hostages and took their name from Domhnaill, which means "world mighty." The Gaelic spelling is O'Domhnaill. They primarily lived in Donegal where they built strongholds to defend first against the O'Neills and later against the Tudors, although that was a losing battle. All of their chiefs were inaugurated at the Rock of Doon near Letterkenny. When Red Hugh (1571-1602) was very young, he was imprisoned in Dublin Castle because he was the heir to the O'Donnell clan. A great Irish saga was written of his escape from the castle, his hazardous trek over the snow-covered Wicklow mountains, and his leadership in the battle of the Yellow Ford. He died in Spain after he fled Kinsale. Mary Stuart O'Donnell ran off with her maid to escape an arranged marriage; dressed as soldier and carrying a sword, she offered to fight duels to allay suspicion.

**O'Donovan** This family clan traces its ancestry back to Donnabhain, son of the tenth-century King Ceallachan of Munster. The Gaelic name O'Donnabhain is derived from *o,* meaning "son of," *dubhann,* meaning "black," and *donn,* meaning "brown." These chiefs of Carberry had territory that followed the River Maigue in Limerick. Their stronghold was called Brugh Riogh (Royal Residence). The Normans drove them south into Cork where they established new holdings. They lost their wealth and became outlaws when they backed the doomed Stuarts. The ones who went to France suffered during the French Revolution. A second O'Donovan family, which came from Kilkenny, traced its ancestry back to Eoghan, who was a third-century king of Munster.

**O'Dowd** Spelled O'Dubhda in Gaelic, this surname means "black." They claim descent from the Celts who came from Spain and Niall of the Nine Hostages. Peadar O'Dubhda (b. 1881) translated the Douai Bible into Irish. The family primarily lived in Mayo, Sligo, and Galway. Variants are DODD, DOODY, and DUDDY.

**O'Dwyer** In Gaelic this surname is spelled O'Duibhir and is derived from the Old Irish word *dubh,* which means "black shirt." The family lived in Sligo and Mayo. Bill O'Dwyer, one of eleven children, emigrated to the United States, where he became a lawyer, an attorney-general of Brooklyn, a mayor of New York, and a U.S. ambassador to Mexico. His brother Paul O'Dwyer (b. 1907) also emigrated to the United States and became a lawyer and politician.

**O'Farrell**   The original Irish Gaelic name was O'Fearghaill, which means "man of great valor." Their base was Longphuirt Ui Fhearghaill (O'Farrell's Fort) near Longford. As this family grew, they divided into two main branches: O'Farrell Boy (*buidhe,* meaning "yellow") and O'Farrell Ban (*ban,* meaning "white"). Their intermarriage with the Moore clan started another branch, the More O'Ferralls. Ceadagh O'Ferrall was killed at the battle of the Boyne in 1690.

**O'Flaherty**   This family clan traces its ancestry back at least 3,000 years. Sea-farers of Connacht, they were the enemies of the Fourteen Tribes of Galway, who called them the Ferocious O'Flahertys. They constantly warred against the Burkes and O'Conors. After they soundly defeated the Burkes, they controlled much of the land between Lough Corrib and the Atlantic Ocean, and were called Lords of the Iar (West) Connacht. Many of their revenge killings were centered around Aughnanure Castle near Oughterard in Galway. Because in Ulster a slightly different form of the Irish language is spoken, the name O'Flaherty there is pronounced O'Laverty. Variants are FLAHERTY and O'FLAVERTY.

**O'Flanagan**   This family from Connacht at one time used the Gaelic spelling of O'Flannagain, which means "red," for their surname. The priest Michael O'Flanagan was an active member of *Sinn Fein.* He left quite a trail of incidents in the United States. A variant is FLANAGAN.

**O'Gara**   Spelled O'Gadhra in Gaelic, this surname means "a mastiff (dog)." The family lived in Sligo and Mayo.

**O'Gorman**   Spelled O'Gormain or MacGormain in Gaelic, this surname is derived from the word for "blue." The family lived in Leix, Monaghan, and Clare. Variants are MACGORMAN, GORMAN, and GRIMES.

**O'Grady**   The original Gaelic name was O'Gradaigh, which means "illustrious." They were of the Dalcassian family and related to the royal O'Briens. Their fortress was on Inis Cealtra (Holy Island) on Lough Derg, but they also had settlements in Clare and Lough O'Grady near Scarriff. There was a name change from O'Grady to

Brady by at least one of this family during the bloody rule of Henry VIII. This action enabled the family to keep their lands and have a son become the first Protestant bishop of Meath. Donough O'Grady had his confiscated lands restored when he married Faith, the only daughter of Sir Thomas Standish. The names Standish and Faith have been used in every generation since. An American O'Grady was the great-grandfather of Cassius O'Grady Clay, now known as Muhammed Ali.

**O'Halloran** The Gaelic spelling for this surname is O'hAllmhurain, which means "stranger beyond the sea." The family primarily lived in Clare and Galway. Sylvester O'Halloran was a distinguished eye surgeon and one of the founders of Dublin's Royal College of Surgeons in 1784.

**O'Hara** In Gaelic this surname is spelled O'hEaghra. The family lived in Sligo and Antrim. John O'Hara in 1934 wrote the novel *Appointment to Samarra.*

**O'Hegarty** In Gaelic this surname is O'hEigceartaigh, which means "unjust." The family lived primarily in Donegal, Derry, and Cork. Sairseal O'hEigeartaigh was a Gaelic scholar who founded a publishing company to print books in the Irish language. A variant is HAGGERTY.

**O'Keeffe** The original Irish Gaelic form of this name was O'Caoimh. The personal name Caom means "noble." The family clan traces its ancestry to Art O'Caom, the son of Fionghuine, who was the king of Munster. Their ancient land-holdings were around Glanmore and Fermoy in Cork until the Normans drove them south to the Duhallow country. Several of the O'Keeffe men were officers in the French armies, where the surname became corrupted to Cuif. An O'Keeffe heiress married John Lanigan of Tipperary and produced the combined name of Lanigan O'Keeffe. Many of the family with this name went to Australia and Zimbabwe. Georgia O'Keefe (1887-1986) was a famous painter in New Mexico, in the United States.

**O'Leary** In Gaelic this surname is O'Laoghaire and means "calf keeper." The family lived primarily in Cork. Art O'Leary, who had been a colonel in the Austrian army, was killed in Ireland in 1773 when he refused to sell his horse to an English soldier.

**O'Malley** The original surname of this very old family from Mayo was O'Maille, which is believed to have come from *maglios*, the Celtic word for "chief." They primarily lived in Burrishoole and Murrisk as they made their living from the sea. One of their most famous members was Grace O'Mally (also known as Granuaile or Grania), the Irish pirate queen, who preyed on English ships at every opportunity. Daughter of Owen O'Malley, a chief of this clan, she was married at age fifteen to a Donal O'Flaherty, who was soon killed in battle. Then she married a Burke. Although Grace was captured several times and sentenced to death by hanging, she managed to escape and live to a ripe old age. When the Irish clans were broken up by the English invaders, many of the O'Malleys went abroad to fight in foreign armies. A variant name is MELIA.

**O'Meara**   In Gaelic this surname is spelled O'Meadhra. The family resided in Tipperary.

**O'Neill**   The family has been a predominant Irish clan for at least 1,000 years. They claim Niall of the Nine Hostages as their ancestor, but their name was taken from Nial Glun Dubh (Black Knee), a king of Ireland killed by Norse Vikings in 919. The clan was so powerful in Ulster that Elizabeth I ordered their coronation stone destroyed. By the fourteenth century the family separated into two branches: the Princes of Tyrone and the Clanaboys of Antrim and Down. Famous members of the O'Neill family in the United States are Eugene O'Neill, the dramatist, and Thomas P. "Tip" O Neill (1912-1994), the politician. Variants are CREAGH, NEILL, and NIHILL.

**O'Reilly**   The original Irish Gaelic surname of this family was O'Raghailligh. This name is derived from the personal name Ragheallach, meaning "gregarious race," the name of the great-grandson of Maolmordha, a descendant of the O'Conor kings of Connacht. At one time their territory extended from around Lough Oughter in Cavan into Westmeath. There are descendants of the O'Reilly family also living in Havana. As financiers, the Irish O'Reillys cast their own coinage in the fifteenth century. In the twentieth century, an O'Reilly headed the family brewing industry. Tony O'Reilly, a former rugby champion, was chief executive of the American Heinz company. Variants are REILLY and O'RAHILLY.

**O'Riordan**   The Gaelic version of this name is O'Riordain, which means "royal bard." The family lived in Tipperary and Cork. Don Jacques Alferez Rirden served in the Spanish Netherlands in 1660.

Members of an O'Riordan family were created peers of France in 1755. Variants are RIORDAN and REARDON.

O'Rourke   This surname may have been derived from the Norse-Viking name Hrothrekr. The Vikings who stayed in Ireland after the invasion were called Lords of Breffny and produced three kings of Connacht. From their stronghold at Dromahair on Lough Gill, they ruled over Cavan and Leitrim. In the O'Rourke clan there have been nineteen chiefs all having the same personal name of Tiernan. The most notorious of these chiefs was the Tiernan whose actions caused the Anglo-Normans to invade Ireland. The trouble began when he invaded Meath and encountered Dermot MacMurrough who was also raiding there. MacMurrough abducted Tiernan's wife, Dervorgilla. In retaliation, Tiernan joined with the O'Conor King of Connacht and deposed MacMurrough. MacMurrough fled to England where he invited the Anglo-Normans to invade Ireland. During the ensuing struggles, Tiernan was killed by Hugo de Lacy. When their lands and titles were taken by the English Crown, most of the O'Rourkes fled to Europe. Descendants of this Irish clan still live in Russia and Poland. Variants are ROARK, ROOKE, ROURKE, and RORKE.

O'Shaughnessy   This family of Galway, Clare, and Limerick at one time used the Gaelic spelling of O'Seachnsaigh. They claim descent from Daithi, the last pagan king of Ireland, about 500 C.E. Dermot O'Shaughnessy (d. 1559) betrayed the Irish cause to gain a knighthood from Henry VIII. Variants are SHAUGHNESSY and SANDYS.

O'Shea   The Gaelic version of this surname is O'Seaghada, which means "dauntless." The family lived in Kerry and Kilkenny. This family was a member of the Ten Tribes of Kilkenny. Today, Milo O'Shea is a famous actor on stage, film, and TV. Variants are SHEA and SHEE.

O'Sullivan   There is disagreement about the meaning of the original Irish name O'Suileabhain. Some authors think it means "one," while others say it means "hawk-eyed." This Celtic clan traces their ancestry to Olioll Olum, the third-century king of Munster. They began in Tipperary, but spread out into Cork and Kerry. The chief O'Sullivan Mor lived in his stronghold at Kenmare Bay in Kerry, while Donal O'Sullivan Beare (1560-1618) was in Dunboy on Bantry Bay. Because of James I's hatred of the Irish, O'Sullivan Beare and his family left for Spain where many of them served in the army and navy of Philip III. General John O'Sullivan (1744-1808) fought in the American War of Independence. In the eighteenth and nineteenth centuries, however, this clan began to produce literary talent instead of military fodder. and Sir Arthur O'Sullivan wrote the music for Gilbert and Sullivan operas.

**O'Toole**   The original Gaelic form of this surname was O'Tuathail, taken from the personal name Tuathal, who was a tenth-century king of Leinster. Some sources think the name means "mighty people," while others believe it means "prosperous." This clan began in Kildare, but is usually associated with Wicklow where the members built their castles. From these strongholds, the O'Tooles attacked their neighbors as well as the English. The patron saint of Dublin is Laurence O'Toole, who spent his youth as a captive to Dermot MacMurrough. After his release he joined the church and was made the first Irish archbishop of Dublin in 1161. Peter O'Toole is a famous screen and stage actor. Variants are TOAL, TOOL, TOOLE, TOOHILL, and TWOHILL.

**Phelan**   The Gaelic spelling is O'Faolain or O'hAoileain. It means "wolf." The family was spread through Waterford, Kilkenny, Wexford, and Carlow. Variants are WHELAN, HEELAN, and HYLAND.

**Plunkett**   The ancestors of this family clan came from Denmark before the Normans arrived in Ireland and married into the Irish clans. Their name is derived from a French word for "white" or "blonde." The family ruled over vast tracts of land in Meath and Louth and, by the sixteenth century, had a number of titles. The nineteenth Baron Dunsany still lives his estate in Meath, while the seventeenth Lord Louth lives in the Channel Islands. The Plunketts sided with the Catholic Stuarts and many of them had to flee to France later. During the eighteenth century, they changed to Protestantism to save their lands, but returned to their original faith when religious persecution died down. Joseph Plunkett signed the Proclamation of the Irish Republic and was executed in 1916. A variant is PLUNKET.

**Power**   The original Norman surname of this family was le Poer, which means "poor." They came into Ireland with the Norman invaders and owned estates in Wicklow and Waterford. Margaret Power married the earl of Blessington. A beautiful woman, she took up with Count D'Orsay after her husband's death. Between this painter-dandy and her improvident family, she lost all her money and died in Paris, pursued by creditors. Catherine Power, countess of Tyrone, fought for the right of Irish heiresses to inherit property through the female line. Tyrone Power was a famous American movie actor. The Powers Distillery in Dublin was established by Sir James Power in 1791.

**Quigley**   The Gaelic spelling of this surname was O'Coigligh. It means "untidy hair." The family was spread throughout Mayo, Donegal, Derry, Sligo, and Galway. Dr. James Quigley (d. 1915) was a bishop of Buffalo, New York in the United States. He took an interest in trade unions and helped settle many strikes. Variants are COGLEY and COIGLEY.

**Quinlan**   This family from Munster at one time spelled their name as O'Caoinleain, which means "gracefully shaped." Variants are KINDELLAN and QUINLEVAN.

**Quinn**   The original Gaelic spelling of this surname was O'Cuinn, and it means "intelligent." The family lived in Antrim, Longford, and Clare. This family was of the Dalcassian group with their original headquarters at Inchiquin. The Inchiquin family of County Clare were styled earls of Dunraven. A variant is QUIN (a Protestant spelling).

**Rafferty**   This family from Connacht originally spelled its name O'Raithbheartaigh (prosperity wielder) or O'Robhartaigh (flood tide). In records of 1663, the name is spelled O'RAVERTY. Another variant is O'RAFFERTY.

**Redmond**   This Norman surname was adopted into the Irish Gaelic as Reamonn and originated with Raymond le Gros, a leader of the Normans who invaded Ireland about 1169. John Redmond (1856-1918) and his brother William Redmond (1861-1917) were politicians who worked for Home Rule. The family lived in Wexford and Wicklow.

**Regan**   In Ireland, this surname is pronounced Reegan and originated from more than one ancestor into several separate families. The original Gaelic name was O'Reagain or O'Riagain. The name goes back a thousand years to Riagain, a nephew of Brian Boru. The O'Riagains in Meath and Dublin belonged to the Fourteen Tribes of Tara. They were powerful defenders against the Vikings, but were defeated by the Normans and driven to Leix. An unrelated family of this surname descended from one of Brian Boru's brothers, Donnchadh. They belonged to the Dalcassians and ruled in Clare, Leinster, and Tipperary. Many Reagans emigrated to the United States before the Famine. Ronald Reagan was one of the presidents of the United States.

**Rice**    This is the Irish adaptation of the Welsh name Rhys; it entered Ireland with Welsh immigrants. The family mainly lived in Kerry, Louth, Dublin, and Ulster.

**Roche**    This surname probably came from Flanders and was introduced into Ireland along with the Norman invaders. Their Pembrokeshire fortress was called Roch Castle. Eventually, they separated into five family branches. The first viscount Fermoy in 1570 was David Roche, an ancestor of Diana, Princess of Wales.

**Rooney**    The Gaelic spelling of this name was O'Ruanaidh, which means "hero." The family began in Down and spread throughout Ireland. Ceallach O'Ruanaidh (d. 1079) was the chief poet of Ireland, and Eoin O'Ruanaidh (d. 1376) was the chief poet to the MacGuinnesses of Iveagh.

**Ryan**    The Gaelic surname of this family was O'Riain or O'Maoilriain, meaning "follower of Riain," which is possibly derived from a personal name meaning "illustrious." They trace their ancestry to a second century king of Leinster, whose name was Cathaoir Mor. There are two separate branches of this family: the O'Riains of Idrone in Carlow, and the O'Maoilriains of Tipperary and Limerick. As with many Irish families, the Ryans went abroad and served in the armies of other nations. In the United States, Thomas Fortune Ryan began as a penniless orphan and became a multi-millionaire. A variant is MULRYAN.

**Scanlan**    Originally, this surname was spelled O'Scannlain or Mac-Scannlain. The family lived in Kerry, Limerick, and Cork, with a few of them in Connacht. Dr. Lawrence Scanlan (1843-1915) was bishop of Salt Lake City.

**Scully**    The Gaelic name of this family, who lived in Tipperary and Leinster, was O'Scolaidhe, which means "crier."

**Shannon**    The original Gaelic of this surname was O'Seanain, meaning "old" or "wise." The family primarily lived in Clare and Ulster. Edward Shannon (c. 1790-1860) was a poet whose writing was sometimes mistaken for Byron's.

**Sheehan**   The Gaelic form of this name was O'Siodhacain, which means "peaceful." The family lived in Munster. Ronan Sheehan (b. 1953) won the Hennessy Award for young writers in 1974. A variant is SHEAHAN.

**Sheehy**   Another family based in Munster, they originally spelled their name as Mas Sithigh. They came as mercenary soldiers from Scotland (clan MacDonald) in the fourteenth century. A variant is MACSHEEHY.

**Sheridan**   The Gaelic surname of this family was O'Sirideain. Of obscure origins, they lived in Cavan. This clan tended toward pursuits in the church and the arts instead of on the battlefield. One member helped translate the Bible into Irish. A Thomas Sheridan was the close friend of James II and fled with him into exile. His son, also named Thomas, fought at Culloden. Joseph Sheridan Le Fanu (whose mother was a Sheridan) wrote tales of the supernatural.

**Taaffe**   This family came to Ireland from Wales in 1196 and settled in Louth. They still own Smarmore Castle near Ardee. Taaffe is the Welsh equivalent of the personal name David. Many of this family went into the church, including one renegade priest Father James Taaffe who forged a Papal Bull. After the mysterious death of Prince Rudolph, the Hapsburg heir, Count Taaffe was entrusted with the investigation documents. This family is still involved in horsebreeding.

**Tierney**   The original Gaelic name was O'Tighearnaigh. It means "lordly." The family lived in Mayo, Donegal, and Tipperary. A variant is TIERNAN.

**Tobin**   This name was originally de St. Aubyn, a Norman name that entered Ireland with the French Norman invaders. Families with this name are found both in Brittany and in the Irish county of Munster. A variant is TOIBIN.

**Treacy**   The Gaelic spelling was O'Treasigh, meaning "fighter." The family primarily lived in Galway, Cork, and Leix.

**Tully**   Originally, the Gaelic spelling of this surname was Mac an Tuile or O'Taicligh, which means "flood." The family lived throughout Connacnt, Cavan, Longford, and Westmeath. The family were hereditary physicians to the O'Reillys and the O'Connors. They were also among the leading Galway families during the seventeenth century. When the English surpressed all Gaelic language in Ireland, this family changed their name to Flood. Variants are FLOOD and MACATILLA.

**Twomey**   The Gaelic version of this name was O'Tuama. The family lived in Cork, Kerry, Clare, and Limerick. A variant is TOOMEY.

**Wall**   The original Norman name was de Bhal. The name entered Ireland with the French Norman invaders in the twelfth century. The family settled in such areas as Carlow, Kilkenny, Waterford, Limerick, and Cork. Many of this family emigrated to France and Russia.

**Walsh**   Since all Welshmen were called by this name when they entered Ireland with the Norman invaders, there is no common ancestor. The Gaelic version is Breathnach, which is an Irish word for "Welshman." Two brothers, Philip and David, who arrived in the twelfth century, are said to be the ancestors of the Walsh families living in Dublin, Kilkenny, Leix, Waterford, and Wicklow. Members of this family were active in both the Catholic and Protestant churches. Nicholas was the bishop of Ossory in about 1567. Peter Walsh, a Franciscan friar in the 16th century, was excommunicated because he preached against papal infallability. Maurice Walsh of Kerry wrote the famous book *The Quiet Man*, which was made into a popular movie. Variants are WALSHE and WELSH.

**Ward**   The original Gaelic version of this surname was Mac an Bhaird, which means simply "bard." The family lived in Ulster and Connacht. General Thomas Ward (1749-1794) served in the French army.

**Woulfe**   The French Norman invaders brought the original of this name—de Bhulbh, meaning "son of Ulf"—into Ireland. The family lived primarily in Kildare, Limerick, and Cork. General James Wolfe (1727-1759) was responsible for the taking of Quebec. Variants are WOLFE, WOOLEY, and WOOLFE.

# Scotland

The Scots and the Irish are very similar in language and history, for the Scots originally came from Ireland to settle in the north of Britain. Many of their personal and surnames have been influenced by political allies as well as invaders—the Romans, Vikings, Normans, Anglo-Saxons, and the French, to name a few. The earliest record of any tartan is 1597, although there may have been use of such clan identity before this date. This list does not include all the possible Scottish surnames. Whenever a clansman was the head of a clan, he was called the Bruce or the Campbell. However, it is also correct to speak of the man as, for example, Robert Bruce.

**Abbot**  This surname is probably a version of Macnab, which in Gaelic means "son of the abbot." Alexander Abbot signed the Band of Dumfries in 1570. A variant is ABBOTSON.

**Abercrombie**  This surname began with William de Abercromby in 1296. His territory was in Fife. This particular line died out about the middle of the seventeenth century, and the Abercrombies of Birkenbog now represent the family name. Many bearing this name served in the Scots Guards in France in the 1500s, where the name is recorded as Abre Commier. Variant spellings are ABERCROMBY, EABERCROMBIE, and ABIRCROMBY.

**Abernethy**  The origins of this surname are uncertain, but documents show that they were lay abbots of the Culdee Monastery of Abernethy in Strathearn in the twelfth century. The death of Hugh Abernethy, the first record of this family, appears about the middle of the twelfth century. His son Orm succeeded him as lay abbot.

Orm was the first of this family to use de Abernethy (Abirnythy), denoting a territory. He may have been given the lands of Ormiston, which is near Salton, East Lothian. By the thirteenth century, the Abernethies are shown in Upper Lauderdale, probably as vassals of the de Morevilles.

**Adam**  Adam, the sub-prior of Melrose, became abbot of Cupar in 1189. Andrew Adam was a representative of Lanark when the burghs were paying ransom for King James I. This family is allied with the Gordon clan. James Adam (1730-1794) was a renowned architect.

**Adamson**  This surname means "son of Adam." Records show that Adam, son of Ade, son of Phillippi, was a burgess in 1261. John Adamson, a Scot, had safe conduct to go to Bruges from England in 1433. This family is allied with the Shaw and Mackintosh clans. Robert Adamson (1821-1848) was a chemist and pioneer in photography. Variants are ADEMSON and ADAMESOUNE.

**Adie**  A name derived from a diminutive of Adam. It was common in Edinburgh and Aberdeenshire in the seventeenth century. This family is allied with the Gordon clan. Variant spellings are ADDIE, ADDY, EADIE, EDDIE, and EDIE.

**Agnew**  The first record of this Norman name in Scotland was in Liddesdale about 1190. One branch of this family moved to Ulster, Ireland, settling on lands near Larne, where the ruins of their Kilwaughter Castle still stand.

**Alaister**  Derived from the Gaelic version of Alexander, the variant spelling is Alastair. This family is allied with the MacDonald clan.

**Alcock**  This is a diminutive of Allan. Records show William Alkok was a witness in Aberdeen in 1281. This family is allied with the MacDonald clan.

**Alexander**  This Greek name was brought into Scotland from the Hungarian court by Queen Margaret, wife of King Malcolm Ceannmor. A variant is MacAlexander; the *mac* was dropped near the end of the seventeenth century. This family is allied with the MacDonald and MacArthur clans. A nickname for Alexander is Sandy.

**Alison**  Possibly a version of Allanson, a variant spelling is ALLISON. This family is allied with the MacDonald clan.

**Allen**  This family is allied with the MacDonald and MacFarlane clans. Sir Hugh Allan (1810-1946) emigrated to Canada where he became a prominent shipbuilder and founder of the Allan Line of steamers. A variant is ALLEN.

**Alpin** The name comes from Kenneth MacAlpin who united the Picts and Scots into one kingdom around 850. He made his capital at Dun Add in Dalriada, which is beside Loch Crinan. Other clan-families that claim descent from MacAlpin are MacGregor, MacAulay, MacDuff, MacFie, MacKinnon, MacNab, and Mac-Quarrie. Variants are MACALPINE (son of Alpine) and MACALPIN.

**Anderson** Also known as MacAndrew, this surname comes from Andrew, the patron saint of Scotland, and means "son of Andrew." The name is very common in Aberdeenshire. This family is allied with the MacDonald and Ross clans.

**Andrew** This family is allied with the Ross clan.

**Angus** This name came from Ireland into Scotland and comes from the god Aonghus mac Og. In the nineth century an Angus was king of Dalriada in western Scotland. This family is allied with the MacInnes clan.

**Anstruther** This name comes from the lands of Anstruther in Fife. In the twelfth century the barony of this family was held by the de Candelas, a Norman family with lands also in Dorset. William de Candelas (or de Candela), who died in 1153, took the name Anstruther. Records show that a David Anstruther was in the Scots Guards in France; his descendants are the barons of Anstrude.

**Arbuthnott** This surname originated in Berwickshire. Duncan, the son and heir of Hugh of Swinton, adopted the name in the twelfth century. The family received the lands of Arbuthnott in Kincardineshire from Walter Olifard, who was granted them by William the Lion about 1175. The name is quite common around Peterhead and Grampian.

**Armstrong** In the French-Norman language this surname originally was Fortenbras. Legend says the armor bearer to a king of Scots got this name after he rescued the monarch in the middle of battle when the king's horse was killed under him. Because of his strength, he became known as Armstrong, literally meaning "strength of the arm." The family grew quite powerful in the Borders, frequently making raids into England. They were so warlike, they became known as the Reivers. An American descendant, Neil Armstrong (b. 1930), was the first man to walk on the moon on July 21, 1969.

**Arthur** This name comes from the Old Irish word *arth,* and means "bear." In the Shetland Islands, this personal name is a corruption of the Norse-Viking name Ottar. Aedan mao Gabrain, king of Dalriada, married a British princess and named his first son Arthur. The United States President Chester Arthur (1830-1886) was descended from a Scottish minister in this family. The family is allied with the Campbell and MacArthur clans.

**Ayson**   Also known as EASON, EASSON, and ESSON, this is a very old family. This family is allied with the Mackintosh clan.

**Baillie**   This surname is a variant of the English Bayliss, which means "son of the bailiff." Prominent families of this line are those of Lamington, Polkemmet, Jerviswood, and Dochfour. Dame Isobel Baillie (1895-1983) was a great oratorio soprano.

**Bain**   The De Bayns lived in England in the thirteenth century, but this Scottish surname is widespread. There were several families bearing this name in St. Andrews in the sixteenth century. The name also occurs in seventeenth-century records in Edinburgh, Dysart, and Aberdeen. This family is allied with the Mackay and MacBain clans.

**Baird**   This surname is derived from the word "bard," which means "poet." Folk history says that a Baird rescued William the Lion, a Scottish king, from a wild boar and was given land grants as a reward. John Baird of Kirkintilloch, who died in 1891, built the New York elevated railroads.

**Balfour**   This name comes from the lands and barony of Markinch in Fife. James de Balfure in 1304 is the first with this name to be listed in records. At one time more than twenty branches of this family held lands in Fife. Arthur James Balfour (1848-1930) was a statesman and philosopher who served under Lloyd George as foreign secretary, and was responsible for the Balfour Declaration that favored establishing Palestine as a national home for Jewish people.

**Ballach**   Donald Balloch is mentioned in records of 1476, and a Robert Balloch was in Edinburgh in 1598. The name sometimes appears in sixteenth century records as Bello, Belloch, and Bellocht. The family is allied with the MacDonald clan.

**Bannatyen**   This name comes from a place called Bennachtain. Old documents show that William de Bennothine witnessed a grant by William de Moravia. The spelling changed at the time of Charles II, when it became BANNATYNE or BALLENTYNE. The Bannatynes of

Bute were followers of both the earl of Argyll and the Stewarts of Bute. This family is allied with the Campbell clan.

**Bannerman**   Legend says that this name came from a standard-bearer of one of the early Scottish kings. The first record of a family with this name is in the reign of David II, who gave a charter and lands to Dovinaldus Bannerman, his physician. They are allied with the Forbes clan.

**Barclay**   Both the Scottish and English families of this name are of Norman descent. The surname comes from Roger de Berkeley, who came into England with William the Conqueror and was given a castle and lands in Gloucestershire.

**Bartholomew**   A biblical name that means "son of the twin." An Alisaundre Bertholmeu lived in Edinburgh in 1296. In the old marriage records of Edinburgh, this name is variously spelled BARTELMEW, BARTILMO, BARTLEMO, and BARTILMEW.

**Baxter**   This surname is derived from the Old English *baecestre,* meaning " a female baker." Later, in Middle English the name changed to the masculine *Baxster.* In old Scottish Latin records, the name is listed as *Pistor.*

**Bayn**   This surname is derived from the Gaelic word *ban,* meaning "white." The name has no connections with the English Bayne, which came from a Norman name. Sometimes written as BAYNE, the family is allied with the Mackay clan.

**Bean**   Derived from the Gaelic word *beathan,* meaning "life," this name was sometimes written as Macbean. In old seventeenth-century records in Edinburgh this name is written as BEANE, BEAN, and BEAINE. This family is allied with the MacBain clan.

**Beath**   This name comes from a place-name: Beath, in Fife. They are allied with the MacDonald clan.

**Beaton**   Two families practicing medicine to the chiefs of the Mac-Donalds and MacLaines in the sixteenth and seventeenth centuries were members of this family: Macbeth (in Islay and Mull) and Beaton (Skye). This family is allied with the MacDonald, Macleod, and Maclean clans.

**Bell**   There are three possible origins for this name: Peter le Bel, meaning "handsome," John atte Belle (a Middle English name), and Robert, son of Bel or Isabel. The name was quite common on the Borders for centuries. They are allied with the Macmillan clan.

**Bethune**   This name first appears in Scottish records between 1165 and 1190, when a Robert de Betunia was a witness in court. The name possibly comes from a town in Pas de Calais. Variants in documents are BETUN and BETON, which caused confusion with BEATON in the sixteenth century. The family is allied with the MacDonald clan.

**Bisset**   This name is a diminutive of the Old French word *bis,* meaning "rock dove." William the Lion, when he was released from English captivity in 1174, brought back young Englishmen, including the Biseys, with him. Records show that the Bissets of Aird and Lessendrum are some of the oldest families in Aberdeen.

**Black**   There seems to be no agreement among authorities as to the origin of this name. It could derive from the Old English *blaec,* or *blac,* meaning "black," or the Old English *bla'c,* meaning "bright," "white," or "pale," or may come from the Gaelic names *M'Ille dhuibh* or *Mac Gille dhuibh,* which mean "son of the black lad." Blaecca was also a well-known Old English personal name. In early Scots charters, the name was listed as Niger. The Clan Lamont Society says the Blacks were originally Lamonts who changed their name. This family is allied with the Maclean, Lamont, and MacGregor clans.

**Borthwick**   This name comes from the old barony of Borthwick along Borthwick Water in Roxburghshire. Folk legend says that a Borthwick who was in the Crusades recaptured the heart of Robert the Bruce from the Saracens.

**Boswell**   This name first appears in old Scottish records during the time of William the Lion, when a Robert de Boseuille came from Normandy. By the twelfth century, the family was established in Berwickshire. The biographer of Samuel Johnson, James Boswell, was born in Edinburgh in 1740.

**Bowie**   A John Boye, alias Bowy and Boee, was a Scotsman living in Yarmouth in 1481. The family is allied with the MacDonald clan.

**Boyd**   This surname may derive from the place name Bute, which in Gaelic is *Bod* or *Bhoid.* The first records of the Boyds show them as vassals to the De Morevilles and probably of English descent.

**Boyle**   Some sources believe this surname comes from the Irish O' Baoghail, while others say it goes back to the De Boyville family who came from Normandy with William the Conqueror and originated in Boyville or Beauville near Caen.

**Brodie**   This family traces its ancestry back to one of the Pictish tribes of Moray. The name itself comes from the ancient Thaneage. Michael de Brothis was given a charter by King Robert Bruce just before the battle of Bannockburn in 1311. This family is allied with the MacDonald clan. Variants are BRODY, BRYDE, and BRYDIE.

**Broun**  This surname is a variant of *Brown*, a very common Scottish name. A Broun family owned estates in Cumberland before the Norman Conquest in 1066. The branch of this family in East Lothian claim descent from the royal house of France. They also trace their ancestry to George Broun, who married Jean Hay, daughter of the third Lord Yester, in 1543. Jean Hay's dowry was the renowned Coulston Pear, which her ancestor, Hugo de Gifford of Yester (a magician), was said to have empowered with magic to provide the family with constant prosperity. One branch of this Coulston family became merchants in Helsingor, Denmark.

**Brown**  They are allied with the Lamont clan. James Gordon Brown (b. 1951) was a politician who entered the House of Commons in 1983.

**Bruce**  This name is derived from the family de Bruis who came from Normandy with William the Conqueror in 1066. They were given the lordship of Annandale in 1124 by King David I. Robert Bruce (1274-1329), took the Scottish throne in 1306, and fought the battle of Bannockburn. When he died in 1329, his heart was carried to Jerusalem during the Crusades, later to be brought back and buried at Melrose Abbey. After the death of his son, the throne went to the Stewarts. A variant is BRUSI.

**Buchan**  This family traces its name and ancestry to the Pictish Mormaers of Buchan who became the earls of Buchan in the twelfth century. Although an individual clan, this family is allied with the Comyn or Cumming clan.

**Buchanan**  This family is of Pictish origin, the pre-Scottish people who held land on the east side of Loch Lomond. They claim descent from the Ancient Britons of Strathclyde. However, one source relates a legend in which the name MacAuselan is derived from the Irish prince Anselan O'Kayn. Another source says the clan took the name from the district of Buchanan. Branches of this family are Arnprior, Auchamar, Carbeth, Drumakill, Leny, and Spittal. James Buchanan was the fifteenth president of the United States. Variants are MACCALMAN and MACCAMMOND.

**Burnett** The Burnetts of Barns claim descent from Robertius de Burneville in the reign of David I. In their Crathes Castle on the River Dee in Aberdeenshire can be seen the Horn of Leys, an ivory horn presented to Alexander Burnett by Robert Bruce in 1323. This family is allied with the Campbell clan. A variant is BURNET.

**Burns** They are allied with the Campbell clan. Robert Burns (1759-1796) was a famous poet.

**Cameron** This surname is derived from the Gaelic word *cam-shron,* meaning "crooked nose" or "hooked nose." At one time, there were three branches of this clan: the MacSorleys of Glen Nevis, the Mac-Martins of Letterfinlay, and the MacGillonies of Strone. Throughout all the troubles with the English, the Camerons always supported the royal Stuarts.

**Campbell** This name comes from the Gaelic word *cam-beul,* meaning "crooked mouth." Family tradition says that this powerful clan originated from the marriage of Eva O'Duibhne and Colin Campbell, the first recorded Campbell in the thirteenth century. Colin's son Neil supported Robert Bruce, by which the family gained extensive grants of land. The Campbells of Trachur are descended from Colin's cousin, and from the Campbells of Loudon from his younger son.

**Carmichael** This name comes from the name of a barony in Lanarkshire. In 1250, Robert de Carmitely had lordship of the land of Cleghorn. In the fourteenth century, John de Carmychell had the lands of Carmychell. In Holland this name appears as Carmiggelt.

**Carnegie** The name is derived from the lands of Carryneggy in southwest Angus. John de Ballinhard was given these lands by King David II in 1358. Andrew Carnegie (1835-1918) was born in Dunfermline, Fife, and emigrated with his family to the United States in 1848. At one time, he was the richest man in the world.

**Cathcart** This surname comes from the lands of Cathcart in Renfrewshire. This family came north with Walter Fitz Alan, the first of the Stewarts, and was probably of Breton origin.

**Charteris** Thomas de Longueville, who founded this family, was given the lands of Kinfauns by King Robert Bruce. Later, Francis Wemyss took the name and arms of Charteris of Amisfield under the entailment from his maternal grandfather.

**Chattan** This clan name comes from Gillichattan Mor, the Great Servant of St. Catan of the ancient Culdee Church. Sometime after

1291, when Eva Chattan married Angus Mackintosh, this clan name was used to describe a tribal federation. They were a powerful force in the Highlands for nearly five centuries. A variant is CATTANACH.

**Cheyne**  The ancestors of this family were Normans, who came from Quesney near Coutances. Reginald de Chesne became chamberlain of Scotland in 1267.

**Chisholm**  Originally, this surname was De Chesholme and came from a Norman family in Roxburghshire. Both the Highland and the Lowland Chisholms descended from one ancestor, who married Margaret, lady of Erchless. Sir Robert de Cheseholme was constable of the royal castle of Urquhart in 1359.

**Cochrane**  This surname was taken from the lands of Cochrane (Coueran) near Paisley in Renfrewshire. William Cochrane was created the first earl of Dundonald in 1669.

**Cockburn**  This name is derived from a place-name near Berwickshire. The Cockburns were ancient vassals of the earls of March. Because the clan supported Mary, Queen of Scots, their castle at Skirling was demolished in 1568.

**Colquhoun**  This surname (pronounced Cohoon) comes from the barony of Colquhoun in Dunbartonshire. They trace their ancestry to Humphrey de Kilpatrick or Kirkpatrick, who received a land grant from Alexander II. Sir John Colquhoun was the last known person to openly practice witchcraft in Scotland.

**Colville**  It is possible that this surname came from the town of Coleville in Normandy. Scottish records of the twelfth century list Philip de Coleuille as having the baronies of Oxnam and Heiton in Roxburghshire. He had been a hostage of William the Lion in 1174.

**Cranstoun**  Descended from Elfric de Cranston, a tenth-century Norman, this family owned land in Edinburgh and Roxburghshire.

**Crawford**  This surname comes from the barony of Crawford in the upper ward of Clydesdale. Sir Archibald Crawford of Loudoun (who was murdered by the English during a banquet) came from a branch of this family. Archibald's sister married Malcolm Wallace and was the mother of Sir William Wallace, the patriot.

**Crichton**  The name is derived from an old barony in Midlothian. Old records show that in 1128 Turstand de Crectune was in Scotland.

**Cumming**  They trace their beginings to the Norman king Charlemagne through Robert de Comyn who was appointed governor of

Northumberland in 1068 by William the Conqueror. During the reign of Alexander III they had the earldoms of Atholl, Menteith, and Buchan. John Comyn (the "Red" Comyn), lord of Badenoch, had a strong claim to the Scottish throne through descent through King Duncan. His mother was the sister of King John Balliol. Variants are CUMMINGS, COMYN, COMMON, and CUMMIN.

Cunningham    This family traces its ancestry to the Warnibald family who settled in Ayrshire in the twelfth century. Alexander III presented the lands of Kilmaurs to Harvey de Cunningham after the battle of Largs.

Dalrymple    Old records state that this family held a charter for lands in the fourteenth century. James Dalrymple was made a baronet in 1164. His son, later the first earl of Stair, issued notorious letters that led to the massacre of MacIan Macdonalds in Glencoe.

Dalzeil    The origins of this family go back to the barony of Dalzell in Lanarkshire. Folk legends tell of King Kenneth II who offered a reward to any man who was brave enough to retrieve the body of his hanged kinsman. A man shouted, "Dal Zell," which in Old Scots means "I dare."

Davidson    This surname originated from Donald Dhu of Invernahavon, chief of the Davidsons, who married a daughter of Angus, sixth Mackintosh before 1350. This family maintained an on-going feud with the Macphersons regarding precedence in the Clan Chattan. Variants are DAVEY, DAVIS, DAVISON, MACDADE, MACDAID, and MACDAVID.

Douglas    The first record of this family is of William de Douglas (known as the Black Douglas), in Lanarkshire in the twelfth century. In the thirteenth century, the Red Douglases were established at Dalkeith and Angus. Because of this clan's wealth, strength, and influence, they were a threat to the royal Stewarts, thus causing them to lose their title and lands in 1455. A variant is DOUGLASS.

Drummond    This surname is derived from a place name, the lands of Drummond, or Drymen, near Loch Lomond in Stirlingshire. The first records of this clan begin with Malcolm Beg, the little. His son took the name of Drummond. This clan supported the royal Stuarts.

Dunbar    This family traces its ancestry to Crinan the Thane and Seneschal of the Isles, who was the father of King Duncan I and of Maldred. Maldred's son, Gospatric, was deprived of his title of earl by William the Conqueror. He fled to Scotland and was made earl of Dunbar by King Malcolm III.

**Duncan** The name comes from a chief of Clan Donnachaidh, "Fat Duncan," who led his clan at Bannockburn. They held lands in Forfarshire, including the barony of Lundie and the estate of Gourdie.

**Dundas** Old documents show Serle de Dundas in the reign of William the Lion. This family obtained its lands during the reign of Malcolm IV. They were prominent in the legal affairs of the nation. Henry Dundas, the first Viscount Melville, managed Scotland for William Pitt. He used his office to restore many estates that had been forfeited after the 1745 Rebellion. The Dundas family of Virginia trace their ancestry to a member of this family who emigrated in 1757.

**Elliott** One of the great Border clans of southern Scotland, this surname appeared in the thirteenth century at Arbirlot (Aber-Eliot). When James VI banished and executed many of the Border clans for their lawlessness, the Elliotts of Stobs took over the chiefship. A variant is ELIOT.

**Elphinstone** This surname is derived from a place name, the village of Elphinstone in East Lothian. The sixteenth baron married Lady Mary Bowes Lyon, a sister of Elizabeth, the Queen Mother.

**Erskine** This name comes from Henry de Erskine, who had lands in Renfrewshire in the reign of Alexander II. His son Robert became chief of the ancient Tribe of the Land of Mar. A descendant, Gratney of Mar, married the sister of Robert Bruce; their son Donald was regent of Scotland.

**Farquharson** The ancestor of this clan was Farquhar, son of Alexander Ciar, the third shaw of Macintosh of Rothiemurchus in Strathspey. His son Donald married Isobel Stewart. Farquhar's son, Finlay Mor, died at the Battle of Pinkie in 1547. Branches of this family are Inverey, Finzean, Monaltrie, and Balmoral.

**Fergusson** Tradition says that this family first settled at Kintyre. The seat of the Fergusson chiefs, Kilkerran in Ayrshire was named after St. Ciaran of Ireland who came to Daruadhain in the sixth century. The family branch of Kilkerran are descended from Fergus in the time of Robert Bruce. Variants are FERGUSON, FERGUS, FERRIES, and FORGIE.

**Fleming** Originally meaning "one from Flanders," old Scottish records first show this name in the twelfth century. Jordan Fleming was taken prisoner along with William the Lion in 1174.

**Fletcher**    Meaning "arrow maker," the Fletchers followed the clans and made arrows. They are associated in Argyll with the Stewarts and Campbells, and in Perthshire with the MacGregors.

**Forbes**    This family traces its history to Ochonochar. Legends say that this man killed a bear and took over the previously uninhabitable Braes of Forbes or Forbois in Aberdeenshire. Alexander de Forbes fiercely fought against King Edward I of England and died defending Urquhart castle near Loch Ness. A variant is FORDYCE.

**Forsyth**    This name may be derived from the Gaelic word *fearsithe,* meaning "man of peace." In 1296 Robert de Fauside signed the Ragman Roll. Later chiefs of this clan were members of the royal Stewart household at Falkland.

**Fotheringham**    This surname is believed to be a corruption of Fotheringhay in Northamptonshire, which held the royal house of Scotland in the twelfth century. Henry de Fodringhay was given lands near Dundee by Robert II.

**Fraser**    This family traces its ancestry back to Anjou and Normandy, and to the name de Friselle or Fresel, then Fraisier. This name is derived from *fraises,* meaning "strawberry flowers." They probably sailed to England with William the Conqueror in 1066. Variants are FRESER, FREZEL, FRISELL, and FRIZELLE.

**Fullerton**    The first record of this family was of Alanus de Fowlertoun, who founded a convent of Carmelites (or White Friars) at Irvine. In the fourteenth century, a branch of this family settled in Arran.

**Galbraith**    In Gaelic this surname means "Briton's son." The family appears to have originated from the Britons who settled in Strathclyde. They were connected with the island of Gigha and the Clan Donald.

**Gardyne**    This name comes from the barony of Gardyne in Angus and is very common in the Arbroath area.

**Gayre**    This family was in Cornwall during the twelfth century. A branch of the family migrated to Yorkshire, then after destroying a castle there fled to Scotland in the sixteenth century. They married into the Mowe and MacCulloch families. Variants are GAIR, GEAR, GAIRN, GEIR, GAIRE, GARRISON, GARSON, MCGAIR, and MCGEIR.

**Gillies**   This surname comes from Badenoch and the Hebrides and means "servant of Jesus." Uhtred, son of Gilise, had lands in Lothian during the twelfth century.

**Gordon**   The first record of this family in Scotland is in the late twelfth century. The sixth Lord Byron, George Gordon, was a poet.

**Graham**   William de Graham, a member of an Anglo-Norman family, is the first of the family to be listed in records of the twelfth century. Folklore says they are descended from Gramus, who tore down the wall built by the Emperor Antoninus. The fourth marquis, named James, helped to restore the tartan. Variants are GRAEME and GRAHAME.

**Grant**   This family is the main branch of the Siol Alpine of the Clan Gregor as chief. They trace their ancestry to Normandy where their name came from the French *grand*, meaning "big" or "eminent." Most of the clan were loyal to the Stewarts. General Ulysses S. Grant (1822-1885), was the eighteenth United States president.

**Gray**   Scottish records of the thirteenth century list a Hugo de Gray from Normandy. This is now a very common name in Scotland.

**Grierson**   This family traces its ancestry to Gilbert, second son of Malcolm, and to Dominus de MacGregor of the fourteenth century.

**Gunn**   There are two opinions as to the origin of this clan. One is that this family is descended from Gunni, grandson of Sweyn Asleifsson, the Ultimate Viking who died at Dublin in 1171. The other is that they were Pictish, and the name came from the Welsh word *gwynn*. They were a warlike clan who held the northern areas of Caithness and Sutherland and constantly feuded with the Keiths and MacKays. When the Highland Clearances occurred in Sutherland, many of this family emigrated to New Zealand and Canada. Variants are GANSON, GALDIE, GALLE, and GAUNSON.

**Guthrie**   Tradition says this family is descended from Guthrum, a Scandinavian prince. In 1299, Squire Guthrie brought William Wallace back to Scotland from France.

**Haig**   Records of the twelfth century list a Petrus del Hage. Alexander Haig was secretary of state under United States President Nixon.

**Haldane**   Some sources believe this surname is derived from the Old English *healf-dene*, or the Old Danish *half-dan*, meaning "half

Dane." Others think it comes from a member of the Border house of Hadden or Howden who acquired the estate of Gleneagles through marriage.

**Hamilton** This family traces its ancestry to Walter Fitz-Gilbert of Hameldone, 1295, who was given the lands of Cadzow by Robert Bruce. The name may have originated in Yorkshire or Lancashire.

**Hannay** This family originated in the ancient province of Galloway. The earliest owners of Sorbie Tower were a powerful Anglo-Norman family named the Viponts, in 1185. The Hannays gained the estate through marriage.

**Hay** This surname is listed in French records of the eighth century. La Haya de Puits was a high leader with William the Conqueror's army. William de Haya was butler to William the Lion. William de Haya's son was a hostage of William the Lion in England. When the men returned to Scotland, de Haya was given a manor in Errol.

**Henderson** Tradition says that Eannig Mor Mac Righ Neachtan (Big Henry), son of King Nectan who ruled Caledonia in the eighth century, was the founder of this name. However, a 1450 manuscript states that the clan descended from the Scottish tribe of Loarn. The Hendersons were hereditary pipers to Clan Abrach. A variant is MACKENDRICK.

**Hepburn** This surname derives from the place-name Hebburn in Northumberland. Adam de Hepburne was taken prisoner by the Earl of March, who gave him lands when he saved the earl from a savage horse. James Hepburn (1536-1578), the fourth earl of Bothwell, escorted Mary, Queen of Scots, to Scotland from France. He took part in the murder of Lord Darnley, Mary's husband, but later married the queen. When Mary was granted a divorce in 1570, the earl of Bothwell fled to Denmark where he was imprisoned and died insane.

**Home** Pronounced Hume, this name comes from Aldan de Home of Berwickshire in the twelfth century. A variant is HUME.

**Hope** Records show a John Hope of Peebles-shire in the thirteenth century. The earls of Hopetoun trace their ancestry to John de Hope, one of the retinue of Queen Magdelen, wife of James V.

**Hunter** This family came to Scotland from Normandy about 1110. Aylmer le Hunter signed the Ragman Roll in 1296. The family acquired their lands from Robert II in 1374.

**Innes**   Derived from the Gaelic word *innis,* this name means "islet." This family originated in Moray in 1160 during the reign of Malcolm IV. The lands of Innes were given to Berowald, a man from Flanders. A variant is INCH.

**Irvine**   This surname comes from two place names: Irving, an old parish in Dumfries-shire; and Irvine in Ayrshire. William de Irwyne received the Forest of Drum in 1324 from Robert I.

**Jardine**   At the battle of Hastings, this surname is listed as du Jardin. The family settled first near Kendal in the twelfth century, then moved to Lanarkshire in the thirteenth century. Finally they settled in Dumfries-shire early in the fourteenth century.

**Johnston**   This powerful Border clan held the central area of Annandale. Tradition says that the name derived from John, a twelfth-century holder of Annandale lands, who gave his name to his citadel or "toun." Legend says that the chief of the Johnstons heard of the English king's treachery to depose Bruce in favor of Baliol while he was at the Scottish court. He sent Bruce a spur with an attached feather, meaning "flight with speed." Thus Bruce avoided the plot. This family had a deadly feud for years with the Maxwells, but finally resolved the problem in 1623. A variant is JOHNSTONE.

**Keith**   Hervey de Keith held half of the lands named Keith in the reign of King David I. A very powerful family, it received the lands of Kintore for supporting Robert Bruce. They were created earls of Marischal in 1458.

**Kennedy**   One source says this family traces its ancestry to Duncan of Carrick who lived in the twelfth century. Another source states that Henry Cinnidh or Kennedy was a younger brother of William the Lion and founded this clan. Bishop James Kennedy and his daughter Kate founded a college at St. Andrews University in 1455.

**Kerr**   This family is possibly of Viking descent, first settling in France, then in the Scottish Borders in the twelfth century. They were early sheriffs of the Marches but also part of the Border Reivers. Variants are KER and CARR.

**Kilpatrick**   The first of this family to appear in Scottish records was Roger de Kirkpatrick. A Roger de Kirkpatrick was with Robert Bruce when he stabbed the Red Comyn in the thirteenth-century Franciscan friary.

**Lamont**   This surname comes from the Old Norse word for

"lawman." Tradition says the clan originated in Ferchar in the thirteenth century. When they opposed Robert Bruce, they lost much of their land and influence. Variants are LAUMON, LAMBIE, LAMMIE, LAMOND, LAMONDSON, and LEMOND.

Lauder   Old documents show that this family originated with a Norman Baron de Lavedre during the time of Malcolm Canmore. Robert de Lawedre fought for William Wallace and later became ambassador to England for Robert I.

Lennox   The first Celtic earl of this name was Alwin MacMuredach MacMaidouern, Mormaer of the Levanach in the twelfth century. Lord Darnley, who married Mary, Queen of Scots, was the son of the fourth earl of Lennox.

Leslie   One source says this surname came from Bartolf, a Hungarian nobleman who was chamberlain to St. Margaret, queen of Malcolm Canmore. Another source lists the origin as the lands of Leslie in Garrioch, Aberdeenshire. These lands were granted to Malcolm, son of Bartholf, under King William the Lion.

Lindsay   A Norman, Baldric de Linsay, is the first person recorded with this name in Scotland. The name means "isle of the lime trees" and is a place near Rouen. Sir Walter Lindsay settled his family at Tweedside when David I was king of Scotland. David, the thirteenth lord, married a daughter of Robert II. Lord Lindsay of 1740 was the first Colonel of the Black Watch. Variants are LIMESAY and LINDESEY.

Livingston   Old twelfth-century records show that Leving, a Saxon, held lands in West Lothian. This family was prominent in Scottish history from 1300 until 1715. The Highland branch of this clan originally had a Gaelic name that they spelled many ways, including MacDunsleinhe, Mac-an-Leigh, and Maclea. David Livingston, the explorer, came from this Highland clan.

Lockhart   The ancestor of this family came from Flanders and settled in Lanarkshire in 1272. They gained the name Lockhart when, during the Crusades, Simon Locard carried the key to the casket that contained Robert the Bruce's heart.

Logan   There are two distinct families with this clan name, one of the Highlands, the other of the Lowlands. The MacLennans of the north trace their ancestry to the Logans of Drumderfit. Their name means "son of Finnan's servant." A variant is MACLENNAN.

**Lumsden**   This surname originated from a place name on the coast of Berwickshire. The first mention of this family is in a charter signed by Edgar, king of Scots in 1098.

**Lyle**   During the thirteenth century, a family bearing this surname were barons of Duchal in Renfrewshire. The name appears to have originated with Ralph de Insula, who followed Steward from Northumberland.

**Lyon**   Thomas Lyon, who was in the pay of Edward II in the fourteenth century, is the first Lyon mentioned in old records. Some sources say the lineage is Norman, while others believe it is of Celtic origin. The wife of John Lyon, sixth Lord Glamis, was accused of witchcraft by James V and burned alive outside Edinburgh Castle.

**MacAllister**   This family is a branch of Clan Donald that traces its ancestry to a great-grandson of Somerled, Allister (or Alexander). They held lands in Kintyre and Knapdale. After Bruce attacked their Castle Sweyn in Knapdale, the clan seat was moved to Ardpatrick, then to Loup in Kintyre. Variants are ALASTAIR, ALEXANDER, ALISON, ALLISTER, and MACALASTER.

**MacArthur**   This is one of the oldest Argyllshire clans. They backed Robert Bruce and, as a reward, were given the lands of the MacDougalls who had opposed him. General Douglas MacArthur (1880-1964) was a famous American soldier. Variants are ARTHUR, ARTHURSON, MACCAIRTER, and MACCARTER.

**MacAulay**   This surname means "son of Aulay." The MacAulays of Lewis were of Norse ancestry and followers of the MacLeods of Lewis. Another unrelated branch of this family was part of the Clan Alpine. The branch that moved to Loch Fyne took the name MacPhedran, which became Paterson. Variants are AULAY, MACALLEY, MACPHEIDRAN, PATERSON, and MACCAULEY.

**MacBean**   Believed to have originated in Lochaber, this family settled in eastern Inverness-shire. As a member of Clan Chattan, Myles MacBean supported Clan Mackintosh against the Red Comyn. Variants are MACBAIN, BEAN, BINNIE, MACBEATH, MACBETH, MACVAIN, MACVANE, and MACVEAN.

**MacCallum**   This surname means "son of the gillie of Calum." Before 1850, the head of the branch in Poltalloch changed the name to Malcolm.

**MacColl**   A branch of the Clan Donald, this family settled around Loch Fyne and joined in the feud with the MacGregors.

**MacCorquodale**   A distant branch of the MacLeods of Lewis, this family lived on lands on the north side of Loch Awe. These lands had been given to their ancestor Torquil by King Kenneth MacAlpine.

**MacCulloch**   This family is descended from Lulach, who was the King of Scots after Macbeth, and who was killed by Malcolm Canmore. The Highland MacCullochs owned much land in the province of Ross. The MacCullochs of Argyllshire were associated with the Clan MacDougall. The history of the Galloway MacCullochs before 1296 is vague.

**MacDonald**   This surname means "son of Donald." Clan Donald is an important clan, and the largest Highland clan. At one time, this clan controlled the entire western Scottish coast from the Butt of Lewis to the Mull of Kintyre, and also had lands in Ireland and in the Isle of Man. The MacDonalds trace their ancestry to Conn of the Hundred Battles, the High King of Ireland in the first century. The name Donald actually comes from Donald of Islay, grandson of Somerled, lord of Argyll. From Donald came the Clan Alister, the MacAllisters of Loup. Variants are MACDOMHNALL, MACDONNELL, DONALD, DONALDSON, MACDONELL, and DONNELL.

**MacDougall**   This name means "son of Dougal." They trace their ancestry to Dugald, a son of Somerled and Ragnhildis who was the daughter of Olaf, king of Man. They lost all their land during the feud between Robert Bruce and the Comyns. They later supported the Stuarts. Variants are MACDUBHGALL, DOUGALL, DUGAL, and DUGALD.

**MacDowall**   This family claims descent from the ancient lords of Galloway. In 1312, Dugald McDowall was sheriff in Dumfries.

**MacDuff**   The name means "son of Duff." As descendants of the clan Alpin, this clan held the very old privilege of crowning Scottish kings. MacDuff, who was the first earl of Fife, is thought to be connected to Macbeth. An older spelling is MacDhuibh. A variant is DUFF.

**MacEwen**   Old documents show that Ewen of Otter lived in the thirteenth century. Elspeth MacEwan was the last witch executed in Scotland in 1698.

**MacFarlane**   A Parlan or Bartholomew lived during the reign of King David Bruce and had lands at the head of Loch Lomond. This man is claimed as ancestor of this clan. They also claim descent from the ancient Celtic earldom of Lennox. Variants are MACPARLAND, MACPARLANE, and MACPHARLAN.

**MacFie**   This family is a branch of Clan Alpin. Their ancestor MacDuffie of Colonsay was the hereditary Keeper of the Records for the Lords of the Isles. The MacFies held Colonsay until the seventeenth century, but were later scattered during the Highland Clearances. Variants are DUFFIE, DUFFY, FEE, MACCAFFIE, MACVIE, MACVEE, MACPHEE, and MACDUFFIE.

**MacGillivray**   This family originally came from Morvern and Lochaber and was one of the great MacDonald clan. In the thirteenth century they became identified with the Clan Chattan. Variants are GILRAY, GILROY, GILVRAY, MACGILROY, and MACILROY.

**MacGowan**   This surname is derived from the Gaelic word *gobha*, meaning "blacksmith." The family traces its ancestry back to a king of the Britons who died in 1018. A variant is GOW.

**MacGregor**   This name means "son of Gregor." This family traces its ancestry back to Griogar, the third son of Kenneth MacAlpine, King of Scots in the ninth century. They are the senior clan of Clan Alpine. Their lands were taken by the Clan Campbell, so they became raiders and killers. They were outlawed, hunted down, and executed. Those who escaped this persecution were forced to change their name. After fighting under the standard of Charles I in 1644, they were pardoned, but it took until 1775 for the clan name to be fully restored. The most famous of this name was Rob Roy MacGregor (1671-1734). Variants are GREER, GREGG, GREGORSON, GREGORY, GREIG, GREYSON, GRIER, and GRIGG.

**MacIain**   This name means "son of John." The MacIaians of Ardnamurchan trace their ancestry to a son of Angus Mhor, who was Lord of the Isles in the fourteenth century.

**MacInnes**   This name means "son of Angus" and arose from the Gaelic pronunciation of the name MacAngus. They originated from the Dalriads, who were hereditary bowmen to the chief of Mackinnon. Variants are MACAINSH, MACANISH, MACCANSH, and MACMASTER.

**MacIntyre**   This name means "son of the carpenter." They came from the Isle of Skye in the Hebrides and settled in Lorn in the fourteenth century, where they became Hereditary Foresters to the Stewarts of that region. Variants are MACINTIRE, MACTEAR, and TYRE.

**MacKay**   This clan traces its ancestry to the Royal House of Moray through the line of Morgund or Morgan of Pluscarden. In 1160, Malcolm IV moved them to Ross and Sutherland. Other MacKays settled in Galloway and Kintyre. Variants are KAY, KEY, MACCAW, MACCAY, and MACKIE.

**Mackellar**   This name means "son of Ealair," which is the Gaelic form of Hilarius. This was the name of the bishop of Poitiers. By the thirteenth century they were well established in Argyllshire.

**Mackenzie**   At one time this clan's territory probably included most of mid-Ross and Muir of Orde. However, William the Lion moved them to Wester Ross (Kintail) in the twelfth century. John, the son of Alexander "Ionraech," who was the seventh chief of Kintail, fought at Flodden. Variants are KENNETH, KYNOCH, MACKENNA, MACKENNEY, and MACKINNEY.

**Mackie**   This name can be traced back to Stirlingshire in the fifteenth century. The clan living in mid-Galloway was powerful in the sixteenth and seventeenth centuries. They also supported the Covenanters.

**Mackinley**   The records of this Lennox district clan are obscure, but they claim descent from Findlay, a son of Buchanan of Drumikill. They were associated with Clan Farquharson. The name is also found in Ireland and originated with the Scots who were taken there to inhabit Ulster. Variants are DONLEAVY, FINLAY, FINDLAY, FINLAYSON, MACINALLY, and MACCINFHAOLAIDH.

**MacKinnon**   This branch of Clan Alpin is descended from Fingon, great-grandson of King Kenneth MacAlpine. They were vassals of the Lords of the Isles. For generations a branch of this family were standard bearers to the MacDonalds of Sleat. Variants are MACKINNING, MACINNON, and MACKINVEN.

**Mackintosh**   This name means "son of the Thane." This family claims descent from a son of MacDuff. They became associated with the Clan Chattan when Angus, the sixth chief, married into that clan in 1291.

**MacLachlan**   This family traces its ancestry to Ferchar of Anrothan, prince of Aileach, one of three brothers who were related by marriage to the kings of Ireland and to the Somerled Lords of the Isles. Variants are MACLAUGHLAN, LACHIE, LACHLAN, and MACLAUGHLIN.

**MacLaine of Lochbuie**   Eachin Reganach, the elder brother of

Lachlan Lubanach, was the ancestor of this clan. His son Charles began the line of Macleans of Glen Urquhart and Dochgarroch, who were associated with Clan Chattan. The MacLaines followed the Lords of the Isles.

**MacLaren** There are two distinct families of this surname: one in Perthshire, and the other (the Maclaurins) who once owned the Isle of Tiree. This clan was also known as Clan Labhran.

**Maclean** This family traces its ancestry to Gilleain-na-Tuaighe (Gillean of the Battle Axe), who lived in the eleventh century and was a relative of the kings of Dalriada. They supported Bruce and fought at Bannockburn. Their enemies, the Campbells, forced the Macleans to mortgage much of their land, but were prevented from taking it by force of sword by their fall from grace in 1681. Variants are MACLANE, MACLAINE, and LEAN.

**Maclellan** This name means "son of the servant of St. Fillan." This family was quite numerous in Galloway in the fourteenth century. Some of the Maclellans of Perthshire claim to be a branch of the Clan MacNab.

**MacLeod** This name means "son of the ugly man." They are descended from Leod, the son of Olaf the Black, who was king of the Isle of Man. Tormod, Leod's oldest son, inherited Dunvegan and the Isle of Harris. He adopted the title MacLeod of Dunvegan. The second son, Torquil, inherited Lewis. The MacLeods held high rank under the Lords of the Isles. A variant is MCCLOUD.

**MacMillan** This clan of Moray came from the ancient people of Kanteai, who were of the northern Picts. The Lord of the Isles gave Malcolm Mor Macmillan a charter in 1360, but these lands were lost by the end of the fifteenth century. Kirkpatrick Macmillan, who invented the bicycle, was born at Keir. When he rode his bicycle to Glasgow, he was fined for knocking down a pedestrian.

**MacNab** This family traces its ancestry to the hereditary Celtic abbot of Glendochart in the reign of David I. In 1823, descendants emigrated to Canada and settled in MacNab near Ottawa. Some of them returned at a later date and settled at Killin. Variants are NAB, ABBOT, and ABBOTSON.

**MacNair** This name means "son of the heir." A variant is MACNAIR.

**MacNaughton** During the thirteenth century this clan lived in Lochawe, Glenaray, Glenshira, and Loch Fyne. In the fourteenth century Dundarave became the clan's stronghold. They lost their lands in 1700 after a marriage debacle with the Campbells. Mac-Naughton of Dundarave was drunk when he married the wrong daughter of James Campbell of Ardkinglas. The next morning, when he discovered his mistake, he fled with the daughter he intended to marry, leaving behind a pregnant wife. Variants are MACNACHTAN, MACNAUCHTON, and MACNAUGHTAN.

**MacNeill**    This family traces its ancestry to Niall of the Nine Hostages, High King of Ireland, who came to Barra in 1049. A variant is MACNIALL.

**Macpherson**    This name is derived from Duncan, Parson of Kinussie in the fifteenth century. This Duncan was a descendant of Muriach, chief of Clan Chattan in 1173. Three Macpherson brothers (Kenneth, John, and Gillies) of the fourteenth century are claimed as ancestors of the Macphersons of Cluny, Pitmain, and Invershie. Variants are MACPHERSON and PEARSON.

**MacQuarrie**    This family is a branch of Clan Alpin and held land on the islands of Mull and Ulva. Unfortunately, most of their family papers were burned in a fire in 1688.

**MacQueen**    This family traces its ancestry to Conn of the Hundred Battles and to the Isle of Skye. Although they became associated with Clan Chattan through marriage, they kept close ties with Clan Donald. The name may have been derived from the Norse name Sweyn. Variants are MACSWAIN, MACSWAN, MACSWEEN, and MACWHAN.

**MacRae**    In Gaelic, this surname means "son of grace." They settled in Kintail in the fourteenth century and became chamberlains of Kintail under the Mackenzies. Variants are MACRAY, MACCRAY, MACCREA, MACCRAE, MACCRAITH, MACCREE, and MACCRIE.

**MacThomas**    Tomaidh Mor, a Gaelic-speaking Highlander, was a descendant of the Clan Chattan Mackintoshes who lived in the fifteenth century. When the Clan Chattan became too large, Thomas took his followers to Glenshee. Variants are MCCOMAS, MCCOMB, MACCOMBIE, THOMAS, and THOMSON.

**Maitland**    A Lowland family, they rose to become dukes of Lauderdale. Because John Maitland supported the queen in 1567, he lost his office, but became secretary of state for life in 1584.

**Malcolm**    This surname means "devotee of St. Columba." It was the name of four Scottish kings, one of whom signed a charter in 1094. An old variant of this name is Maiklum, which was found in Strathblane. Variants are CALLUM and MACCALLUM.

**Marjoriebanks**    When Walter, High Steward of Scotland, married Marjorie, the only daughter of Robert Bruce, the king gave his daughter the barony of Ratho in Renfrewshire. These lands were called Terrae de Rath Marjorie banks, from which this surname comes.

**Matheson**    This surname means "son of the bear." They were an early branch of the Celtic earls of Ross and came from Lochalsh. Variants are MATHIESON, MATTHEWSON, MASSIE, and MASSEY.

**Maule**    This family traces its ancestry to the de Maules from France. Robert de Maules came to Scotland with David I and was given land in the Lothians. The second son of the eighth earl of Dalhousie changed his name to Maule in 1831.

**Maxtone**    This name can be traced back to the barony of Maxton in Roxburghshire and probably originated with Maccus, son of Undewyn, who took lands there during the reign of David I. A Hungarian family of similar name is related to one who emigrated from Scotland.

**Maxwell**    The chamberlain of Scotland in the thirteenth century, John Maxwell, is the first of this name to be recorded. For many years this family were wardens of the West March. Caerlaverock Castle, south of Dumfries, was their stronghold.

**Melville**    This family originated in the barony of Malaville in Normandy. Old records list Galfridus de Malveill in Scotland in the twelfth century. Andrew Melville (1542-1622) was a scholar and theologian who spent four years in the Tower of London. He lived the rest of his life in France as a professor at the University of Sedan and often spelled his surname MELVILLE or MELVIN.

**Menzies**    This Norman family came from Mayneris near Rouen. The earliest chief listed was Robert de Maygners who was chamberlain of Scotland in 1249. Variants are MACMENZIE, MACMIN, MEANS, and MINNUS.

**Moncreiffe**    Matthew Moncreiffe was given the lands of Moncreiffe by Alexander II in 1248. Matthew may have been a descendant of Maldred, Duncan I's brother.

**Montgomerie**    When William the Conqueror invaded England in

1066, Roger de Montgomerie was joint regent of Normandy and earl of Arundel. The first mention in old records of this family is of a Robert de Mundegumerie, who died in 1177.

**Morrison**   Tradition says that this family is descended from a natural son of a king of Norway who was cast ashore on the Isle of Lewis. They were Judges of the Island until 1613. They were also deadly enemies of the Lewis MacAulays.

**Mowat**   This Norman family settled in northeast Scotland, Orkney, and Shetland during the reign of David I. Old documents show that a Robert de Montealto moved from Wales to Scotland. The family had a bitter feud with the Camerons.

**Muir**   Thomas de la More's name appears as executor of the will of Dervorguilla de Balliol, daughter of the earl of Galloway, and the mother of John Balliol who was appointed king by Edward I of England. The family held lands in Ayrshire, Lanarkshire, and Berwickshire.

**Munro**   This family originally came from North Morady and were vassals of the earls of Ross. Historical records of the twelfth century list Hugh as their first chief. The clan lands near Dingwall were called Ferindonald. A variant is MONROE.

**Murray**   This family traces its ancestry back to Freskin de Moravia, a Fleming of Duffus in Moray, where he was chieftain of the Duffus branch of the Royal House of Moray. Other branches of this family are the Murrays of Blackbarony, Dunerne, Ochtertyre, and Abercairney. Variants are MORAY and MURRIE.

**Napier**   Old records show that this family was in Scotland as early as 1140. Their heraldry points to a descent from the Lennox family. Tradition says they took their name from a statement by Alexander III, "Lennox had na peer," meaning "no equal."

**Nicholson**   This name came from the Lowlands of Scotland around Dumfries, but it is also found in the islands of Skye and Lewis as MacNicol. The MacNicols trace their ancestry back to the Vikings and are a very ancient family. A variant is MACNICHOL.

**Nisbet**   This name comes from the barony of Nesbit in Berwickshire. The first record of this family is a Philip Nesbit who was a sheriff in 1493. In the sixteenth century, some of this family went to Sweden.

**Ogilvy**   The family traces its ancestry back to Gillibride, the second son of Ghillechriost, earl of Angus. He was given the barony of Ogilvy in about 1163. Family branches include those of Inverquharity and East Lothian.

**Oliphant**    This family is of Norman origin. William Holifard saved David I at the rout of Winchester in 1141. Later, a David Olifard was the godson of David I. William Oliphant held Stirling Castle against the siege of Edward I of England.

**Preston**    This family is related to the de Preston family of Ireland. Old documents show that Alured de Preston was in Scotland in the thirteenth century.

**Pringle**    This name was taken from the name of lands in Roxburghshire. The family first appears in records in the reign of Alexander III. They were one of the Riding Clans of the Scottish Borders.

**Ramsay**    Simon de Ramsay, an Anglo-Norman, was the first of this family recorded in Scotland. He received lands from David I. After the Battles of Marston Moor and Philiphaugh, William Ramsay was made the first earl of Dalhousie in 1633.

**Rattray**    This family traces its ancestry to Adam de Rattrieff of the thirteenth century. They were followers of the Murrays of Atholl, but not a branch of the family.

**Robertson**    The ancestor of this family was Duncan or Donnachaidh Reamhair who led the clan for Robert Bruce at Bannockburn and was himself descended from the Celtic earls of Atholl. The name Robertson came from a later chief, Robert, who lived during the reign of James I. They fought with the Stuarts and in the Jacobite risings. Variants are DONNACHAIDH, DOBINSON, MACROBBIE, MACROBERT, MACROBIE, ROBERST, and ROBSON.

**Rollo**    John Rollo received the lands of Duncrub in 1380. Robert, the fourth baron, supported James Francis, the Old Pretender, in 1715 but was forced to surrender.

**Rose**    The Roses of Kilravock were in Nairn during the reign of King David I. Hugh Rose built Kilravock Castle in 1460. Prince Charles Edward Stuart stayed at this castle before the Battle of Culloden in 1745.

**Ross**    This family claims to be of Norman descent and is possibly descended from Gilleon na h-airde. One of his descendants was Fearcher MacinTagart, who helped put down a rebellion for the

Crown in 1215. The Ross family who held lands in Ayrshire and Renfrewshire in the twelfth century and may be descended from Godfrey de Ros from Yorkshire. Variants are VASS and WASS.

**Russell**   This family surname is connected to the French name Rosel. The Russells of Aden in Aberdeenshire trace their ancestry to an English baron who came with Edward III of England and who, after the siege of Berwick, decided to stay in Scotland.

**Rutherford**   This once rich and powerful Border family took their name from the lands of Rutherford in Roxburghshire. This name appears in old documents of William the Lion and Alexander II. Daniel Rutherford, born in Edinburgh in 1749, discovered nitrogen.

**Ruthven**   This family traces its ancestry to Swan, son of Thor, son of Swein, who held lands in Perthshire and Clydesdale. Thor took the name de Ruthven. One of the Scottish lords involved in the murder of David Rizzio, secretary to Mary, Queen of Scots, was Patrick Ruthven. In what is known as the Ruthven Raid, his son, the first earl of Gowrie, kidnapped the young king and held him for ten months. The king escaped and Gowrie was executed in 1584. Because of the later Gowrie Conspiracy, the name was proscribed for forty years and not reinstated until 1641.

**Schaw**   This Lowland surname is recorded in the thirteenth century. The northern branch of this clan is descended from Shaw, son of Gilchrist, grandson of the sixth chief of Clan Mackintosh. The other branch is descended from Adam, the second son of Rothiemurchus. A variant is SHAW.

**Scott**   A Border clan, this family traces its ancestry to Uchtredus filius Scoti, who lived in the twelfth century. His two sons, Richard and Michael, were the heads of two branches of this family. They were linked by marriage to the duke of Monmouth and the powerful Douglas dukes of Queensberry. The family of Sir Walter Scott, the writer, was connected with Hugh Scott of Polwarth. The Scotts were a powerful Border clan during the sixteenth century, able to raise 600 warriors for a battle.

**Scrimgeour**   The first mention of this surname is in thirteenth-century documents of Fife. Two documents of 1298 grant to Schyrmeschur, son of Colin, son of Carun, the honor of carrying the king's banner in war, and made him constable of the Castle of Dundee.

**Sempill**    This family came from Renfrewshire and traces its ancestry to Robert de Semple, who lived around 1280. They were hereditary sheriffs of Renfrew.

**Seton**    William the Lion gave land charters to Philip de Seton in 1169, and Robert Bruce gave more lands to Alexander Seton in 1321. This family played an important role in Scottish affairs and built several splendid houses, including Seton Castle, where Mary, Queen of Scots, went to live after Rizzio's murder.

**Sinclair**    The founder of this clan was William Saint Clair, the son of Robert de Saint Clare of Normandy. Records show that a Henry de Sancto Claro supported Robert Bruce and signed a letter to the pope in 1320. Tradition says that William St. Clair built Roslin Castle. The Highland Castle of Mey was a Sinclair stronghold built in 1568.

**Skene**    The ancestor of this clan received the barony of Skene from Malcolm Canmore. The Skenes of Skene died out in the nineteenth century. A variant is SKEEN.

**Somerville**    This surname is derived from a town in Normandy. David I gave lands in Lanarkshire to William de Somerville when he came to Scotland with him. Folklore says that another William de Somerville got the lands for killing a monster that was terrorizing the area.

**Spalding**    This name comes from the town of Spalding in Lincolnshire. The first record of this name in Scottish documents is in the thirteenth century. Peter de Spalding, a burgess, helped the attackers of Berwick in 1318. Robert Bruce gave him lands in Angus.

**Spens**    Family tradition says that this family is descended from Duncan, the fourth earl of Fife. A Patrick de Spens had lands in Berwickshire in the fifteenth century, and John de Spensa of Perth had land in Menteith.

**Stewart**    The Royal House of Stewart has a family tradition that they are descended from Banquo, thane of Lochaber. However, the family has been traced to Alan, Seneschal of Dol, a Celtic noble, and are essentially a Lowland family. His third son, Walter Fitz Alan, was High Steward of Scotland under David I. Walter's grandson, also named Walter, adopted the title Steward as a surname. Bruce's grandson, Robert Stewart, was the first of the Royal House of Stewart. This family was very prolific, with many legitimate and illegitimate offspring. Prince Charles Edward, son of James Francis, the Old Pretender, was known as Bonnie Prince Charlie; he is the best known of the Stuarts. His uprising was crushed at Culloden Moor in 1745, and he died in Rome in 1788. The name Stewart was changed to Stuart after Mary Stuart, Queen of Scots. Variants are STUART, STEUARD, and STEUART.

Stirling   This surname first appears in records of the twelfth century. John Stirling of Moray swore fealty in 1291, and the Stirlings of Keir were established there in the twelfth century.

Sutherland   This name is derived from the place name Sutherland, which the Norsemen of Caithness and Orkney called Southland. The family traces its lineage to the Celts who retreated before the Norse invaders. Hugh Freskin received the lands of Sutherland from King William the Lion in 1197. The first duke of Sutherland, George Granville Gower, built the town of Golspie. He is blamed for excessive Clearance evictions that drove most of his tenants overseas.

Swinton   This family is possibly of Anglian origin. Hugh of Swinton and his son Duncan received the thanedom of Arbuthnot from Walter Olifard. A Henry de Swyntone of Berwickshire made forced allegiance to Edward I of England in 1296. In the fifteenth century, some of this family went to France, where the name changed to Vincton.

Trotter   This name means "messenger." Trotter of Prentannan was head of the Border clan with this name in Berwickshire. Those associated with Morton Hall in Midlothian date their origin back to the reign of Robert II.

Turnbull   Tradition says this name came from William of Rule, who saved Robert Bruce from a wounded bull. Because of this incident, he became known as Turn-e-bull.

Tweedie   Family tradition says this old clan originated from a water spirit of the river Tweed. This family held their lands of Drumelzier for 300 years until their lands were taken away by Charles I.

Urquhart   This surname comes from the lands of Urquhart on Loch Ness. William Urquhart, who was sheriff of Cromarty, married a daughter of the earl of Ross in the fourteenth century. Their family-seat at Craigston Castle has been held since 1604.

**Wallace** This name means "Strathclyde Briton" and is a native Gaelic name. It was well known in Ayrshire and Renfrewshire in the thirteenth century. The first record of this surname mentions a Richard Wallace (or Wallensis) in the twelfth century. Malcolm Wallace was the father of the patriot William Wallace (1274-1305) who led the revolt against the English. Tradition says that William Wallace took up arms after his wife was murdered.

**Wardlaw** This family is probably of Anglo-Saxon origin, although their name was taken from Wardlaw near Beauly. Henry Wardlaw of the fifteenth century was bishop of St. Andrews and founded the University of St. Andrews.

**Weir** This Norman name came from a place called Vere in France. The first Scottish record with this name mentions a Radulphus de Ver, who was captured at Alnwick with William the Lion. His descendants, the Weirs of Blackwood, only appear in records in 1400. Some of the Macnairs in Cowal anglicized their name to Weir.

**Wemyss** This surname derives from a place name, the lands of Wemyss in Fife. Michael de Methkil, also known as Michael de Wemy, is the first recorded name of this family.

**Wood** This name means "one living near a wood." It is very widespread in Scotland. The most important branches of this family settled in Morayshire and in the Borders near Lanarkshire.

# Wales

The number of surnames in Wales compared to the total population is very small. Some sources believe there are fewer than one hundred authentic Welsh surnames, although the list has been augmented by the Norman and English invasions. Since Wales has few occupations, there are not many surnames based on trade or skills. Because of ancient Wales' lack of any great number of towns, the original Welsh naming system was primarily based on relationship to the father.

**Ace**   This is an English surname, found in the Domesday Book, and did not appear in Wales until 1293. Variants are WACE, ASSE, BADHAM, and BADDAM.

**Adams**   A biblical name, this surname was common in England long before it entered Wales. Adda is the more popular Welsh version of this name. It is found primarily in Pembrokeshire and Castlemartin. Variants are ATHOE, ATHA, BATHA, and BATHOE.

**Adda**   The Welsh version of the surname Adams. The variant Athoe appears in south Pembrokeshire. Both Batha and Bathoe come from the Welsh word *ab,* added to Adda. Other variants are ATHA, BATHA, and BATHOE.

**Ajax**   This is a classical name found only in one part of Cardiganshire and seems to belong to only one family.

**Alban**   Occasionally used during Tudor times, this surname came from the name of the first British Christian martyr. It first appears in Pembrokeshire. The surname slowly spread into Pembrokeshire, south Cardiganshire, Carmarthenshire, and Glamorgan.

**Allen**  This English surname was brought into Britain with the Norman invaders, and comes from the personal name Alan. By 1853, this name was quite common in both England and Wales. During Tudor times, the surname was common in Pembrokeshire.

**Andrew**  The biblical name of a disciple, this surname is not common in Wales, although it is found in southeast Wales and in Powys Fadog. The greatest concentration of this name is found in Montgomeryshire. Variants are BANDRA and BANDREW.

**Anthony**  This surname comes from the Roman name Antonius, and was also the name of an early saint. It is found in south Wales in scattered numbers.

**Anwyl**  This name is derived from the Welsh word *annwyl*, which means "dear, beloved, or favorite child." It is found primarily in north Wales. Variants are ANWELL, ANWILL, and ANNOIL.

**Arthur**  For many centuries this name was considered too holy to use as a first name. It comes from the legendary hero, King Arthur. It became popular both as a personal and surname after Henry VII gave it to his eldest son. The greatest concentration of this surname appears in Glamorgan.

**Ashton**  Chiefly found in Montgomeryshire and north Radnorshire, this surname appears in the early seventeenth century in Trefeglwys. Variants are ASHE, ASTON, and ASH.

**Astley**  This is an English location name that was adopted by the Welsh. In 1574, records show three men with the surname Asteley living in Montgomeryshire.

**Augustus**  Taken from the Latin *augustus*, which means "great" or "magnificent." This surname was never widespread in Wales; only a small number of people living in southwest Wales have it.

**Austin**  This English surname, which was derived from the Middle English name Augustine, made its way into Powys and southeast Wales in the fifteenth century. Records show that an Austen ap David lived in Montgomeryshire in 1574. This surname is primarily found along the coast of south Wales from Carmarthen to Chepstow.

**Awbrey**  The Welsh adaptation of the Norman surname de Alberico that arrived in Wales shortly after the Conquest. Documents show two prominent families with this surname: the Awbreys of Abercynrig, and those of Ynyscedwin. This surname is concentrated in Glamorgan and south Wales. Variants are AUBREY and OBRAY.

**Bach** This surname means "small" or "little." It is a variation of the surname BAUGH.

**Bamford** A place name in Derbyshire and Lancashire that became a surname. It was taken into Wales by John Bamford of Derbyshire, who settled in Llangurig, Montgomeryshire in 1576. Variants are BAMPFORD, BAMFORTH, BUMFORT, BUMFORD, BOUNDFORD, BAMFORD, and BUMPFORD.

**Barry** This name comes from *ap Harry* and means "son of Harry."

**Baskerville** This surname arrived in Britain during the Conquest with Normans from Boscherville. It has a long history of use on the border between England and Wales. Records show a family of Baskervilles living in Aberedw, Radnorshire. It is also found in a few families in Glamorgan. A variant is BASKETFIELD.

**Bateman** Used first as a personal name, it was widely used as a surname in Pembrokeshire. It is derived from the name Bartholomew, which was often shortened to Bate or Batte. The addition *man* at the end means "servant of."

**Baugh** Although this surname is derived from *bach,* which means "small" or "little," it is rare in Wales and more frequent across the border into England. This may be an indication of a Welshman who took a new name when he moved into English territory. Variants are BACH, BEACH, and BATCH.

**Bebb** Long associated with Montgomeryshire, this name is listed in records dating back to 1596. Families with this name emigrated to the United States. One of their descendants was William Bebb (1802-1973) who was a governor of Ohio. Variants are BEBBE, BABB, BABBS, BIBB, and BIBBS.

**Bedward** This name means "son of Edward." A variant is BEDWARDS.

**Beedle** Some sources say this surname is derived from the Middle English word *bedele,* meaning "town crier," while others believe it is connected with the place names of Bedwell in Hertfordshire Essex, and Bidwell in Bedfordshire, Northamptonshire, Devon, and Somerset. It is chiefly located in Llanidloes, Montgomeryshire.

**Belth** This is a rare surname and comes from the Welsh place name Buallt or Builth. In early northern Pembrokeshire records the name Buelth is found. By the seventeenth century, the name Bealth is found. Variants are BEALTH, BUELTH, and BELT.

**Benbow**   This English surname, which comes from *bendbow,* meaning "archer," moved into Wales from the midlands. It is believed that all Welsh families with this name can trace their ancestry back to William Bendbowe, who was born about 1510 in Prees, Shropshire. A variant is BENBOUGH.

**Bengough**   This surname is composed of two corrupted words, *pen,* meaning "head" and *goch* or *coch,* meaning "red." A variant is BANGOUGH.

**Benjamin**   A biblical name that was used in Wales as a surname after the Reformation. It was spread throughout Wales, but only in small numbers, except for Glamorgan.

**Bennett**   This family name probably originated with the sixth-century St. Benedict. Although such men as Nicholas Bennett of Derbyshire moved into Wales in 1576, a very few Welsh families were already using this surname when the English arrived. Benedict or Bennet of Penclawdd in Gower, lord of Kilfiggin, was said to be the father of William Bennet of Gower, 1302-1350. The name is most common in Pembrokeshire, west Glamorgan, and along the English border.

**Bevan**   A surname derived from *ap,* meaning "son of," and Evan, a personal name. Most families bearing this name lived in Breconshire, south Radnorshire, and west Glamorgan. Variants are BEVANS and BEVIN.

**Beynon**   A surname derived from the Welsh name ab Eynon, which itself comes from the word *einion,* meaning "anvil." Widely used in Wales by the thirteenth century, it is concentrated in west Glamorgan, west Carmarthenshire, Radnorshire, and Pembrokeshire. Variants are BEINON, BENNION, BAYNHAM, BEYNAM, BUNYAN, BEYNON, and AB ONION, which is a variant of EYNON.

**Bidder**   This family name comes from an English surname, which some sources say means "a bidder," or someone who tells assemblies of people when to stand. Other authors suggest that the name comes from "beggars," or those who made a trade begging. Records of 1292 show an Iduan ap Budur. This surname is primarily found in west Glamorgan. Variants are BYTHER, BYDDER, BYDDIR, and BUDDYR.

**Blackwell**   An English location name, especially prevalent in neighboring Derbyshire, it probably came into Wales with families who can be traced back to that region. These families were strongly connected with lead mining.

**Blayney**　Derived from rare Welsh location names, *blaenau,* meaning "uplands," and *blaen,* meaning "a river source." One source says it may be connected with Castle Blayner in Ireland. A variant is Blaeny, which is found in old records in Montgomeryshire and Radnorshire. By the sixteenth century the name was changed to BLAYNEY.

**Bonner**　Records of the thirteenth century show the personal name ab Ynyr, which comes from the Latin name Honorius. Gradually, this name changed to a surname that rhymes with "honor." It is chiefly found in north Cardiganshire. Variants are BUNNER, BUNNA, BINNER, BUNNELL, and BINNELL.

**Bonsall**　This surname came into Wales with lead miners from Derbyshire. Thomas Bonsall of Bakewell in Derbyshire came to Cardiganshire in the last part of the eighteenth century. It is found in small areas of north Cardiganshire, Pembrokeshire, and Monmouthshire.

**Boulter**　This English surname is derived from a word that means "someone who makes bolts." Families with this name primarily lived in Radnorshire. Variants are BOLT and BOLTER.

**Bound**　Some sources believe this name comes from "bondsman," while others say it is derived from the Old Danish personal name Bundi, which was still being used after the Norman Conquest. This surname is primarily found in Llangurig and Llandinam in Montgomeryshire and in Radnorshire. Variants are BOND, BOUNDS, and BOWND.

**Bowdler**　This surname originated with an old Shropshire family and is primarily found in middle Wales along the border.

**Bowen**　Derived from ab Owen or Owain, meaning "son of Owen." This surname is spread throughout Wales but is absent from Anglesey in Caernarfonshire.

**Bown**　Often a variant of Bowen, although some sources list it as derived from Bohun or Boon.

**Brace**　Derived from the Welsh word *bras,* meaning "fat." In 1670 there were three distinct families having this surname in Narberth.

**Breese**　Some sources believe this surname is derived from the name ap Rhys or Rees. However, others list it as coming from Norfolk and Yorkshire in England, saying it is derived from the Old

English word *breosa*, meaning "gadfly." This surname is primarily found in Montgomeryshire. Variants are BRYSTE, BRYSE, and BREEZE (pronounced brees).

**Brigstocke**  An English location name in Northamptonshire, this surname entered Wales through marriage. A John Brigstocke of Surrey married the daughter of Morris Bowen of Llechdwnni in 1626. Variants are BRIGSTOCK, BRICKSTOCK, BRIGSTOCKE, and BRIDGESTOCK.

**Brooks**  Derived from an English surname meaning "one who lives at the brook," this name is found primarily along the English border. Variants are BROOK and BROOKE.

**Brown**  A very common surname in both England and Wales in 1853. It is derived from an Old English word *brun*, which means "brown hair or skin." Records of the late thirteenth century list families with the names Bron, Broun, Brown, and Brun.

**Bufton**  Derived from an Old English word meaning "upon the hill," there are places with this name in Cornwall, Leicestershire, and Hertfordshire.

**Bulkeley**  A powerful family of north Wales, its ancestry can be traced back to northeast Cheshire. It was established in Anglesey and Conwy before 1450.

**Button**  This surname is derived from either "one who makes buttons," or a nickname for someone who had a wart or growth. Button Gwinnett signed the American Declaration of Independence.

**Bythell**  A variant of the name Ithell, which means "son of Ithell."

**Caddock**  This Welsh name comes from the personal name Cadog. There was a Saint Cadog (more popularly known as Caedfael) who lived in the fifth century. A variant is CADDICK.

**Cadogan**  The modern spelling of this surname is derived from the old Welsh name Cadwgan. Some of these families may have had Irish roots. Variants are CARDUGGAN, CARDIGAN, GUDWGAN, DUGGAN, and KDUGGAN.

**Cadwalader**  This surname is derived from the personal name Cadwaladr, which itself is derived from *cad*, meaning "leader," and *gadwaldr*, meaning "battle." It is mostly found in north Wales, with a few families in Radnorshire, Merionethshire, and Caernarfonshire. Variants are COEDWALLIDER, CADWALADR, and WALLITER.

**Cantington**  This surname began as an English location name and appeared primarily in Pembrokeshire.

**Canton**  This name is first recorded in Cemais, where it arrived with the Anglo-Norman invaders. Descendants with this name are related to the Coedcanlas family of 1670. Variants of this surname are CAUNTON and CAENTWN.

**Cardiff**  A Welsh place name that has become a surname.

**Cardigan**  A Welsh place name that has become a surname. It means "one from Cardiganshire."

**Carew**  A Welsh place name that has become a surname.

**Charles**  This surname came from the Latin name Carolus or perhaps the Old English word *ceorl,* meaning "man." Although this name came into England with the Norman invaders, it did not become popular until the Stewart kings took power. However, the name appears in Welsh records in small numbers in the fifteenth century.

**Christmas**  This surname was originally a personal male name given to a boy born on or near Christmas Day. It became a surname late in Wales as shown by old records.

**Clayton**  This name means "great." There are several place names in English counties that were probably brought into Wales with English settlers. It was popular in Llandinam in the 1590s, and is most frequent in Montgomeryshire. Variants of this surname are CLEATON (pronounced CLEE-ton) and CLETTON.

**Clement**  This name was a popular first name in England in the twelfth century, but shows up as an English surname in the twelfth and thirteenth centuries. By the fifteenth century, Clement is used as a surname in certain parts of Wales. It is primarily found in west Glamorgan and eastern Carmarthenshire.

**Clocker**  This Cornish surname came into Wales with a lead mining family just prior to 1800. It is found only in north Cardiganshire and south Pembrokeshire.

**Clougher**  Although pronounced similarly to Clocker, this surname likely came into Wales with a family of stationers from Ireland where it is a place name.

**Cole**  Some sources say this surname is derived from the Old English *col,* meaning "coal," while others believe it is a diminutive of Nicholas. It arrived in the border counties from England with the Cole family who came into Cemais with the Martins. The family eventually divided into three branches with different names: Cole, Younge, and Mathias. The name is concentrated in Pembrokeshire.

**Connah**    This surname comes from the Welsh family names Cwna and Cwnws. A variant spelling is CUNNAH.

**Conway**    Spelled Conwy in Wales, this name may have come from Ireland, where it means "wolf" or "hound of the plain."

**Coslett**    This surname arrived in Wales in about 1568 with a man named Corslett. A smith skilled in working with osmond iron (a soft iron), he worked for the Mineral and Battery Company, who had a license from the queen to make iron wire. Records show that many men with the surname Coslett worked in the metal trade from the late 1700s into the early 1900s. The name is found primarily in Gwent and Glamorgan. A variant is COSSLETT.

**Craddock**    This surname is derived from the Welsh personal name Caradog, which is the same as the Latin version of the name Caractacus, which in turn comes from the British name Caratacus. Mostly a surname in the English border counties, it appears only once in fifteenth-century records.

**Crowther**    This surname comes from the Welsh word *crythor*, meaning "a player of the *crwth* (an early fiddle)." The same word and meaning appeared in Middle English as *crouthe* or *croude*. The name is concentrated to Radnorshire.

**Crunn**    This name is derived from the Welsh word *cron*, meaning "round," but was at first added to a personal name for description. It began appearing as a Welsh surname in the 1600s. The name was confined to Pembrokeshire.

**Cunnick**    A variant spelling of the Welsh surname Cwnic and the personal name Cynog, it was the name of a saint in the sixth century. It is found almost exclusively in Pembrokeshire and Carmarthenshire along the border. Variants are CONNICK and CWNIC.

**Daniel**    Both a biblical name and a form of the Welsh name Deiniol, the name of a sixth-century saint. It was probably adopted under the English spelling in the post-Reformation period. This name is found throughout Wales, but only in small numbers. A variant is DANIELS.

**David**    A biblical name that was adopted by early Welsh Christians. It is popular because the patron saint of Wales is named Dewi or David. The Latin version is Davidus, which led to the Welsh Dewydd and Dewi. However, Dafydd is more widely used. The use of this surname is mostly concentrated in Carmarthenshire, south

Cardiganshire, north Pembrokeshire, and the Vale of Galmorgan. Variants are DAVIES, DAI, DEI, DYAS, DYOS, DEW, DAKIN, DAYKYN, DEAKYN, DACKINS, DAVIS, and DYKINS.

**Dawkins**  Derived from the name Dafydd or David. A Thomas Daukyn lived in Castlemartin in 1480. It is usually found in south Wales. Variants of this surname are DAWE, DAWES, DAWSON, and DAUKYN.

**Deere**  This name is derived from the Old English personal name Deora, meaning "dear." The surname has long been used in Glamorgan.

**Devonald**  It is derived from the Welsh surname Dyfnallt. It is primarily found in southwest Wales. Variants are DAVENOLD and DEVENALLT.

**Dodd**  This was originally an English surname derived from the personal names of Dudde, Dodda, and Dudda, which were still widely used during the fourteenth century. Members of this family trace their ancestry back to Cadwgan Dod who settled in Cheshire in the reign of Henry II. This name is most prevalent in Denbighshire.

**Edmunds**  This is an English personal name that comes from the Old English words *ead,* meaning "rich," and *mund,* meaning "protector." It appears in fifteenth-century records only in small numbers in Wales, most of them in Monmouthshire. In Pembrokeshire, the name was changed into Emment. A variant is EDMONDS.

**Edwards**  This surname comes from the Old English personal name, compounded of *ead,* meaning "rich," and *weard,* meaning "ward" or "guardian." Because this name was used by both kings and saints, it remained popular with the people after the Norman Conquest. The Welsh personal name Iorwerth is an equivalent of Edward, thus helping its acceptance by the Welsh people. By the fifteenth century this surname appears frequently in records. This surname is found throughout Wales. Variants are EMMENT, KEDWARD, KEDWARDS, and EMONT.

**Elias**  A biblical name, this surname came into Wales after the Reformation. It is found primarily in Cardiganshire and Glamorgan. A variant is ELISHA.

**Ellis**  This name is derived from the Welsh personal name Elisedd, which is found frequently in old records. In time the final *dd* was dropped, producing Elise, Elisa, and Elisha. The name is mostly found in north Wales. Other variants are ELLICE, ELIS, BELLIS, BAYLISS, ELIZA, ELLISA, and HELIS.

**Emanuel**   This biblical name may have entered Wales from Cornwall where it is listed in fifteenth- and sixteenth-century records. The largest concentration of this name is in Montgomeryshire. A variant is MANUEL.

**Ephraim**   This biblical name was not popular with the Puritans and came into use primarily during the eighteenth and nineteenth centuries. Although records list one family with this name in Hayscastle, Pembrokeshire in 1851, it is confined to Merionethshire.

**Esau**   This biblical name, which means "hairy," was not popular in Wales. It is found only along the Cardiganshire-Carmarthenshire-Pembrokeshire border. A variant is ESAY.

**Evans**   Derived from the Welsh name Ieuan or John, this name originated when the "u" was changed to a "v." This surname is most frequent in south Cardiganshire. Variants are IEFAN, IFAN, EVAN, EVANCE, BEVAN, JEAVANS, JEVONS, JEAVINCE, and HEAVENS.

**Eynon**   This surname has evolved from the Welsh name Einion or Einon, which means "anvil." Before the fifteenth century it was one of the most common personal names in Wales. It is found primarily in south and southwest Wales. Variants are BEYNON, ONIONS, ENIAN, EINON, and INIONS.

**Faithfull**   An English surname and a popular first name with the Puritans, this name was used very rarely, and then only in south Wales.

**Felix**   Derived from the Latin name which means "lucky," it was also a saint's name. It was particularly found in Cardiganshire and areas of east Glamorgan in the eighteenth century.

**Fenna**   This surname may have come from the Welsh name *Fenn* meaning "a person who lives in a marshy area." It is primarily found along the border of northeast Wales. Variants are FENNER, PHENNA, FENNAH, and PHENNAH.

**Folland**   This is the Welsh version of the name Valentine and is basically found in Pembrokeshire. Variants are FOLANT and VALLANT.

**Foulkes**   This English personal name, which comes from the German *folc*, meaning "folk," was introduced into Wales by the Normans. In Wales this name is often spelled FFOULKES. This family name is primarily found in Denbighshire and Flintshire. Variants are FFOWKES, FUGE, and VOLK.

**Francis**  Although this name was introduced into England in the early sixteenth century, it was already known in Wales in the fifteenth century. Variants are FRENCHMAN and FFRANCH. Some registers in Glamorgan in the seventeenth century list the name as PHRANCIS.

**Gabriel**  This biblical name was rarely used as either a personal or surname and was primarily only found in north and south Wales.

**Gadarn**  Hu Gadarn was the name of a forest deity worshipped by the Welsh druids. He is very similar to the Celtic god Cernunnos.

**Games**  This rare surname was derived from the Welsh word *gam* or *cam,* which means "crooked" or "bent." It was primarily added to personal names for description. This surname is almost totally confined to east Breconshire and a very small area of Pembrokeshire.

**George**  This name in its personal form was introduced into England by the Crusaders and did not become popular until the Hanoverian kings. It does not appear as a surname in Welsh records until the early eighteenth century, although it does appear as a personal name in records of the fifteenth century. It is found throughout Wales.

**Gethin**  This family name is derived from the Welsh word *cethin,* meaning "ugly" or "hideous." A variant shown in old records is KETHIN.

**Gibbs**  This English surname came from a diminutive of the name Gilbert. Records of fifteenth-century Wales list Gibbon as a personal name in small numbers. The variant Gibby may be derived from the Welsh personal name Cybi. The surname Gibbs is almost entirely confined to the coastal areas of south Wales. Variants are GIBB, GIBBON, GIBBONS, GIBBY, and GIBBAH.

**Gittins**  This surname comes from the nickname for Gruffydd (Griffiths). These surnames are found along the northern border of Radnorshire. Variants are GTUO, GUTYN, GITTAH, GITTOES, and GITTINGS.

**Goodwin**  An English surname derived from the Old English name Godwine, meaning "good friend." It was popular as a personal name before the Norman Conquest as it was the name of the father of King Harold. The surname is confined to the Welsh border counties. Variants are GOODWYN and GOODIN.

**Gough**  This surname is derived from the Welsh word *goch* or *coch,* meaning "red," thus meaning "one with red hair or a red complexion." Found only in small numbers and then in Montgomeryshire and Monmouthshire. Variants are GOGH, GOCH, GOFF, GOUDGE, GOODGE, and GOOCH.

**Gravenor** This name comes from the Old French for "great hunter." The first English record of this name was Gilbert le Grosvenor, a kinsman of William I. The name probably entered Wales from Cheshire where it was a family name of the dukes of Westminster. It is primarily found in Radnorshire. A variant is GROSVENOR.

**Griffiths** A surname that comes from the Old Welsh name Grippiud, which later became Gruffudd. In modern Welsh it is Gruffydd. History shows it was frequently the name of Welsh princes and leaders. It was a common name in north Wales in the fifteenth century. In many old documents the name is commonly abbreviated to Gr'. It is found throughout Wales, but is particularly concentrated on the Llyn peninsula and in north Pembrokeshire. Variants are GRIFFITH, GRIFFIN, GRIFFIES, GRIFFIS, and GUTO.

**Gronow** This is a form of the Welsh personal name Goronwy, which appears in fifteenth-century records. Along the border with England, however, variants are GRONO, GRONNAH, GRUNNA, GRUNNAH, GREENAWAY, GREEN, GREENHOW, and GREENO. This surname is found only in south Wales.

**Gunter** Based on a German personal name that means "battle-army," this name entered Wales with Peter Gunter, who was a follower of Bernard de Neufmarche in the conquest of Brycheiniog; he named his early Welsh family home Tregunter. This name is most common in Breconshire and Monmouthshire.

**Guy** This name is derived from the Old English word for "guide." This surname never spread in Wales beyond west Glamorgan.

**Gwalchmai** This early personal name comes from the Welsh words *gwalch*, meaning "hawk," and *mai*, meaning "field." It is often translated as "hawk of May." Gwalchmai fab Gwyar was a character in the Arthurian sagas, and Gwalchmai ap Meyler was a twelfth-century poet. By the Middle Ages, it had changed from a personal name into a surname, although rare. It is also an Anglesey place name. This name is local to Montgomeryshire.

**Gwilt** Derived from the word *gwillt*, meaning "wild," this surname was most common along the border with England. A John Gwilt of Cardiganshire gave his name to a place, Banc Sion Cwilt (Quilt). This name is found primarily in Montgomeryshire. Variants are QUILT and GUILT.

**Gwynne** This name is derived from the Welsh word *gwyn*, meaning "white" or "fair hair" or "fair complexion," and was first used as a personal name. It is primarily found in south Wales. Variants are GWYN, GWYNN, GWINNETT, GWYNETT, GWYYNS, GWYNNE, WYN, WYNN, and WYNNE.

**Gwyther**    This name comes from the Welsh name Gwythur, which itself is derived from the Latin word *victor*. This name is primarily found in Pembroke, although occasionally in south Carmarthenshire and southwest Wales. Variants are GUYTHER, WITHER, and WITHERS.

**Haines**    This surname may be derived from either the personal name Einws or the adjective name Hen. It is primarily found in southeast Wales.

**Hall**    This is a common surname in both England and Wales. Originally it meant "one who works at or lives in a hall." It is found in small numbers in south Wales.

**Hamer**    This surname comes from a place name in Lancaster and has been a surname in that area since before the 1700s. This surname is mostly found in Montgomeryshire and Radnorshire.

**Harries**    This name may derive from the Welsh name Harri, which was an early pronunciation of the personal name Henry. It means "son of Harry or Henry." This surname is largely confined to Pembrokeshire, Carmarthenshire, and Monmouthshire. Variants are HARRIS and HENRY.

**Harry**    Derived from the Welsh name Harri, this was first popular as a personal name because of Norman and English kings. By the fifteenth century, Harri or Henry was common in Wales. Found in Carmarthenshire, Glamorgan, and east Monmouthshire. Variants are HENRY, HARRHY, PARRY, PENRY, PENDRY, and HENDRY.

**Hatfield**    Both an English place name and a surname, it appeared in Montgomeryshire about 1576. It is primarily found in north Radnorshire. Variants are HATFELD and HATTEFELD.

**Havard**    This surname entered Wales when Bernard de Neufmarche, the Norman conqueror, gave the manor of Pontwilyn to Sir Walter Havard, or as some historians record his name, Walter Havre de Grace. Descendants of a Breconshire family with this name were the Havards of Glamorgan. This name has two distinct and separate clusters in southwest and southeast Wales.

**Heilyn**    A surname of Welsh origin, it only appears rarely in the fifteenth century. Variations are HEYLYN and PALIN.

**Herbert** This surname includes the earls of Pembroke and the earls of Powis, which have offshoots in many parts of Wales. One Welsh book of genealogies has fifty-nine pages of different families with this name. This family name is most prominent in Cardiganshire and Radnorshire.

**Hier** This name is derived from the Welsh *hir,* meaning "tall" or "long." A variant is Hire, which is listed in records of 1613. It is primarily found in Pembrokeshire and parts of Monmouthshire. Variants are HYER and HIRE.

**Hooson** Mainly found in Flintshire, this surname is a variant of the English Hughson.

**Hopkins** Primarily a name of Glamorgan, this English surname was widely adopted in Wales. It is derived from the diminutive Hob (Robert) and the ending *kin.* It was a common name when listed in Glamorgan records of the seventeenth century. Although this surname appears infrequently in other parts of Wales, it is primarily found in Glamorgan and the Usk area of Monmouthshire. Variants are HOPKIN, POPKIN, and POPKINS.

**Hoskin** This surname is of English origin. In the fifteenth century, the variant Hoesgyn is listed in Caernarfonshire and Anglesey. In 1481, Reece ap Hoskin is listed as portreeve of Manordeifi. The name is basically found in east Denbighshire and west Glamorgan. In Monmouthshire variants are HOISKIN, OISKINS, HODGE, HOSKINS, HODGKIN, HOSKYN, and POISKIN.

**Howard** A surname that is derived from an Old Norse name. Variants are HAWARD and HERWARD.

**Howe** This surname is derived from the English name Hugh, and includes variants of How and Howes. Mostly confined to Monmouthshire and Glamorgan.

**Howells** This name comes from the Welsh personal name Hywel and has been anglicized into Howell. It is sometimes pronounced as rhyming with towel; other times it is hew-el, as in Hugh. This surname is found throughout Wales. Variants are HOWELL, HYWEL, HOWES, HOWEL, HOEL, HOELL, HOLL, HOLE, and POWELL.

**Hughes** The Germanic name of Hugh came into England with the Norman Conquest. The greatest number of families having this surname live in northern Wales, especially in Anglesey. Variants are HUWS, and in some parts of Wales HULLIN.

**Hullin**　This name is derived from Hugh and appears to be a variant of Hughes. It was a common sixteenth-century name in parts of Glamorgan. Other variants are HOELL, HULLYN, and AP HULLIN.

**Humphreys**　This surname is not found in early Wales and only shows up in small numbers in the fifteenth century. It is primarily found in Merionethshire, Montgomeryshire, north Cardiganshire, and the Llyn peninsula. Variants are PUMPHREY, BUMFREY, BUMPHREY, and WMFFRE.

**Husband**　This name comes from the English word for "householder" or "husbandman." It is widespread in Pembrokeshire with the first records of this name in 1532. It is also found in west Carmarthenshire.

**Hussey**　This family name is probably derived from the Middle English word *huswif,* meaning "mistress of a household." It is primarily found in Glamorgan and Monmouthshire. Variants are HUSSEYS, HUZZEY, and HUZZY.

**Isaac**　The most prominent biblical name in Wales, it came into the country with the Reformation. It is found over most of south Wales.

**Ithell**　In Old Welsh, the personal name was Iudhael. It is found in several areas of Wales, but only in small numbers. Variants are BEETHEL, EATHELL, ETHELL, BETHELL, ITHAEL, ITHEL, BITHELL, BYTHELL, and ABETHELL.

**Jacob**　A biblical personal name that came to Wales with the Reformation. It may come from the Latin name Jacobus. It is found over a large part of southwest Wales. A variant is JACOBS.

**James**　A non-Welsh personal name, it appeared in the twelfth century. It was the name of several saints and kings. This name is found throughout Wales.

**Jarman**　This surname is derived from the Latin *germanus,* meaning "kinsman." It is very prominent on the border between Montgomeryshire and Radnorshire. Variants are JERMIN, JERMYN, and JERMYNE.

**Jasper**　Derived from the English name Caspar. By the fifteenth century in northwest Wales, this name is listed, but in small numbers. This name is almost totally confined to southeast Wales.

**Jeffreys**　Derived from the personal name Geoffrey, this name was brought to Wales by the Normans. Thomas Jefferson's family had connections with seventeenth-century Wales. The name is found extensively throughout Wales, but particularly in Denbighshire and Flintshire. Variants are GREGORY and JEFFERSON.

**Jehu**   Almost totally found in south and southwest Wales, this name is a nickname for John. Variants are JENKINS and JANKIN.

**Jervis**   This surname is derived from Gervaise, a personal name introduced by the Normans. It is mostly found in Montgomeryshire and Flintshire. A variant is JARVIS.

**Job**   This biblical name became widespread from the medieval passion plays or dramas in England. It first came into Wales as a personal name with the Reformation and later was used as a surname. It is found in small numbers throughout Wales.

**John**   This is a biblical name that first came to Wales as the Latin Johannes and became the Welsh Ieuan. The name John was used after the Normans arrived. Since the letter "j" is absent in the Welsh alphabet, the name was most frequently written as Sion or Shone. The use of this surname is mostly concentrated in Carmarthenshire, south Cardiganshire, north Pembrokeshire, and the Vale of Galmorgan. Variants are JONES (son of John), SHONE, and EVANS.

**Jones**   This is one of the most common surnames in Wales, especially in the north. It may be derived from both John and James. Jones literally means "son of John" in Welsh. A variant is JONE.

**Joseph**   A biblical name that was unknown in Wales until the Reformation. It is found all across south Wales with the exception of Pembrokeshire.

**Kendrick**   This surname comes from the popular medieval Welsh personal name Cynwrig. In the fifteenth century it was found only in north Wales. It is primarily found along the border with England.

**Kinsey**   This English surname is derived from the Old English words *cyn* and *sige,* which mean "royal victory." It is mostly found in Montgomeryshire and Breconshire.

**Kneath**   This surname is pronounced as rhyming with "great." It comes from the Welsh personal name Cynaethwy, which led to the variants Cnaitho, Cneitho, and Cnaith. It changed to Kneath under the English influence. It is found only in a small part of west Glamorgan.

**Knethell**   This surname comes from the Welsh personal name Cynddelw. It is sprinkled through many sections of Wales.

**Kyffin**   This name is derived from the Welsh word *cyffin* (pronounced cuffin), which means "border" or "boundary." It is primarily found in northeast Wales. Variants are CUFFIN, KEFFIN, KEPHIN, KIFFIN, CAFFYN, and COFFIN.

**Landeg**    This name is a mutation of the word *glandeg* which means "handsome," and is found in limited areas in west Glamorgan and east Carmarthenshire.

**Laugharne**    This surname is derived from a Welsh place name and was the anglicized version of Talacharn, Carmarthenshire. It is pronounced Larne. Records show Richard de Thallazharne in the late thirteenth century. Variants are DE LACHARN, DE TALACHARN, and DE LAGHAM. By the fourteenth century it became Lacharn and Lagharn. Still later the family is listed as Laugharne of St. Bride's. It is more prominent in Pembrokeshire and west Glamorgan than anywhere else in Wales.

**Lewis**    This surname came from an English approximation of Llewellyn. However, the English already had the personal name derived from the French Louis and the German Ludwig. In the fifteenth century, the Welsh spelling was Lewys. Although this name is found concentrated in certain small areas, it is more prominent in south and middle Wales.

**Leyshon**    This is derived from the Welsh personal name Lleision. It is found in parts of Breconshire, Monmouthshire, Glamorgan, and Carmarthenshire. A variant is LEY.

**Llewelyn**    This is a very ancient Welsh personal name and was quite popular as the name of princes in medieval times. By the fifteenth century it was found in all parts of Wales. Some sources believe it is derived from the British names Lugobelinus and Cunobelinus, while others say it comes from the Welsh word *llew,* meaning "lion." The nickname Llelo is found in fifteenth-century documents. Found only in south Wales, it is absent in the north. Variants are LEWELIN, LEWHELLIN, LLEWELIN, LLEWELLIN, LLEWELLING, LLEWELLYN, LLEWELYN, LLEWHELING, LLEWHELLIN, LLEWHELLING, WHELLIN WELLING, WELLINS, HILLIN, HILLING, LELLO, LELLOW, FLELLOS, and FLELLO.

**Lloyd**    This surname is derived from the Welsh *llwyd,* meaning "gray-brown." This was used as surname very early in Wales and only occasionally as a personal name. It is found primarily in Monmouthshire. Variants are LOYD, LLWYD, FLOYD, and FLOOD.

**Llywarch**   A Welsh surname that is found in early records. In the fifteenth century it is listed in only one place: Deheubarth. It is found in very small numbers in Montgomeryshire.

**Lodwick**   This name comes from the Latin name Ludovicus. It is largely confined to Cardiganshire and found only occasionally in Carmarthenshire.

**Lougher**   This name comes from a Welsh place name, such as the river Llwchwr. It is found only in Glamorgan. Variants are LOUGHER and LOCKER.

**Lucas**   This is a biblical name that is quite common in England. In the second half of the fifteenth century, records show a Lucas family of Gower. It is mostly found in Monmouthshire and Glamorgan. Variants are LUKE and LICAS.

**Lumley**   This comes from an English place name in county Durham. An English family there traces its ancestry to Ligulf of Northumberland at the time of the Conquest. Robert de Lumeleye is the first record of this name in the twelfth century. A branch of this family moved into Wales in the sixteenth century and intermarried with the family of Williams of Denbigh and the Salusbery family. It is mostly found in Montgomeryshire, Merionethshire, and Cardiganshire.

**Mabe**   Derived from the Welsh word *mab,* meaning "son," it was first used as a personal name before becoming a surname. It is also a place name.

**Maddocks**   This surname is derived from the Welsh personal name Madog, which was the name of princes and leaders. It is more common in north Wales than in the south. Variants are MADOCK, MADDOCK, MADDY, and MADDOX.

**Mason**   A widespread English surname that entered Wales with immigrant families. It is found in small areas throughout Wales, with the greatest number in Cardiganshire. A variant is MASSON.

**Matthews**   Derived from the biblical name Matthew, this name was popular in medieval Wales. It is found in records of the fifteenth century in south Wales. It is found in small numbers throughout Wales, especially in Glamorgan. Variants are MATHEW, MATHEWS, MATTHEW, and MATHIAS.

**Maybery**   This name entered Wales with a Worcestershire family who worked in the South Wales iron industry. This surname occurs in small numbers in Monmouthshire and the valleys of Glamorgan. A variant is MAYBERRY.

**Mendus**    Folklore says that this name came into Wales at the time of the Spanish Armada. The Spanish names Mendes and Mendoza are very similar. This name is primarily found along the Pembrokeshire-Carmarthenshire border. Variants are MENS, MEANDS, MENDAY, MEANDS, MENDE, MENDS, and MEANS.

**Meredith**    The Welsh personal name Maredudd is very ancient. In Welsh, *udd* means "lord," with the emphasis in pronunciation of Maredudd on the middle syllable. The surname Meredith is mainly found in south Radnorshire, while the variant Beddow is along the Glamorgan-Carmarthenshire border. Variants are BEDO, PREDITH, and PREDDY.

**Meyler**    The Welsh personal name was Meilyr, as in Meilyr Brydydd, a medieval poet who lived from 1100-1137. As a surname, this name appeared in only small numbers in the border areas. It is primarily found in Pembrokeshire and scattered throughout southeast Wales.

**Meyrick**    This surname is derived from the Welsh personal name Meurig, which has been anglicized as Maurice and Morris. The Meyrick family of Anglesey was prominent in Tudor times. This name is centered in southeast Wales, with a few in Pembrokeshire and Glamorgan.

**Michael**    This biblical name has been associated with Welsh churches since the Norman times. In the fifteenth century, this rare surname appears in small numbers in northeast and southwest Wales. It is found in small numbers in Anglesey, Radnorshire, Cardiganshire, and Caernarfonshire. Variants are MEJANGEL, MIHANGEL, and FIHANGEL.

**Miles**    This Germanic name came into England with the Norman invaders and enjoyed some popularity during the Middle Ages. It appears in the records of southeast Wales in the fifteenth century. A variant is MILO.

**Mills**    This is a place name common in southern England which means "one who works or lives by a mill." Welsh records of the early sixteenth century show families with this surname living in Montgomeryshire. Variants are MILL, MILLE, and MYLLE.

**Morgan**    This Welsh surname has been popular for many centuries. By the fifteenth century this name appears in all parts of Wales.

Folklore says it was the original name of the heretic Pelagius. The Welsh Morgans of Monmouthshire managed to regain their prominence after the Norman Conquest. It is found in south and middle Wales.

**Morris** This surname is derived from the Welsh personal name Meurig and the Latin name Mauricius. This spelling is from England, and is a more popular spelling than Maurice in Wales. It is found throughout Wales, but is more frequent in the north. Variants are MORUS, MAURICE, and MORYS.

**Morse** This is a variant spelling of the surname Morris. This name is primarily confined to Pembrokeshire.

**Mortimer** This surname comes from an influential Norman family of this name who lived in Wales in medieval times. The name is plentiful in south Cardiganshire and north Pembrokeshire in the eighteenth century.

**Mostyn** This was a Welsh place name that became a surname. It is mostly found in northeast Wales.

**Nanney** This Welsh place name is an anglicized version of Nannau, the name of the estate of the powerful Merioneth family, who adopted it as a surname in the sixteenth century. It is found only in Merionethshire and Caernarfonshire.

**Narberth** This Welsh place name comes from Narberth (Welsh Arberth) in Pembrokeshire. This surname is confined to south Pembrokeshire and west Carmarthenshire. A variant is NARBETT.

**Nash** This surname is both an English and Welsh place name, which means "at the ash tree." It was very common in Pembrokeshire in the seventeenth century. This name is primarily found in southwest and southeast Wales.

**Nevett** This surname is derived from the Welsh personal name Ednyfed. A separate English form of this name is derived from the Old English word *cniht,* meaning "knight." The name Ednyfed is also abbreviated to Eden, which has led to the name Bennet in some areas. It is found only in small numbers. Variants are KNEVETT, EDEN, and NEVET.

**Newell** This English surname may have been derived from Nevill, Nowell, or Noel. A family of glovers in Shrewsbury were called either Newell or Newill and were wardens of the Glover Company. This name is primarily centered in Montgomeryshire.

**Nicholas**    This personal name was popular as a saint's name in the English Middle Ages and is related to the name Cole. The name is mostly found in south Wales, particularly in Pembrokeshire. Variants are CULE, CULL, NICOLAS, NICHOL, and NICHOLLS.

**Nock**    Some sources believe this surname came from England, while others say it is from Scotland or Ireland. It means "one who lives by an oak tree." It is widely found in Pembrokeshire. Variants are NOKE and OAKLEY.

**Nuttall**    This surname derives from a place name in either Lancashire or Nottinghamshire and entered Wales with migrating families from those areas. It is almost totally confined to Flintshire.

**Oliver**    This personal name was brought into England by the Norman invaders and may be a form of the name Olaf. In the fifteenth century it appears in Wales as a surname. This name is found throughout the country. Variants are BOLVIER and BOLVER.

**Owen**    This personal name is very old and may come from the Latin Eugenius or Audoenus. It has long been used as the name of princes and leaders. By the fifteenth century it was common throughout Wales. A variant is BOWEN, which comes from ap Owen, meaning "son of Owen." The greatest number of families having this surname live in northern Wales. Another variant is OWENS.

**Parker**    This English surname means "keeper of the deer park." It is found along the English border with Wales and some in south Wales, as in west Glamorgan.

**Parry**    This surname is derived from ap Harry, and means "son of Harry." It is the second most common surname and is found throughout Wales.

**Pask**    This surname came to Wales from England and Cornwall. It comes from the name of Pascall, a ninth century saint and pope. The original name may be derived from the Latin word *pascha,* meaning Easter. It is only found in the southeast corner of Wales. Variants are PASCOE and PAISH.

**Paskin**    A similar name to Pask, this surname is derived from the Old Welsh personal name Paskent or Pascen.

**Peate**    This English surname is derived from the Middle English for "pet" or "darling." It reached Montgomeryshire before the 1600s. From there, it entered Breconshire where it became Pate. A variant spelling is PEAT.

**Peregrine**  This surname may come from either the Latin word *peregrinus,* meaning "pilgrim," or the anglicized Perkin. It is almost totally confined to south Wales.

**Perkins**  This surname comes from the personal names Piers and Peter. It is widely found in south Wales. In medieval times in Pembrokeshire, Perkyn appears as a personal name, then gradually became a surname. A variant is PERKIN.

**Peters**  This personal name became a surname late in Welsh history, with only small numbers shown in records of the fifteenth century. It is found throughout Wales, but only in small numbers.

**Phillips**  Derived from the Greek name Phillippos meaning "lover of horses," this was the name of several early saints. It was quite common in Wales by the late thirteenth century. This surname is found throughout Wales, but is more common in the south and west. Variants are PHELPS, PHILPIN, and FILPIN.

**Picton**  This surname comes from Picton Castle in Monmouthshire, built by William de Picton, a follower of Arnulph de Montgomery. This name is mainly confined to Pembrokeshire and Carmarthenshire.

**Pierce**  This name is derived from the Old French name Piers. In the fifteenth century only small numbers of this name appear in old records. This family name is found primarily in Denbighshire. Variants are PEARCE, PEARSON, PIRS, and PYRS.

**Powell**  This surname is derived from ap Howell, or "son of Howell." It is most common in Breconshire.

**Price**  It comes from ap Rhys or ap Rees, which means "son of Rhys." This surname is found on the border between Wales and the English areas of Herefordshire and south Shropshire, but is most frequent in Breconshire and Radnorshire.

**Pritchard**  This surname is derived from ap Richard, meaning "son of Richard." It is primarily found in Anglesey and Caernarfonshire. Variants are PRICKETT and UPRICHARD.

**Probert**  It is derived from ap Robert, meaning "son of Robert." This surname is found on the border between Wales and the English areas of Herefordshire and south Shropshire, primarily in Radnorshire and Breconshire. Variants are PROBART, ROPPERT, and PROPERT.

**Probyn**  This name is derived from ap Robin, meaning "son of Robin," a diminutive of Robert. It is mainly found in Monmouthshire and east Glamorgan.

**Profit**  This name may come from the Old French word *prophete,* meaning "prophet," a name the Welsh would have heard in the medieval mystery plays. It is entirely confined to Flintshire. Variants are PROPHET and PROPERT.

**Prosser**  This surname is derived from ap Rosser, meaning "son of Rosser." It is found on the border between Wales and the English areas of Herefordshire and south Shropshire, basically in Beconshire, Radnorshire, and Monmouthshire.

**Prothero**  It comes from ap Rhydderch, meaning "son of Rhydderch." This surname is found on the border between Wales and the English areas of Herefordshire and south Shropshire. Variants are ROTHERO and PRYDDERCH.

**Pugh**  This name comes from ap Hugh, meaning "son of Hugh." Mostly concentrated in west Merionethshire. A variant is TUGH.

**Rees**  This surname comes from the Welsh medieval personal name Rhys, which was the name of several princes and leaders. Found in south Wales, this surname is concentrated on the Carmarthenshire-Glamorgan border. Variants are PREECE, CREESE, RHYS, RICE, RESEUS, RHESEUS, and RICEUS.

**Reynolds**  This name is derived from the Germanic personal name Reynold that came in with the Normans. Its Welsh version is Rheinallt. It is found extensively across south Wales. Variants are REYNOLD, RYNALT, RYNALLT, and RHEINALLT.

**Rhydderch**  This ancient Welsh personal name was the name of a sixth-century leader, Rhydderch Hael, which means "liberal." During the Middle Ages it was a very common name in Wales. The small numbers of this surname are almost entirely confined to south Wales. Variants are RUDDZ, RUTHER, ROTHERO, and RUDDOCK.

**Richards**  This surname is derived from the Germanic personal name, which itself comes from *ric,* meaning "power," and *hard,* meaning "strong" or "hardy." It is connected with Prichard and Pritchard. It is found throughout Wales. Variants are CRICHETT and CRICHARD.

**Roberts**  This Germanic personal name came in with the Normans and is derived from *hrod,* meaning "fame," and *berht,* meaning "bright." It is connected with Probert. This surname is found in north Wales, especially in Caernarfonshire, Denbighshire, and Merionethshire. Variants are ROBIN and ROBLIN.

**Roch**   This is a Welsh place name that became a surname. The Anglo-Norman Roch Castle was built on a prominent rock in Pembrokeshire. This name went into Ireland when the Normans invaded that country; the name there is Roche.

**Roderick**   The Welsh personal names connected with this surname were Rhodri and Rhydderch. The name Roderick, however, is of Germanic origin. It is found throughout middle and south Wales.

**Rogers**   This name is derived from the German personal name Roger, which comes from *hrod*, meaning "fame," and *gar*, meaning "spear." It entered England and Wales with the Norman invaders. It is found throughout Wales, but has the greatest numbers on the borders with England. Variants are ROSIER, PRODGER, and ROSSER.

**Rowlands**   This surname comes from the German personal name Roland (*hrod*, meaning "fame," and *land*, meaning "land" ) that was brought in by the Normans. There are traces of the name in fifteenth century Wales. A variant is ROWLAND.

**Salmon**   This post-Reformation name is derived from the personal name Solomon. It is found in small numbers in north Pembrokeshire.

**Salusbury**   This surname comes from an English place name. William Salesbury (1520-1584) translated part of the Bible into Welsh. This name mostly occurs in the north. Variants are SALESBURY, SALBRI, and SALEBIRI.

**Sambrook**   This surname began as an English place name. In the early 18th century it is found in south Cardiganshire and north Pembrokeshire. Later it was occasionally used as a personal name. One document shows a Samrook living in Glamorgan in 1721. Variants are SANDBROOK, SHAMBROOK, and SAMBROTH.

**Samuel**   A biblical name, this surname began as a personal name. Old documents show that Christmas Samuel lived in Carmarthenshire from 1674 until 1764. It is common in Monmouthshire, Glamorgan, and Carmarthenshire. A variant is SAMWELL.

**Savage**   This surname began as a descriptive nickname. A family with this name moved to Montgomeryshire in the sixteenth century. They trace their family line back to the Rock Savage family in Cheshire and tended to use the personal name Rock. This name is found along the border, particularly in Flintshire and Montgomeryshire. A variant is SAYVAGE.

**Sayce**   This name is derived from the Welsh word *sais,* meaning

"English-speaking." It is found in the border country and Pembrokeshire. Variants are SAER, SAISE, SAIES, SAIS, SAYS, SAYSE, and SEYS.

**Sheen**    This surname comes from the Old English word that means "fair" or "handsome," and is also an English place name. It is mainly confined to south Radnorshire.

**Sheldon**    This name came into Wales from Derbyshire in the late eighteenth and early nineteenth centuries. It is found in the lead mining areas of Wales, such as Flintshire, Cardiganshire, Monmouthshire, and Pembrokeshire.

**Smith**    Sources claim that this surname is the most common in both England, Wales, Scotland, and the United States. It was the fifth most common name in Ireland in 1890. It is an occupational name that is found in small to moderate numbers throughout Wales, particularly in Radnorshire, Monmouthshire, and Pembrokeshire.

**Smout**    This name very likely came into Wales from Derbyshire and may be a variant of Smith. The variant SMOUT is often found in Scotland. This surname is primarily located in Montgomeryshire. Variants are SMOTH, SMOOT, and SMUTH.

**Stephens**    This surname comes from the Greek word *stephanos,* which means "wreath," "garland," or "crown." It was used by early popes and brought into England by the Normans. Many Welsh emigrants to the United States changed the spelling to Stevens. It is mostly found in the south and middle Wales. A variant is STEVENS.

**Stradling**    The original Tudor family of this name helped Robert fitz Hamo conquer Glamorgan. They trace their ancestry to John de Estatlinges from Strattligen, Switzerland in the reign of Edward I. This name is confined to east Glamorgan and a little of west Monmouthshire. A variant is ESTATLING.

**Swancott**    This surname is primarily confined to Montgomeryshire. Originally, this was an English place name from Shropshire.

**Tannatt**    A gentry family took this surname in the sixteenth century from the river Tanad or Tannat in Montgomeryshire. It is found in small numbers only in parts of Montgomeryshire and Denbighshire. A variant is TANAT.

**Taylor**    This English occupational name was listed as the fourth commonest surname in England and Wales in 1853. The greatest concentration of this name is in Gower, Monmouthshire, and Glamorgan.

**Teague**   This surname may have two origins: one, the Irish personal name and surname Tegan; and two, derivation from the Welsh word *teg,* meaning "fair" or "beautiful." Variants are TEGAN, DEAGE, DEGG, TEAGE, TECKA, TEGG, and TEGUE.

**Tew**   Found primarily in Pembrokeshire, this surname is derived from the Welsh word *tew* or *dew,* which means "fat."

**Thomas**   This is a biblical name that is derived from the Greek word *didymos,* meaning "twin." In England it was known only as a priest's name until the Norman Conquest. It became very popular after the era of Thomas à Becket. The surname is not listed in Wales until the fifteenth century. This surname is found primarily in south Wales and Monmouthshire.

**Tibbot**   This surname came from the personal name Theobald, originally the French Thibaud. It came into Wales from England. The name is also found in Anglesey. Variants are TIBBETT, TIBBETTS, TIBBITT, and TIBBITTS.

**Timothy**   This biblical name comes from the personal Greek name Thimotheus, which means "honoring God." It was not used in Wales until the post-Reformation era. It is found in only very small numbers in Monmouthshire, Glamorgan, Carmarthenshire, and south Cardiganshire.

**Treharne**   This surname is an anglicized version of the Welsh personal name Trahaearn, which is taken from *tra,* meaning "over" or "excessive," and *haearn,* meaning "iron." This name is found in certain areas of Glamorgan and Carmarthenshire and across south Wales.

**Trevor**   This is an early Welsh place name, usually connected with estates. This name is concentrated in north Wales.

**Trewent**   This surname derived from a Welsh place name is recorded from medieval times into the twentieth century. The name is confined to just one part of Pembrokeshire.

**Trow**   Some sources say this surname is derived from the Old English word for "faithful" or "true," while others insist it began as a Devon place name or from the Old English word *trog,* meaning "trough." Edward Trow manufactured flannel in Montgomeryshire in 1838. This name is particularly concentrated in Montgomeryshire.

**Tucker**   This surname comes from an English occupational name, which means "one who fulls cloth." Therefore, it is interchangeable with the name Fuller. It is found in the southern parts of Wales that were subjected to the greatest English influence.

**Tudor**  This surname is derived from a north Wales personal name. Famous people bearing this name were the Tudor monarchs. Henry VII's grandfather's name was actually Owain ap Meredith ap Tudor, known as Owain Tudor. This name is often confused with Tewdwr, which is derived from a separate first name. The greatest number of families with this name are found in Montgomeryshire. Variants are TUTOR, TIDDER, TEWDWR, and TITHER.

**Turner**  This surname comes from an English occupational name, which means "one who works with a lathe." Variants are TURNOR and TYRNO'R.

**Vaughan**  This surname is derived from the Welsh word *bychan,* which was mutated to *fychan,* meaning "younger." It was a descriptive name used to distinguish father from son. In English, the word *fychan* became *vychan.* Sometimes the old name Fychan or Vychan is used. It is found throughout Wales except in Anglesey and west Caernarfonshire. Variants are FYCHAN, VAIN, VAYNE, VANE, BAUGHAN, and BAWN.

**Voyle**  This name comes from the Welsh word *moel,* which was mutated to *foel,* meaning "bald." Sometimes the older spellings of *Moel* and *Foel* are used as variants. It is primarily confined to Pembrokeshire.

**Walbeoff**  This surname is derived from an Anglo-Norman family who held land in Brycheiniog as followers of Bernard de Neufmarche. The name Waldebeuf is listed in Breconshire from the middle of the twelfth century. It is found only in east Monmouthshire.

**Walters**  This name is derived from the German personal name Walter (from *wald,* meaning "rule," and *heri,* meaning "warrior" ) brought in by the Normans. The Welsh adopted the personal name as Gwallter according to very early records. It occurs in south Wales. Variants are WALLITER, WATERS, WATTARS, and WATT.

**Warlow**  This surname is derived from the Middle English word warloc meaning "warlock" or "wizard." Variants are WARDLOW, WARLACH, and WARLAZ.

**Warren**  This name comes from the German personal name Warin, which in Old French was Guarin or Guerin. It became Gwaren in Wales. It is found in Monmouthshire.

**Watkins** At one time, this was used as a personal name in some parts of Wales. It is a diminutive of the name Walters. In the fifteenth century, it was found everywhere except northeast Wales. This family name is found throughout Wales. Variants are GWATKIN and WATKISS.

**Watts** A diminutive form of the name Walter, this surname is found in both Wales and Scotland. Small numbers of this name are found in south Wales.

**Weal** This is an English place name, which refers to one who lives by the waterwheel. However, the Cornish version is *whel*, which means "mine-working." This surname is confined to Radnorshire. Variants are WHEAL, and WHEELS.

**Weaver** This English occupational name comes from the Old English word *wefan*, meaning "to weave." This surname is found only in the borderlands, especially in Montgomeryshire.

**Whittal** This surname is derived from a place name, such as White Hill or Whitwell. This name is found only in Pembrokeshire and Radnorshire. Variants are WHETTAL and VITTLE.

**Wigley** This name comes from a Derbyshire place name and appeared in Wales as a surname. It is found in very small numbers in various parts of Wales.

**Wild** Derived from the English surname Wilde, this name means "one who lives in wild places." Old documents show a Wilde family in 1292. It is found in very limited areas of Radnorshire, east Glamorgan, and Monmouthshire. A variant is WILDE.

**Wilding** This name comes from the Old English name, which was either a personal name or a nickname. It is confined to Radnorshire and a small part of Montgomeryshire.

**Williams** This surname comes from the German personal name Wilhelm ( a combination of the words "will" and "helmet" ) and was brought in by the Normans. The Welsh adopted it as Guilielm and Gwilym, then it became Gwilliam and Gullam. The name is found throughout Wales. The greatest concentration of this surname is in north Wales, on the Llyn peninsula of Caernarfonshire, and around south Breconshire. A variant is WILSON.

**Wogan** Some sources believe this name came into Wales with migrating Irish families, while others say it is derived from the Welsh Gwgan. It is primarily concentrated in south Pembrokeshire.

**Woosencraft**   This name is derived from a Lancashire place name Wolstencroft, which comes from *Wulfstan* (a personal name) and *croft,* meaning "enclosure." This name is found in small numbers in Radnorshire. A variant is WOOSENCROFT.

**Woosnam**   This surname comes from the Lancashire place name Wolstenholme, which is derived from *Wulfstan* and *holm,* meaning "a dry land in the fen." It first appeared in Montgomeryshire in 1596, and is nearly totally confined to that area now.

**Worthing**   One source says this surname derives from a Shropshire place name, Worthen. Others believe it comes from the Old English personal name Worth meaning "worthy." It is confined to a small area of Radnorshire.

**Wynne**   This name is a mutated version of the Welsh name Gwynne. It is primarily found in north Wales. A variant is WYNN.

**Yorath**   This surname comes from the Welsh personal name Iorwerth, which itself is derived from *ior,* meaning "lord," and *berth,* meaning "handsome." During medieval times it was quite common. It is found only in Monmouthshire. Variants are IORWERTH, YORATH, and YERWARD.

**Young**   This English surname began as a nickname, meaning "junior." It is found in very early records of Pembrokeshire. It is found in pockets throughout Wales, but not in northwest Wales. Variants are YONG, YONGE, and YONGUE.

# Part III
# Celtic Deities

# Major Celtic Gods and Goddesses

All three Celtic countries knew most of the same deities by the same or similar names. However, they did develop some gods and goddesses that were specifically their own. Scotland, because of its close Irish connections, did not develop different gods in their country of origin.

**Aine of Knockaine**  Ireland. Moon goddess and patroness of crops and cattle, she was associated with the Summer Solstice.

**Angus Mac Og**  Ireland. One of the Tuatha De Danann, his name means "young son." His golden harp made irresistible music, while his kisses turned into birds that carried messages of love. His *brugh* (underground fairy palace) was on the banks of the Boyne River. God of youth, love, and beauty. Variants are ANGUS or OENGUS OF THE BRUGH and ANGUS MAC OC.

**Anu**  Ireland. Goddess of plenty and Mother Earth. The greatest of all the Irish goddesses, she was the deity of cattle, health, fertility, prosperity, and comfort.

**Arawn**  Wales. God of the dead and the underworld or Annwn. Until Christian conversion, the Welsh did not look upon the underworld as hell. God of revenge, terror, and the dead.

**Arianrhod**  Wales. Known as Silver Wheel and the High Fruitful Mother, the palace of this sky goddess was called Caer Arianrhod (Aurora Borealis). She was the keeper of the circling Silver Wheel of Stars, a symbol of time and karma. Her ship, the Oar Wheel, carried dead warriors to Emania (Moon-land). Deity of beauty, fertility, and reincarnation.

**Badb**    Ireland. The sister of Macha, the Morrigan, and Anu, the name of this goddess translates as "boiling," "battle raven," and "scald-crow." In Gaul she was known as Cath Bodva. As a Mother Goddess and Triple Goddess, Badb's cauldron boiled with the ever-producing mixture that produced all life. A deity of life, wisdom, inspiration, and enlightenment. Variants are BADHBH and BADB CATHA.

**Banba**    Ireland. One of a triad of goddesses that included Fotia and Eriu.

**Bel**    Ireland, Wales. A sun and fire god, this deity was closely connected with the Druids and the festival of Beltane (May 1). Deity of purification, fertility, science, healing, hot springs, fire, success, prosperity, crops, and cattle. Variants are BELENUS, BELINOS, and BELI MAWR (Wales).

**Blodeuwedd**    Wales. Known as the Ninefold Goddess of the Western Isles of Paradise and Flower-Face, this goddess was created by Math and Gwydion as a wife for the god Lleu. Her symbols were the owl and the moon. Deity of flowers, wisdom, and lunar mysteries. Variants are BLODWIN and BLANCHEFLOR.

**Boann**    Ireland. Goddess of the River Boyne and mother of Angus Mac Og by the Dagda, this goddess held the powers of healing. Variants are BOANNAN and BOYNE.

**Bran the Blessed**    Wales. A giant god associated with ravens, he was the brother of Manawydan ap Llyr and Branwen. His father was Llyr, a sea god. Deity of prophecy, the arts, war, music, and writing. A variant is BENEDIGEIDFRAN.

**Branwen**    Wales. Known as Venus of the Northern Seas, this goddess was the daughter of Llyr and one of the three matriarchs of Britain. Deity of love and beauty.

**Brigit**    Ireland. Her Gaelic name of Breo-saighead means "fiery arrow" or "fiery power." The Celts often referred to her as being three in one—the Triple Brigits or the Three Mothers. Her nineteen priestesses lived in a sacred temple at Kildare and kept an ever-burning fire in her honor. The temple was after taken over by the Christians. A daughter of the Dagda, she was the deity of poetry, healing, agriculture, inspiration, learning divination, prophecy, smithcraft, fire, and occult knowledge. Variants are BRID, BRIG, BRIGID, and BRIGHID.

**Caillech**    Ireland, Scotland. A Destroyer or Crone goddess, she was also called the "Veiled One." As the Crone, she ruled with the Maiden and Mother. Dogs guarded the gates of her after-world realm where she received the dead. In Celtic myths, her gatekeeper dog is called Dormarth (Death's Door). Irish bards who could curse with satire were often called *cainte* (dog), for this magical power was said to come from the Crone. Deity of disease and plague.

**Cernunnos**    This deity was known in all Celtic areas in one form or another. The Druids knew him as Hu Gadarn, the Horned God. Ancient Celtic images show Cernunnos seated in a lotus position, naked, and with antlers or horns on his head. Such animals as the stag, ram, bull, and horned serpent were sacred to him. Deity of virility, fertility, animals, woodlands, reincarnation, crossroads, commerce, and warriors. Variants are CEROWAIN, CERNENUS, and HERNE THE HUNTER.

**Cerridwen**    Wales. Known in her aspects of moon goddess, Great Mother, and grain deity, this goddess was the wife of the giant Tegrid. She brewed a magical potion of wisdom in her cauldron, forcing the young Taliesin to stir it for a year and a day. When he accidentally swallowed the last three drops, he was transformed into a bard. Welsh bards once called themselves Cerddorion (sons of Cerridwen), meaning they received their initiation from this goddess herself. One of her sacred symbols was the white sow. Deity of death, regeneration, inspiration, magic, and initiation. Variants are CARIDWEN and CERIDWEN.

**Creiddylad**    Wales. Another daughter of the sea god Lir, she was connected with the festival of Beltane and called the May Queen. Deity of flowers and love. Variants are CREUDYLAD and CORDELIA.

**The Dagda**    Ireland. Known as the "Good God," and "Lord of the Heavens," he was one of the high kings of the Tuatha De Danann and had four great palaces under the hollow hills. The most important of his children were Brigit, Angus, Midir, Ogma, and Bodb the Red. His magical cauldron had an inexhaustible supply of food, and his oak harp made the seasons change. Deity of knowledge, magic, prophecy, the arts, regeneration, prosperity, and music.

**Diancecht**    Ireland. The physician-magician of the Tuatha De

Danann, he was god of healing, medicine, regeneration, and magic. His sons were Miach, Cian, Cethe, and Cu. His daughter was Airmid, also a great physician. A variant is DIAN CECHT.

**Danu**   Ireland. May be an aspect of Anu, but there is no agreement on this. Ancestress of the Tuatha De Danann and known as the Mother of the gods, she was a deity of rivers and wells, magic, wisdom, and plenty. Variants are DANANN and DANA.

**Don**   Ireland, Wales. In Ireland, this deity ruled over the Land of the Dead, the entrances to which, tradition says, lies within the burial mounds. In Wales, this was the goddess of sea and air. Deity of the elements and communicating with the dead.

**Druantia**   Known in several Celtic areas, this goddess was known as Queen of the Druids and Mother of the tree calendar.

**Dylan**   Wales. A sea deity and the son of Gwydion and Arianrhod, this god was called Son of the Wave. A silver fish was his symbol.

**Elaine**   Wales, Britain. A Maiden aspect of the Goddess, she was later transformed in the Arthurian sagas.

**Epona**   Britain, continental Gaul. Called Divine Horse and the Great Mare, this goddess of horses was acknowledged and worshipped by the Roman soldiers. Horses and dogs were her symbols. Deity of horsebreeding, healing springs, and prosperity.

**Eiru**   Ireland. A daughter of the Dagda, her alternate name of Erin was given to Ireland.

**Flidais**   Ireland. A shapeshifting goddess, she was deity of forests and wild creatures. She rode in a deer-drawn chariot.

**Goibniu**   Ireland, Wales. One of a triad of Tuatha De Danann craftsmen, this god was called the Great Smith. The weapons he forged always hit their mark and made fatal wounds. The other two craftsmen were Luchtaine the wright and Creidne the brazier. Deity of blacksmiths, weapon-makers, and brewing.

**Gwethyr**   Wales. As King of the Upper World, this god was the opposite of Gwynn ap Nudd.

**Gwydion**   Wales. A son of Donn, the sea goddess, this god was brother to Govannon, Arianrhod, and Amaethon (the god of agriculture). In northern Wales he was known as a great wizard and bard. Many skilled, like the Irish god Lugh, he was a shapeshifter, whose symbol was a white horse. Deity of enchantment, illusion, and magic.

**Gwynn ap Nudd**   Wales. First known as King of the Fairies and

Lord of the Underworld, this god was later said to rule over the Plant Annwn (subterranean fairies).

**Llyr** Ireland, Wales. This god was the father of Manawydan, Bran the Blessed, and Branwen. A sea deity, he may have also ruled over the underworld. Deity of sea and water.

**Lugh** Ireland, Wales. The son of Cian, a Tuatha De Danann, this sun god was a deity of all crafts and arts, journeys, healing, and prophecy. According to legend, his skills were without end. In Ireland he was associated with ravens, while in Wales his symbol was a white stag. He possessed a magic spear and otherworldly hounds. His festival was Lughnassadh or Lunasa (August 1). Variants are LLEW, LUG, LUGUS, LUGH LAMHFADA (of the long arm), and LUG SAMILDANANCH (much skilled).

**Macha** Ireland. Known as Crow, Queen of Phantoms, and the Mother of Life and Death, this goddess was a war deity honored at Lunasa. However, she was also known as a protectress in both battle and peace. Deity of cunning, sheer physical force, war, and death. Variants are MANIA, MANA, MENE, and MINNE.

**Manannan Mac Lir** Ireland, Wales. A shapeshifter deity, this god was the chief Irish sea god whose special retreat was the Isle of Man. In Wales his name was Manawydan ap Llyr. He had several magical weapons and a suit of armor that made him invisible. His swine kept the Tuatha De Danann from aging. Deity of the sea, navigators, storms, rebirth, weather, magic, and commerce.

**Margawse** Wales, Britain. Originally a Mother Goddess, she was transformed in the later Arthurian sagas.

**Math Mathonwy** Wales. Legend speaks of him as a king who was also a god of enchantment and magic.

**Merlin** Wales, Britain. Originally an ancient Welsh Druid, priest of the fairy religion, and great magician, he was transformed in the later Arthurian sagas. Tradition says he learned his powerful magic from the Goddess in her forms of Morgan, Viviane, Nimue, and Lady of the Lake. Legend says he now lies sleeping in a hidden crystal cave. Deity of all forms of magic and prophecy, healing, illusion, and the arts. Variants are MERDDIN and MYRDDIN.

**Morrigan** Ireland, Wales, Britain. A shapeshifter, this war goddess was known as Great Queen, Supreme War Goddess, Queen of Phantoms, and Specter Queen. She kept company with Fea (hateful), Badb (fury), and Macha (battle). Deity of lust, war, revenge, magic, and prophecy. Variants are MORRIGU, MORRIGHAN, and MORGAN.

**Niamh**    Ireland. Possible a form of Badb, this goddess was called Beauty and Brightness. She helped heroes at death.

**Nuada**    Ireland, Wales. At one time a king of the Tuatha De Danann, this god had to step down when he lost his hand in battle. It was replaced by a silver one. Deity of healing, harpers, poets, historians, writing, warfare, and magic. Variants are LUD, LLUDD, LLAW EREINT, NUDD, and NODENS.

**Ogma**    This god invented the Ogam script alphabet and carried a huge club similar to Hercules. Deity of eloquence, poets, writers, physical strength, inspiration, language, magic, and music. Variants are OGHMA, OGMIOS, GRIANAINECH (sun face), and CERMAIT (honey-mouthed).

**Pwyll**    Wales. He was called Pwyll pen Annwn (Pwyll head of Annwn) because he replaced Gwynn ap Nudd as ruler of the underworld at one time. Deity of cunning and virtue.

**Scathach**    Ireland, Scotland. Called the Shadowy One, She Who Strikes Fear, and the Dark Goddess, this deity was a warrior woman and prophetess who live in Albion (probably on the Isle of Skye) and taught the martial arts. Deity of healing, magic, prophecy, and martial arts. Variants are Scota, Scatha, and Scath.

**Taliesin**    Wales. Known as Prince of Song, Chief of the Bards of the West, and Patron of Druids, he was a great magician, bard, and shapeshifter who gained his knowledge directly from the goddess Cerridwen. Deity of wisdom, poety, music, writing, and magic.

**White Lady**    Known to all Celtic countries. Called the Dryad of Death and Queen of the Dead, this goddess was a Crone aspect of the Goddess. Deity of death and destruction.

# Bibliography

Barnes, Ronald. *Great Legends of Wales.* London: Colin Smythe Ltd., 1991.

Beare, Beryl. *Scotland Myths and Legends.* Edison, N.J.: Chartwell Books, 1996.

Bell, Robert. *The Book of Scots-Irish Family Names.* Belfast, Ireland: The Blackstaff Press, 1997.

Black, George F. *The Surnames of Scotland.* Edinburgh: Birlinn Limited, 1996.

Blundell, Nigel. *Ancient Scotland.* Edison, N.J.: Chartwell Books, 1996.

Chant, Joy. *The High Kings.* New York: Bantam Books, 1983.

Coghlan, Ronan, Ida Grehan, and P. W. Joyce. *Book of Irish Names.* New York: Sterling Publishing, 1989.

Colum, Padraic, ed. *A Treasury of Irish Folklore.* Avenel, N.J.: Wings Books, 1992.

Conway, D. J. *Celtic Magic.* St. Paul Minn.: Llewellyn Publications, 1990.

———. *Magick of the Gods and Goddesses.* St. Paul, Minn.: Llewellyn Publications, 1993.

Daiches, David, ed. *The New Companion to Scottish Culture.* Edinburgh: Polygon, 1993.

Davies, John. *A History of Wales.* London: Penguin Books, 1994.

Duffy, Sean, ed. *The Macmillan Atlas of Irish History.* New York: Macmillan, 1997.

Dunkling, Leslie, and William Gosling. *The New American Dictionary of First Names.* New York: New American Library, 1983.

Dwelly, Edward. *The Illustrated Gaelic-English Dictionary.* Glasgow: Gairm Publications, 1994.

Ellefson, Connie Lockhart. *The Melting Pot Book of Baby Names.* Cincinnati, Ohio: Betterway Books, 1995.

Evans, H. Meurig. *Welsh-English, English-Welsh Dictionary.* New York: Hippocrene Books, 1996.

Fisher, Andrew. *A Traveller's History of Scotland.* New York: Interlink Books, 1997.

Flanagan, Laurence. *Favourite Irish Names for Children.* Dublin: Gill & Macmillan, 1993.

Foster, Sally M. *Picts, Gaels, and Scots.* London: B. T. Batsford Ltd., 1996.

Gantz, Jeffrey, trans. *The Mabinogion.* New York: Dorset Press, 1976.

Gerard-Sharp, Lisa, and Tim Perry. *Ireland.* New York: DK Publishing, 1997.

Grehan, Ida. *The Dictionary of Irish Family Names.* London: Roberts Rinehart Publishers, 1997.

Hanks, Patrick, and Flavia Hodges. *A Dictionary of Surnames.* Oxford: Oxford University Press, 1997.

Kenyon, Sherrilyn. *The Writer's Digest Character Naming Sourcebook.* Cincinnati, Ohio: Writer's Digest Books, 1994.

Laing, Lloyd, and Jenny Laing. *Celtic Britain and Ireland.* New York: Barnes & Noble, 1997.

———. *The Picts and the Scots.* London: Alan Sutton Publishing, 1993.

Lansky, Bruce. *35,000 Baby Names.* New York: Meadowbrook Press, 1995.

Lewis, Edwin C. *Welsh Dictionary.* Lincolnwood, Ill.: NTC Publishing, 1992.

MacCana, Proinsias. *Celtic Mythology.* New York: Peter Bedrick Books, 1983.

MacCulloch, J. A. *The Religion of the Ancient Celts.* London: Constable, 1991.

MacKillop, James. *Dictionary of Celtic Mythology.* Oxford: Oxford University Press, 1998.

Maclean, Fitzroy. *Highlanders: A History of the Scottish Clans.* New York: Penguin, 1996.

Macleod, John. *Highlanders: A History of the Gaels.* London: Hodder & Stoughton, 1996.

Mac Mathuna, Seamus, and Ailbhe O Corrain. *Irish Dictionary.* London: HarperCollins, 1997.

Marsden, John. *Alba of the Ravens: In Search of the Celtic Kingdom of the Scots.* London: Constable, 1997.

Martine, Roddy. *Scottish Clan and Family Names.* Edinburgh: Mainstream Publishing, 1992.

Matthews, John. *Classic Celtic Fairy Tales.* London: Blandford, 1997.

Middleton, Haydn, and Anthea Toorchen. *Son of Two Worlds.* London: Century Hutchinson Ltd., 1987.

Parry-Jones, D. *Welsh Legends and Fairy Lore.* New York: Barnes & Noble, 1992.

Philip, Neil, ed. *The Penguin Book of Scottish Folktales.* London: Penguin, 1991.

Room, Adrian. *A Dictionary of Irish Place-Names.* Belfast: Appletree Press, 1994.

Ross, Anne. *Druids, Gods, and Heroes from Celtic Mythology.* New York: Schocken Books, 1986.

————. *The Folklore of the Scottish Highlands.* New York: Barnes & Noble, 1976.

Rowlands, John, and Sheila Rowlands. *The Surnames of Wales.* Baltimore, Md.: Genealogical Publishing, 1996.

Rule, Lareina. *Name Your Baby.* New York: Bantam Books, 1978.

Sierra, Judy. *Celtic Baby Names.* Eugene, Or.: Folkprint, 1997.

Squire, Charles. *Celtic Myth and Legend.* New York: Newcastle Publishing, 1975.

Yeats, William Butler, and Lady Isabella Gregory. *A Treasury of Irish Myth, Legend, and Folklore.* Avenel, N.J.: Gramercy Books, 1986.